Beyond Habermas

BEYOND HABERMAS

Democracy, Knowledge, and the Public Sphere

Edited by
Christian J. Emden
and
David Midgley

berghahn
NEW YORK · OXFORD
www.berghahnbooks.com

Published in 2013 by
Berghahn Books
www.berghahnbooks.com

Library of Congress Cataloging-in-Publication Data

Beyond Habermas : democracy, knowledge, and the public sphere / edited by Christian J.
Emden and David Midgley.
    p. cm.
Includes bibliographical references and index.
ISBN 978-0-85745-721-9 (hardback : alk. paper) — ISBN 978-1-78238-668-1
(paperback : alk. paper) —ISBN 978-0-85745-722-6 (ebook)
    1. Political science—Philosophy. 2. Democracy—Philosophy. 3. Habermas, Jürgen.
I. Emden, Christian J. II. Midgley, David R., 1948–
JA71.B4893 2012
320.01—dc23

                                                                        2012001690

British Library Cataloguing in Publication Data

A catalogue record for this book is available from the British Library

Printed on acid-free paper.

ISBN 978-0-85745-721-9 (hardback)
ISBN 978-1-78238-668-1 (paperback)
ISBN 978-0-85745-722-6 (ebook)

CONTENTS

PART III—DEMOCRACY, PHILOSOPHY, AND GLOBAL PUBLICS

BEYOND HABERMAS?
From the Bourgeois Public Sphere to Global Publics

Christian J. Emden and David Midgley

When Jürgen Habermas introduced the term *bürgerliche Öffentlichkeit*, or "bourgeois public sphere," to post-1945 political theory some fifty years ago, it was quickly adopted as a way of referring to central aspects of modern constitutional and democratic order.[1] That the very idea of a "public sphere" could gain such momentum in the closing decades of the twentieth century suggests that, despite its focus on political developments in the eighteenth century, Habermas's *The Structural Transformation of the Public Sphere*, originally published in 1962, had provided important stimuli for the interpretation of the predicaments of civil society in the twentieth century, torn as it was between a liberal understanding of the constitutional state, on the one hand, and a variety of challenges from both the right and the left of the political spectrum, on the other.

Habermas's book, as much as the topic itself, was very much a reflection of the political culture of 1950s Germany, which had emerged from the Second World War, shouldering responsibility for both the war and for the Holocaust, only to enter a period of dramatic economic growth, the so-called *Wirtschaftswunder*, that was largely marked by an artificial distance toward the Nazi state. While the German *Grundgesetz*, the constitutional Basic Law, constituted a significant improvement over the Weimar Constitution, thus providing the necessary formal conditions for a liberalization of political culture, the dominance of conservative thought in the early years of the Bonn Republic (under the chancellorship of Konrad Adenauer) limited civil society in ways that were not conducive to the formation of a proper public sphere. German political culture during the 1950s, in other words, was far removed from the ideals of the public sphere Habermas attributed to the early eighteenth century, but the political experience of the 1950s also provided the opportunity to critically assess the possibility of the public sphere in the modern democratic polity.[2]

Against this background, Habermas, despite his proximity to the first generation of the Frankfurt School, certainly does not belong to the intellectual context of historical materialism that shaped much debate in Germany during the 1960s, even though the historical materialism of Max Horkheimer and others remained a crucial point of reference for Habermas's early work. Habermas's theory of the public sphere does not represent the generation of 1968, but that of 1958, a generation whose political experiences was still largely marked by the consequences of the disintegration of German democracy in 1933 and the rise of the Nazi state.[3] This is particularly important to keep in mind, because the hope that Habermas invests in the function of the public sphere and of civil society is in many ways a hope that democracy can, in fact, work, as long as it moves along the lines of free and rational debate, opening up spaces for individual autonomy while at the same time providing a normative framework for democratic governance—a normative framework for deliberative and procedural democracy, often on Kantian grounds, which Habermas developed more fully in *Between Facts and Norms*, originally published in 1992.[4]

Although the concepts of *Öffentlichkeit, opinion publique*, and "the public" certainly accompanied philosophical and political discussion about the nature of modern civil society and its democratic institutions on both sides of the Atlantic from the eighteenth century onward, it was in the course of the twentieth century that these concepts gained a new and dramatic relevance: the complexity of decision-making processes in constitutional nation-states, together with the increasing social differentiation that marked their political life, demanded a reassessment of the relationship between the institutions of the state and the public dimension of the political process. Indeed, the discussion of the nature of the public, and of the formation of public opinion, in a number of seminal texts in the history of modern political thought—from the work of Ferdinand Tönnies and Walter Lippmann to Carl Schmitt and Ernst Manheim[5]—pointed to a fundamental ambivalence that could be found at the heart of "the public": while highly heterogeneous, conflictual, and marked by emotional attachments, "the public" was also a necessary ingredient of those political processes that aimed at compromise and, occasionally, even consensus. Deliberative and procedural forms of democracy could neither come into existence nor gain legitimacy without a public, but the same is also true with regard to concepts of radical democracy that, at times, stand in opposition to a deliberative understanding of the political.

Against this background, it is often possible to observe an intersection of philosophical and legal discourses that seek to come to terms with the forms and functions of the public sphere—itself a conceptual construct that, at least since the end of the Cold War, is increasingly seen as in need of pluralism. Habermas's public sphere, in other words, has acquired additional layers and dimensions of complexity that reach far beyond his own account, originally published in 1962.[6] If the public sphere continues to carry weight as an explanatory model it needs to be seen, to borrow a phrase from James Tully, as representing a "strange multiplicity" of publics, of interests, of forms of political and social action as well as forms of representation.[7]

The present volume aims to contribute to the debate about this strange multiplicity by investigating the emergence, interaction, and limitations of public spheres from a number of different perspectives. Focusing on the relationship between philosophy and "the public" as much as on the relationship between theoretical accounts of the public sphere and what Raymond Geuss has termed "real politics,"[8] the contributions in this volume discuss both the actual reach of our talk about "publics" and the historical and social embeddedness of these publics. This is particularly important, we believe, because much of the debate about the role of the public sphere in political theory often proceeds without paying attention to the many contexts and discourses within which publics come into existence. Publics are historically conditioned and socially concrete "things"; that is, they emerge or are dissolved in specific locations, they are shaped by the technologies and material culture to which they are subject, and they also serve the production of knowledge. Knowledge about the world we live in—even if such knowledge is of a highly specialized nature and accessible, initially at least, only to a small group of experts—tends to be public knowledge; that is, it is knowledge that circulates among specific constituencies: political theorists and philosophers as much as scientists in the laboratory, public health officials in the streets of London, Internet geeks in Mumbai, grassroots movements in the Middle East and North Africa that demand participation in governance, and so on. The present volume, therefore, brings together contributions from a number of different fields, from political science and philosophy to anthropology, intellectual history, and—crucially—the practice of politics itself.

Although Habermas's discussion of the public sphere remains the central point of reference for many of the contributions in this volume, we have sought to draw together a range of positions that seek, each in its own way, to move beyond Habermas. Although the latter's notion of the public sphere has proven to be quite controversial, triggering at times heated debates across a number of fields in the humanities and social sciences, it is indeed difficult to overlook the continued relevance of Habermas's original contribution.[9] On the one hand, it is obvious that the fundamental changes in the political and technological environment since the initial publication of Habermas's book in 1962 render it necessary to ask whether it continues to make sense to speak of a "public sphere." The rise of the global firm as the representative manifestation of market economics after the end of the Cold War, together with the commercialization of political citizenship, which effectively devolves central features of the modern state—from information policy to prisons, education, and the logistics of military operations—to private companies, has raised enormous questions about the viability of the public sphere as a domain of free and rational debate based on intersubjective interests.[10] If we truly live in a state of postdemocracy, as Colin Crouch has suggested, then the normative framework in which Habermas has continued to ground his conception of deliberative democracy will have lost its relevance.[11] At the same time, the formation of new social movements and the effects of digital communication technologies, which have combined to generate the widespread phenomenon of cyber protests, are increasingly shaping what is widely perceived as a transnational public space. These developments invite the question of whether there is indeed still a sense in which the public sphere can serve as a counterbalance to the state and whether it can provide an accurate description of the realities of political life.[12]

The very fact that the market economy appears as the central social imaginary of the present has led others to advocate a return to Habermas's model of the public sphere, albeit situating the latter in the wider framework of contemporary critical theory, thus providing, as it were, an update of Habermas's original account. Seen from this perspective, the modern liberal public sphere can still serve as a model for "a future that is guided by an inter-subjective will that has formed itself through processes of critical scrutiny, deliberation, and negotiated consensus-building."[13] Within such a model, Habermas's principles for the critical function of the public sphere would still apply: only the force of the better argument should prevail, few things—if any—can be exempt from public critique, and transparency is a necessary characteristic of an effective political world. Whether such a future still remains open, given the widespread experience of political disaffection and the highly emotional public discourse that has become common across traditional liberal democracies in the West, is unclear. But it should not be overlooked that, as Habermas pointed out with regard to the seventeenth and eighteenth centuries, the public sphere initially emerged as a powerful counterweight to traditional forms of political authority, inserting itself between the private life of the family and the *arcana imperii* of the early modern state apparatus. It was in this sense that the public sphere gave rise to the phenomenon of "civil society," within which the "private autonomy" of the individual—from merchant and university professor to senior civil servant—"stood opposed to the state," questioning the latter's actions on the grounds of an ideal discourse of rational debate.[14] Even if the present state of politics might appear dismal, historical precedents give credence to the potential viability of a public sphere. For Habermas, at least, the public sphere was a corrective to the authority of the state, a corrective that required a specific class of citizens—scholars, capitalist merchants, and civil servants—which were able to put into question the decisions of the state as an institution:

> [T]he "capitalists," the merchants, bankers, entrepreneurs, and manufacturers ... belonged to that group of the "bourgeois" who, like the new category of scholars, were not really "burghers" in the traditional sense. This stratum of the "bourgeois" was the real carrier of the public, which from the outset was a reading public. ... In this stratum, which more than any other was affected *and* called upon by mercantilist policies, the state authorities evoked a resonance leading the *publicum*, the abstract counterpart of public authority, into an awareness of itself as the latter's opponent, that is, as the public of the now emerging *public sphere of civil society*.[15]

The formation of a "sphere of private people" that come "together as a public" is in this respect intimately linked to an idealized model of the Enlightenment that has come under much scrutiny.[16] Some historians have sought to save the general outlines of Habermas's model, filling in the gaps where necessary and rethinking some of the material and social conditions for the emergence of the public sphere.[17] Others have been more critical, asking whether there ever was such a thing as a public sphere of civil society.[18] Indeed, even if one grants the existence of a public sphere in the eighteenth century, this does not necessarily mean that it was democratic in orientation: the criticism of princely absolutism did not always lead to democratic demands, but rather emphasized the importance of the estates, or *Stände*, in an almost Hegelian fashion as an organized counterweight to political power.[19]

Such problems with the concept of a public sphere point to a strange paradox that stands at the center of Habermas's account: the public sphere, once established, always tends to decline. That is to say, as soon as the public sphere becomes sufficiently wide to constitute a model for civil society at large, i.e., as soon as it is properly democratized, it tends to disintegrate and lose its critical function. As Habermas himself noted: "In the hundred years following the heyday of liberalism, during which capitalism gradually became 'organized,' the original relationship of public and private sphere in fact dissolved; the contours of the public sphere eroded." This development was largely due to the enormous success of the public sphere: "While it penetrated more *spheres* of society, it simultaneously lost its political *function*, namely: that of subjecting the affairs that it had made public to the control of a critical public. ... The *principle* of the public sphere, that is, critical publicity, seemed to lose its strength in the measure that it expanded as a *sphere* and even undermined the private realm."[20] Ironically, this also implies that a working public sphere is always limited, that is, it is made up of members that have the time, education, and the financial resources to set themselves in opposition to the state authorities, even if such opposition can be very indirect. In much the same way as Immanuel Kant, in his famous "An Answer to the Question: What Is Enlightenment?" (1784), suggested that—despite the universal claims of reason—the public use of reason was enacted only by "a few who think for themselves," Habermas's public sphere could be most effective only as long as it remained exclusive.[21] As Craig Calhoun has observed: "The early bourgeois public spheres were composed of narrow segments of the European population, mainly educated, propertied men, and they conducted a discourse not only exclusive of others but prejudicial to the interests of those excluded."[22] In a certain sense, this describes the inherently paradoxical relationship between democracy and the public sphere, and it is not surprising that after 1800 Hegel, for instance, was particularly critical of the role public opinion and the public at large was to play in the realm of politics: emotionally charged and with an unclear understanding of the foundations of constitutional order, the public could not entirely be trusted.[23]

The initially exclusive nature of the public sphere, as articulated in the reflections of Kant and Hegel, and as prominently acknowledged in Habermas's historical account, is also confirmed by John P. McCormick's more recent observation about Machiavelli's republicanism and his criticism of elite rule: perhaps it is precisely the fact that "the common people are formally excluded from full political participation in the most powerful and prestigious offices" that provides them with the opportunity to use "more energetically and urgently ... offices and assemblies reserved exclusively for themselves to serve their liberty against the more privileged citizens." What is initially experienced, then, as "formal political inequality" gives rise to "substantive political equality in practice."[24] At first sight, this seems to imply that the efforts of the governed at "rearranging the balances of power" underlines the central importance of the public sphere.[25] On the other hand, McCormick's Machiavellian account also seems to imply that the models of deliberative democracy that Habermas regards as the ideal outcome for the public sphere, and which give civil society its normative framework, ultimately tend to privilege those with the necessary means, financial and otherwise, to exploit this normative framework for their own gain. Is the real paradox of the liberal public sphere, and therefore also of deliberative democracy itself, the increasing growth within it of mechanisms of exclusion? These are important questions that the contributions to this volume seek to address from different perspectives.

A working public sphere requires knowledge about what is relevant to the public, that is, it requires the kind of expertise—about science, about international relations, even about tax law—that most citizens simply do not possess. Indeed, some of the central issues in the debate about the public sphere concern the relationship between knowledge and democracy, and the role that knowledge can play, how it is disseminated and transmitted within different publics that are often in open conflict with each other. These are issues that are rarely discussed in sufficient detail. Within the exploration of the usefulness and the limits of the public sphere as an explanatory model of political action that the current volume conducts, one of the guiding themes is therefore the relationship between knowledge and democracy. Moreover, an underlying premise that unites the contributions in this volume is their emphasis on the need to distinguish between various "publics" in which the interests and concerns of particular groups of people are transacted, and the character of which is inherently dynamic. Individual chapters address aspects of this complexity and dynamism, ranging from the philosophical analysis of concepts and political procedures to the practicalities of implementing governmental policies, and the public communication of knowledge.

The volume begins with three chapters that deal, from different perspectives, with the role of public opinion in the modern democratic polity. Lord Wilson, who, at the end of a long and distinguished career in the British Civil Service, had served as Secretary of the Cabinet and as Head of the UK Home Civil Service from 1998 to 2002, opens this section with reflections on the relation between government action and the various means by which public opinion is shaped. Based on his own experiences and observations during the 1990s and early 2000s, these reflections document and comment upon many significant aspects of the contemporary operation of the public sphere, introducing the range of themes addressed in the following chapters. While Lord Wilson's contribution might initially strike readers as a peculiarly British perspective on the role of the public in modern societies, the broader issues he addresses can be observed across all liberal democracies: the increasing speed, for instance, with which information and policy debates—and leaks—circulate from ministries and parliament to public media and back into the corridors of government clearly alters the relationship between government and governed in fundamental ways. This relationship, of course, cuts both ways: while public discussion and scandal can limit the options available to government, government often has to disregard public opinion in order to remain effective. While public opinion remains an essential ingredient of a working civil society, then, the tensions that can emerge between government and governed are also a frequent feature of the dialogue between the state and its citizens. This is one sense in which the public sphere presents itself as an ever-changing phenomenon, diffuse and dynamic, as different publics come together, disperse, and reassemble around specific shared interests. We are grateful to Lord Wilson for allowing us to publish his impressions, which provide a very suitable introduction to the themes under discussion in this book: the relationship between government and governed, the circulation of knowledge between different constituencies, and the relationship between knowledge and democracy.

Gordon Graham, in his philosophical reflection on the continued usefulness of Habermas's concepts, draws attention to some senses in which the public sphere as Habermas conceived it stands in a relationship of inescapable tension with public opinion as it manifests itself in practice—through pressure groups, the publicity they seek for their own causes, and through opinion polls. He therefore questions whether the formation of public opinion in the public sphere can be seen as carrying rational authority, and he sees this stricture as applying equally to Habermas's model of participatory democracy and to John Rawls's Kantian liberalism.[26] Public opinion and rational scrutiny should, in Graham's view, rather be treated as alternative tests of validity, while any claim of philosophy to a normative role in the domain of politics is open to doubt. As such, the public role of the philosopher—theorizing about the public sphere and intervening in constitutional as well as political debates, as Habermas himself has always done—comes under scrutiny. For Graham, the public role of the philosopher is, and should be, limited; like the public at large, the philosopher lacks the kind of inside information and expert knowledge that are necessary to decide those concerns of government that are discussed most controversially in the public domain. While other contributions to this volume take a very different view from Graham's, at least as far as the role of the philosopher is concerned, this chapter, like Lord Wilson's, raises a crucial issue that anyone has to confront who wishes to enter into debates about the nature of the public sphere: a realist understanding of politics and of the political that inevitably questions the ways in which normative ideals—of the public sphere, deliberative democracy, and morality—relate to human action.[27] In the realm of politics, the normative question as it was outlined by Christine Korsgaard—"Why should I be moral?"—acquires increasing complexity.[28] The demands of real politics, to use Geuss's expression once again, often stand in stark contrast to the normative demands of deliberative democracy. At the same time, however, socioeconomic inequality as a structural problem of modern democracies, coupled with what Machiavelli understood as rule by the few, forces us to rethink the way in which publics, small and large, are able to shape the relationship between government and governed. Public expertise might be limited in a working democracy, but so must the power of government and decision makers outside government be also.

One such practical instance of the demands of real politics, in the shape of the force of public opinion, encountering the normative framework of democracy is the constitutional debate about abortion in the United States. Taking his cue from Habermas's discussion of John Stuart Mill and Alexis de Tocqueville, Gary Wihl argues that in his focus on civil society as striving for rational consensus, Habermas consistently underplays substantive political debates concerning privacy, public opinion, and tolerance. Seen in this perspective, the distinction between public good and private goods cannot exclusively be negotiated within a purely normative framework.[29] This becomes particularly obvious, Wihl points out, if we consider the consequences of the Supreme Court case *Roe v. Wade* of 1973, which legalized abortion in the United States. Although the court's decision clearly reflected, and continues to reflect, a majority public opinion, the emphasis on a right to privacy might actually be better grounded in minority opinion. In a detailed discussion of Ronald Dworkin's and Michael Sandel's positions vis-à-vis these debates, Wihl concludes that conflicts over privacy concern substantive issues—abortion, health care decisions, gay rights, etc.[30] As such, they can be construed as conflicts over the recognition of constituencies that either are minorities or perceive themselves as minorities, such as impoverished women on whom the lack of abortion rights can exert detrimental social and economic effects.

In the next section, the contributions of Christian J. Emden, Anne Hardy, and Christopher Kelty shift the focus of attention from the modern democratic polity to the relationship between knowledge and its publics. Emden argues for an understanding of scientific practice, and of the publics within which scientific practice takes place, that is, at once conceptual and historical. Reaching beyond the straightforward question of how science can be made public, this chapter addresses the way in which the circulation of scientific practices, instruments, and objects among different fields of knowledge generates "epistemic publics." While such epistemic publics are certainly related to, and shaped by, the normative claims that the sciences make, these normative claims cannot seriously be separated from historical context. At first sight, epistemic publics are embedded in the tense relationship between the expert cultures of science and their perception by a broader set of publics outside the sites of scientific investigation, but upon closer inspection the traditional distinction between expert science and lay public appears to be a regulative fiction of heuristic value. Indeed, a historical approach highlights that scientific practice—popularly perceived as a prominent example of experts aiming at rational consensus—gives rise to different epistemic publics with different interests, while the public authority of science is marked by spectacle, secrecy, and dramatic political conflicts over access to resources. To be sure, answering the question what makes a scientific claim merit our consideration can lead us to a normative framework that takes as its model precisely the kind of normative commitments that Habermas regarded as emerging from the liberal public sphere.[31] Drawing on work in the history and philosophy of science, however, Emden concludes that the production of knowledge is inherently dependent on epistemic publics, while the way in which objects, technologies, people, and publications circulate between different publics fundamentally alters their meaning and cultural value.[32] Such publics do not conform to the ideals of the public sphere; rather, the circulation of knowledge among different publics establishes "trading zones" characterized by overlapping and often competing interests.

A particularly interesting example of the complex link between expert knowledge and public opinion—which furthermore directly relates to the political questions raised by the contributions of Lord Wilson, Graham, and Wihl—is the question of public health. Can decisions about health care, or the relationship between physician and patient, be accurately explored from a Habermasian perspective?[33] Tracing the development of the concept of public health in Britain from the nineteenth century to the present, Anne Hardy contends that the notion of public health overriding private interests in the service of population health and state-delivered health services—a particularly timely topic on both sides of the Atlantic—rests on the problematic assumption of a political consensus about what public health entails. Given the history of the concept of public health as it responded to rising levels of infectious disease in urban environments, however, such consensus is remarkably questionable, since the economic dimension of British liberalism, with its emphasis on the individual, often brought public concerns and private interests into conflict. It is this conflict that has continued to shape debate about public health in the twentieth and twenty-first centuries, as can be seen with regard to the introduction of fluoridated water supplies during the 1960s and the recent controversies surrounding a presumed link between the measles, mumps, and rubella (MMR) vaccine and autism. In the latter case—as Emden also points out in his chapter with regard to the public perception of AIDS—scientific knowledge runs into open conflict with public opinion.

Our conceptions of public health, as much as our understanding of what constitutes scientific practice, are in many ways affected by technological change. Such change, of which the most recent example is perhaps the emerging digital culture of the postindustrial world, can have an enormous impact on the constitution of publics. Indeed, technologies can create their own publics, as can be seen with regard to the formation of overlapping publics around the Internet. Christopher Kelty's discussion of "recursive publics" is based on extensive research of communities forged by a common interest in the Internet. The term "recursive" is derived from the mathematical language of computer programming, and is used here to denote a self-sustaining community of creative and autonomous individuals (in this instance, "geeks") that exists independently of, and is capable of functioning as a check on, constituted forms of power.[34] Reflecting on his own experiences of communicating with such communities, and drawing on Charles Taylor's conception of "social imaginaries"[35] in particular, Kelty develops a sense of the nature and operation of a particular variety of public sphere constituted around the technical infrastructure of global communications.

Widening the perspective of Kelty's chapter while also continuing the themes raised in the earlier chapters, Georgina Born opens the final section of this volume, which focuses on both the practical formation of publics in a global environment and the contribution of philosophy to understanding this development. Born notes how the notion of a public sphere has often been used in media theory as an ideal against which to measure the democratic potential of the mass media, and examines the nature of public service broadcasting as a fairly imperfect embodiment of the public sphere. Taking her material above all from recent debates about the future of the BBC, with its long tradition and exceptionally prominent role as a public service broadcaster in Britain and the wider English-speaking world, Born reflects on the complexity of the issues that face official broadcasting in view of the rapid pace of both technical and cultural change in present-day societies.[36] The technical changes are represented especially by the introduction of digital communication and broadband transmission, which bring with them the issues of market competitiveness in the international communication industry, growing consumer choice, and the increasing potential for interactive communication. The cultural changes relate to increasing diversity within societies, the transition from the notion of an identifiable national culture to a more fluid sense of cosmopolitan culture, and the question of enabling effective interaction between subsections of the community, however defined. In view of the role that public service communication can play in fostering the processes that underlie participatory citizenship, and of the potential that different media have for fulfilling specific purposes, Born argues that the debate on the function of public service broadcasting needs to move on from theoretical ideals to considerations of institutional design aimed at meeting a multiplicity of dynamically changing purposes in a global age. This, of course, is particularly important at a time when public broadcasting on both sides of the Atlantic—NPR and PBS in the United States and the BBC in Britain are merely particularly prominent examples—have come under increasing political and economic pressure.

From a more theoretical perspective, and informed by a phenomenological approach to political philosophy, Steven G. Crowell examines the question of political legitimation. Focusing on the writings of Habermas and Hannah Arendt, this chapter takes up themes that are also central to Graham's discussion of public opinion and Wihl's account of rights. Crowell considers the nature of the case that Habermas makes for a rationally founded discourse ethics in light of criticisms and counterarguments that may be made against it, and presents his own argument for a version of Habermas's legitimation strategy that links argumentation to the agonistic processes by which meaning is constituted and rights are asserted—as Arendt recognized in *The Human Condition* (1958) and elsewhere.[37] Just as Born points to the substantive issues and conflicts at stake in the influence of public service communication on political citizenship, Crowell, albeit from a very different perspective, argues that political legitimation is inherently performative, which is to say that it is actualized in very specific contexts and always carries meaning beyond merely normative commitments. The central test case for this claim is Habermas's legitimation of human rights, and of rights in general, which can be seen as the long-term consequence of his earlier work on the public sphere and civil society.[38] The politics of law, Crowell argues, cannot be detached from the politics of meaning, and the normativity of law and rights only comes to the fore once individuals and groups engage in political action. As such, this chapter questions some of the central principles underlying the philosophical formulation of political liberalism as it can be found in Rawls and Habermas.

Having begun with Lord Wilson's discussion of the how the nature of the encounter between government and governed continually shifts as new publics are formed around specific political interests, this volume closes with a substantial reassessment by James Tully of Habermas's theoretical position, from his early reflections on the public sphere to his more recent work on deliberative democracy and the notion of a global domestic politics. More particularly, Tully examines the respective implications of a liberal theory of the public sphere, including Habermas's, which concerns itself primarily with the formal conditions for participation in public discussions, and a democratic model in which a "public" may be said to be formed whenever two or more people come together to discuss a public issue of importance to them. The former is, of its nature, more abstract and unitary in conception, the latter more concrete and differentiated in its focus, and closer to the ethical practice of individuals in their everyday lives. Tully thus establishes what can be understood as a civic model of public discussion that, because of its tendency toward a more radical democratic form, stands in some contrast to the normative principles that mark deliberative and procedural models of democracy. Tully considers the concept of a public sphere—as the sphere in which dialogue between the governors and the governed helps to bring forth good governors and good citizens alike—indispensable to any representation of democratic participation; but he also examines the tensions that exist between the demands of central and peripheral interests, and between the constituent elements in processes of democratization that have taken place throughout the world in recent decades, since the era of decolonization. In his discussion of the relation between the liberal theory and the democratic model, then, he refines the terms of Habermas's argument in ways that make the concept of a public sphere once again fruitful for the understanding of contemporary political experience, as long as such a public sphere is conceived as consisting of a multiplicity of publics that bring local and global interests into conversation.[39]

* * *

Without the generous administrative and financial support of a number of institutions this project could neither have started nor have been brought to a fruitful conclusion. At Rice University, we would like to thank the Humanities Research Center, the School of Humanities, and the Department of German Studies; at the University of Cambridge we would like to express our gratitude to the German Department and the Center for Research in the Arts, Social Sciences and Humanities. We are also grateful to Ludmilla Jordanova, Werner Kelber, Caroline Levander, and Gary Wihl, who supported this project with great enthusiasm right from the beginning, and to Marion Berghahn and Ann Przyzycki, who patiently guided us through the entire publication process, intervening at crucial junctures and rightly reminding us that revisions and rewriting eventually need to come to an end.

Houston, USA
Cambridge, England
May 2011

Notes

1. Jürgen Habermas, *The Structural Transformation of the Public Sphere*, trans. Thomas Burger and Frederick Lawrence (Cambridge, MA, 1989).
2. William E. Scheuerman, "Unsolved Paradoxes: Conservative Political Thought in Adenauer's Germany," in *Confronting Mass Democracy and Industrial Technology: Political and Social Theory from Nietzsche to Habermas*, ed. John P. McCormick (Durham, NC, 2002), pp. 221–42, and the contributions in Jan-Werner Müller, ed., *German Ideologies since 1945: Studies in the Political Thought and Culture of the Bonn Republic* (New York, 2003).
3. Matthew G. Specter, *Habermas: An Intellectual Biography* (Cambridge, 2010), pp. 27–86.
4. Jürgen Habermas, *Between Facts and Norms: Contributions to a Discourse Theory of Law and Democracy*, trans. William Rehg (Cambridge, MA, 1996).
5. Ferdinand Tönnies, *On Public Opinion: Selections and Analyses*, ed. and trans. Hanno Hardt and Slavko Splichal (Lanham, NJ, 2000); Walter Lippmann, *The Phantom Public* (New York, 1925); Carl Schmitt, *The Crisis of Parliamentary Democracy*, trans. Ellen Kennedy (Cambridge, MA, 1985); and Ernst Manheim, *Die Träger der öffentlichen Meinung: Studien zur Soziologie der Öffentlichkeit* (Leipzig, 1933).
6. See, for instance, the discussion in Nick Crossley and John Michael Roberts, eds., *After Habermas: New Perspectives on the Public Sphere* (Oxford, 2004), and Pauline Johnson, *Habermas: Rescuing the Public Sphere* (London, 2006).
7. James Tully, *Strange Multiplicity: Constitutionalism in an Age of Diversity* (Cambridge, 1995).
8. Raymond Geuss, *Philosophy and Real Politics* (Princeton, NJ, 2008).
9. See especially the early assessments of Habermas's position in Craig Calhoun, ed., *Habermas and the Public Sphere* (Cambridge, MA, 1992), in particular the contributions by Calhoun, Peter Uwe Hohendahl, and Nancy Fraser.
10. Colin Crouch, *Post-Democracy* (Cambridge, 2004), pp. 31–53 and 78–102.
11. Habermas, *Between Facts and Norms*, pp. 287–328.
12. See, for instance, the contributions in Crossley and Roberts, eds., *After Habermas*, and Michael Warner, *Publics and Counterpublics* (New York, 2002).
13. Johnson, *Habermas*, p. 14.
14. Habermas, *The Structural Transformation of the Public Sphere*, p. 12.
15. Ibid., p. 23. For a broader contextual account, see James Van Horn Melton, *The Rise of the Public Sphere in Enlightenment Europe* (Cambridge, 2001), and Ursula Golden-

baum, ed., *Appell an das Publikum: Die öffentliche Debatte in der deutschen Aufklärung, 1687–1796* (Berlin, 2004).

16. Habermas, *The Structural Transformation of the Public Sphere*, p. 27. See the overview in Andreas Gestrich, "The Public Sphere and the Habermas Debate," *German History* 24 (2006): 413–30, and John Brooke, "Reason and Passion in the Public Sphere: Habermas and the Cultural Historians," *Journal of Interdisciplinary History* 29 (1998–99): 43–67.

17. See, for instance, Margaret C. Jacob, "The Mental Landscape of the Public Sphere: A European Perspective," *Eighteenth-Century Studies* 28 (1994): 95–113; Anthony LaVopa, "Conceiving a Public: Ideas and Society in Eighteenth-Century Europe," *Journal of Modern History* 64 (1992): 98–115; and Dena Goodman, "Public Sphere and Private Life: Toward a Synthesis of Current Historiographical Approaches to the Old Regime," *History and Theory* 31 (1992): 1–20.

18. Harold Mah, "Phantasies of the Public Sphere: Rethinking the Habermas of Historians," *Journal of Modern History* 72 (2000): 153–82.

19. Rudolf Vierhaus, *Deutschland im 18. Jahrhundert: Politische Verfassung, soziales Gefüge, geistige Bewegungen* (Göttingen, 1987), p. 38, and Georg Wilhelm Friedrich Hegel, *Elements of the Philosophy of Right*, ed. Allen W. Wood, trans. H. B. Nisbet (Cambridge, 1991), pp. 339–52.

20. Habermas, *The Structural Transformation of the Public Sphere*, p. 140.

21. Immanuel Kant, "An Answer to the Question: What Is Enlightenment?" in *Political Writings*, ed. Hans Reiss, trans. H. B. Nisbet, 2nd ed. (Cambridge, 1991), p. 55.

22. Craig Calhoun, "Introduction: Habermas and the Public Sphere," in *Habermas and the Public Sphere*, ed. Calhoun, p. 3.

23. Hegel, *Elements of the Philosophy of Right*, pp. 353–58.

24. John P. McCormick, *Machiavellian Democracy* (Cambridge, 2011), p. 14.

25. Ibid., p. 34.

26. John Rawls, *A Theory of Justice* (Cambridge, MA, 1971) and *Political Liberalism*, exp. ed. (New York, 2005). On the encounter between Habermas and Rawls, see James Gordon Finlayson and Fabian Freyenhagen, eds., *Habermas and Rawls: Disouting the Political* (London, 2011), and Todd Hedrick, *Rawls and Habermas: Reason, Pluralism, and the Claims of Political Philosophy* (Stanford, CA, 2010).

27. See, for instance, Bernard Williams, *In the Beginning Was the Deed: Realism and Moralism in Political Argument*, ed. Geoffrey Hawthorn (Princeton, NJ, 2007).

28. Christine M. Korsgaard, *The Sources of Normativity* (Cambridge, 1996), pp. 7–47.

29. See also Raymond Geuss, *Public Goods, Private Goods* (Princeton, NJ, 2001).

30. Ronald Dworkin, *Life's Dominion: An Argument About Abortion, Euthanasia, and Individual Freedom* (New York, 1994) and Michael J. Sandel, *Democracy's Discontent: America in Search of a Public Philosophy* (Cambridge, MA, 1996).

31. For an examplary discussion of these normative commitments, see Jürgen Habermas, "Discourse Ethics: Notes on a Program of Philosophical Justification," in *Moral Consiousness and Communicative Action*, trans. Christian Lenhardt and Shierry Weber Nicholsen, intro. Thomas McCarthy (Cambridge, MA, 1990), pp. 43–115. Most recently, William Rehg has sought to apply Habermas's argumentation theory to conflicts over scientific theories, both among experts and with regard to their discussion in the wider public. See his *Cogent Science in Context: The Science Wars, Argumentation Theory, and Habermas* (Cambridge, MA, 2009).

32. See, in particular, Joseph Rouse, *How Scientific Practices Matter: Reclaiming Philosophical Naturalism* (Chicago, 2002); Peter Galison, *Image and Logic: A Material Culture*

of *Microphysics* (Chicago, 1997); and Bruno Latour, *Science in Action: How to Follow Scientists and Engineers through Society* (Cambridge, MA, 1987).

33. See, for instance, the discussions in Graham Scambler, ed., *Habermas, Critical Theory, and Health* (London, 2001).

34. See also Christopher M. Kelty, *Two Bits: The Cultural Significance of Free Software* (Durham, NC, 2008).

35. Charles Taylor, *Modern Social Imaginaries* (Durham, NC, 2004).

36. See also Georgina Born, *Uncertain Vision: Birt, Dyke and the Reinvention of the BBC* (London, 2005), and—for a historical account that considers similar questions with regard to an earlier phase of public broadcasting in Britain—Thomas Hajkowski, *The BBC and National Identity in Britain, 1922–53* (Manchester, UK, 2010).

37. Hannah Arendt, *The Human Condition*, 2nd ed., intro. Margaret Canovan (Chicago, 1998).

38. Jürgen Habermas, "Remarks on Legitimation Through Human Rights," in *The Postnational Constellation*, trans. Max Pensky (Cambridge, MA, 2001), pp. 113–29.

39. James Tully, "On Local and Global Citizenship: An Apprenticeship Manual," in *Public Philosophy in a New Key* (Cambridge, 2008), vol. 2, pp. 243–309.

Part I

PUBLIC OPINION IN THE DEMOCRATIC POLITY

Chapter 1

PUBLIC SPHERE AND POLITICAL EXPERIENCE

Lord (Richard) Wilson

I take as my starting point the explanation of the "public sphere" that Christian J. Emden and David Midgley gave in their proposal for the conference out of which this volume grew. It included the phrase "a symbolic site of conversation and public reasoning" and the notion that "it sought to come to terms with the political tensions between state authority and private responsibility." I approach the subject with some diffidence, as someone who is not an academic. But if thirty-six years working inside government can be regarded as a research project, I may have something to contribute.

Governments are surrounded by endless dialogues, cluster upon cluster of conversation and public reasoning. Their contributions to these dialogues may be formal policy statements intended to be of long-term significance. But they may also be tentative interventions that serve some ephemeral purpose such as the need to mediate disagreement, neutralize attack, test out a new idea, propitiate some vested interest, or promote their chances of being reelected. At any one time there are many such dialogues taking place within overlapping circles of government and public institutions, government departments and their client groups and critics, governments and their supporters and, sometimes more important, their enemies, dialogues between all these circles and the wider world, dialogues with media commentators and critics, dialogues with parties and the public, dialogues even with academics. These dialogues do not typically include much artistic activity but they may be theatrical as, say, the Prime Minister's Questions in Parliament and the Hutton Inquiry demonstrate.[1] And they may be the inspiration for much literature, theater, and cinema, not least in Shakespeare's history plays.

It is the essence of government that conflicting interests have to be reconciled, that disagreements have to be resolved, that priorities have to be determined and choices made in a manner that affects many people. All this means that conversation and public reasoning, and the tension between individual freedom and the authority of the state, are central elements in the public sphere. But nothing stays still for long. Just as power moves ceaselessly between people and groups, rarely staying in one place for long, so the topics and issues covered by these dialogues that make up the public sphere are also constantly changing. And it is always important to remember not only the dialogues that take place but also the dialogues that do *not* take place. The things that are not discussed or that occupy very little time and attention in the public sphere can be as significant as those that do, and sometimes more so. Even more important are those areas where governments say one thing and do another.

There are many illustrations one could give of these propositions: for instance, the brilliant presentation of New Labour as a new political force in the 1990s was a remarkable manipulation of perception in the public sphere. However, there are three main points that I want to explore. First, I want to make the point that governments can be as much affected by changes in the public sphere as the other way around. Second, I want to argue that if government is making a great show of using conversation and reasoning in the public sphere it may mean that not much is actually happening. And third, I want to argue that important things may take place in government, not secretly but in relative silence in the public sphere, or the government may do something that is different from what they are saying in the public sphere. I shall take these each in turn.

The Public Sphere Keeps Changing

The ways in which changes in the public sphere may have an impact on government are illustrated by the growth in power of the media, of newspapers and television.[2] In the mid-1960s there were roughly a dozen news reports a day. In the mid-1990s there were 50 news broadcasts, on the hour, every hour of the day and night. Now the reporting of news is virtually continuous, with live news flashes interrupting the 24-hour news programs, while digital television and the Internet make it possible to check the latest news headlines whenever the viewer wishes to do so. This has a considerable impact on the conduct of government. The public sphere never rests. In the late 1990s the UK government set up a team of people to watch the news twenty-four hours a day and to alert departments when a new story of interest appeared so that they could be swift to respond as it gained momentum. Continuous news coverage required a continuous response. The dialogue between government and media never stops.

The nature of the dialogue within this public space also changes. Reporting of facts tends increasingly to be replaced by analysis and comment. There was a time when, if you wanted to know what had been said on the previous day in Parliament, you would be able to find it in the newspapers. Quite often now you are likely only to be able to deduce what was said from an editorial or a semisatirical account written by a Parliamentary correspondent; or by going onto the Internet. In the 1960s, if you wanted to hear the latest developments in government policy you would await the Statement, first business after Questions, in Parliament by the Secretary of State, because convention required that Parliament be told first. This is still the formal position, but in practice you are likely to be able to get a good idea of what is coming from advance trailers in the newspapers or the BBC's *Today* program.

The public sphere has also become bigger and more complex because the number of participants has grown: unofficial briefings and leaks of documents or information mean that in principle anyone who wishes to contribute in the public sphere may do so, anonymously or attributably. Possibly more important, technology and blogs have the potential to allow the individual to participate in the public sphere and to have an impact on it. Citizen journalists are frequently quoted in the media. Consider for instance the private lives of politicians. Forty years ago it was possible for a cabinet minister to have an affair with a member of his staff without attracting public comment, even though it was a matter of common gossip. Contrast that with the present day, where the Guido Fawkes blog discusses similar current affairs with a sharp blend of gossip and shrewdness which in July 2006 had apparently attracted 2,921 hits from the BBC, 3,207 from *The Guardian*, and 18,147 from the Houses of Parliament.[3] In 2008, *The Economist* described the Guido Fawkes blog as one of the most influential political blogs in the UK, and in 2009 *Total Politics* ranked Guido Fawkes as the number one political blog in the UK.[4] There are, of course, many other ways in which developments in the public sphere may affect government. Protests, for instance over the poll tax, and opinion polls are other examples; and certainly the growth of the Internet as a whole.

The code of values in the public sphere is changing and now eschews any hint of deference. Perhaps what is more striking is that so much still manages to remain private within government rather than that so much enters the public sphere. There is an important if ill-defined code of values that, far more than any Official Secrets Act, still limits the information that enters the public domain. Even so, the implications of these changes are important because they represent a shift in power. The influence of the media, the Internet, and opinion polls has to some extent replaced or qualified the power of Parliament. I do not want to exaggerate this. Parliament still exerts huge influence on the behavior of governments. The reputations of government ministers are still only as good or as bad as the last speech they made or the last Parliamentary Questions and Answers they handled. The support of the people on the benches behind the Prime Minister and his ministers are still more important than those of the watching correspondents in the Press Gallery.

But the media in particular are an important adjunct of political life and possess power through their contribution to the public sphere, which can have great influence on events by influencing perceptions and by selectively reporting stories and facts. Government ministers may be as likely to respond to the suggestions of the media in taking a policy initiative as to a proposal from a backbencher or Select Committee. Indeed, the speed of media conversation in the public sphere may influence the very processes of government. Public debate may require a decision to be taken faster than the normal processes of collective government would normally allow and which would involve the preparation of a paper setting out the facts, options, and costs followed by a meeting of a cabinet committee, and so on. There is a price to be paid in terms of governance because of the pressures of the public sphere.

"Spin" needs to be seen in that light. In one interpretation "spin" treats the affairs of the state as soap opera. What a journalist or reporter needs is a "story" that develops day by day in a manner that repeats the same facts but with a new twist: in short, a new episode every day, perhaps for a period of four or five days until the story is exhausted but occasionally for longer. "Spin" is an attempt by government to write the next episode of the "story" for the media, and thereby steer it in a desirable direction from the point of view of the government, rather than let the media determine the next episode and the direction in which it goes.[5] The dangers inherent in this approach, which may set a higher value on the "story" than its truths, are self-evident.

Dialogue between Government and the Governed

I now turn to my second point about the great volume of communication that governments contribute to the public sphere, which may or may not be effective. Communication is a central activity of the state in the modern age. It is the bread and butter of everyday life in government. Consultation with the public is one example of this. Thus, in the late 1990s the government issued a document that stated: "Government departments should carry out a full public consultation whenever options are being considered for a new policy or if new regulation is planned," and there is a *Code of Practice on Consultation* to go with it, which continues to be updated.[6] That was sensible, if unexciting, so far as it went. The question is how far governments listen to what they hear in response. In truth, the effectiveness of consultation from the point of view of those consulted may vary in practice depending on how far the government may be clear in its own mind about what it wants to do. In this as in many things timing is all. If a government is uncertain what do on a particular issue and consults with an open mind, the result may be deeply influenced by the outcome of consultation. But if it knows what it wants to do, it may simply decide that consultation has revealed nothing to deflect it from its proposals.

The point goes further than consultation. Governments have in the past from time to time attempted to use public dialogue as a means of implementing their policies or even defining the role of the state. Let me take a very old illustration of this. In September 1965 the then government issued a document called *The National Plan.*[7] Possibly one of the most ambitious documents ever published by a British government, this was in its own words "designed to achieve a 25 per cent increase in national output between 1964 and 1970," seeking to allocate this growth between different industries in considerable detail. To take a random example, clay brick makers were expected to expand their output of Fletton bricks from 3,216 millions to 4,306 millions over those years, an average annual increase of 5 percent; and other industries were expected to implement similar increases. There was even a "Check-list of Action Required," which included such entries as: "There will be a selective programme of agricultural expansion to meet a major part of the additional demand for food . ... Action: Government; Agricultural industry."

How, you might ask, was this plan to be implemented? The answer lay partly in government action in its own sphere but also partly in dialogue. First Secretary of State George Brown noted in his introduction:

> The Government is discussing with industry the measures needed to implement the plan. Leaders in management and the trade unions have a special responsibility but it cannot be left solely to them. The achievement of these aims will depend on the involvement and acceptance of responsibility by individuals at every level of industry. I hope that the Plan ... will be widely read and discussed throughout the country.

What would happen if they failed to implement the National Plan? It said:

> If an industry falls below projection it will be valuable to discover why. In some cases (eg. if consumers' preferences have been wrongly forecast) no action by Government may be indicated. But in other cases (eg. if it is due to the failure of productivity to rise) it will serve as a useful warning signal for action by industry, by Government, or by both in co-operation.[8]

The National Plan was prepared with great effort and published with tremendous fanfare. It was the centerpiece of a whole new government department, the Department of Economic Affairs. But I know of no commentator who regards it as having had any significant beneficial impact on the economy.

There have been many other examples over the years of governments attempting to implement their policies through conversation and public reasoning in the public sphere: for instance, campaigns on energy efficiency, advertisements on public health matters such as AIDS and diet, campaigns to persuade people to take up social security and tax credits, etc. Advertising campaigns by governments have run into hundreds of millions of pounds sterling a year. What has characterized these interventions over forty years has been a decline in state planning and faith instead in the power of the state to persuade the individual. The trend has been to policies of providing a framework for policy, such as the Energy Policy Green Paper of 1978, which proposed a strategy for the sector, public and private, "developed jointly between the Secretary of State, the Management and the Unions"[9] and to campaigns of the kind I have described.

Mrs. Margaret Thatcher began by envisaging in her manifesto of 1979 that there should be "a more open and informed discussion of the Government's economic objectives (as happens in Germany and other countries) so that there is wider understanding of the consequences of realistic bargaining and industrial action."[10] But by the early 1990s the National Economic Development Council (NEDC)—since 1962 the main channel of dialogue between different sectors of the economy, government, and the unions—was wound up; and the public sphere ceased to be a prime vehicle for extending state control. New Labour in 1997 acknowledged this development, openly avowing in Peter Mandelson's words that its strategy was "to move forward from where Margaret Thatcher left off."[11] In place of centralized planning and state control were partnership and the stakeholder economy, both sound instruments of the Third Way;[12] and, less prominently, the growth in regulation and the use of management targets across a wide swathe of the public and voluntary sectors to achieve state objectives.

What is far less evident is how effective these interventions have been. Even direct appeals to self-interest have been known to fail, as with campaigns to increase the take-up of social security and tax credits. There have been many more attempts to communicate the objectives of government than analysis of the effectiveness of these efforts. It is clear that governments are prolific in their contributions to the public sphere. What is less clear is how effective these contributions are as a way of making things happen.

The Silence of the Public Sphere

This brings me to my third point, which refers to the silences in the public sphere. Let me give an example: constitutional change.[13] A massive program of constitutional change was implemented in the late 1990s with relatively little comment in the public sphere. The British tend to react to constitutional matters as though they were under anesthetic, by denial, by simply ignoring them. We entered the Common Market absentmindedly in the early 1970s and then woke up a couple of decades later to debate whether we meant to do it.[14] The same is true of devolution to Scotland, Wales, and Northern Ireland.[15] Legislation went through Parliament easily in the late 1990s. A decade later we are just beginning to debate the role of Scottish MPs in English affairs. One can draw up a roll call of other constitutional changes:

- Reform of the House of Lords with the reduction in hereditary peers.
- Creation of a Supreme Court and reducing the Lord Chancellor to the role of a departmental secretary of state.
- The Human Rights Act.
- Freedom of Information legislation.
- A proliferation of proportional voting mechanisms.
- A stream of legislation on terrorism, which strengthens the hand of the state against the liberty of the individual.
- The decline of cabinet government in favor of decisions taken by small informal groups.
- The use of the Royal Prerogative to authorize military action in Iraq without any formal requirement for Parliamentary approval.

These developments are a tremendous stew of constitutional issues, simmering but never boiling over. There is no coherence to them. Some changes tend to decentralize, some to centralize. But their potential importance is great. They are directly relevant to the public sphere, to the tensions between the individual and the state. But they are discussed relatively little.

Let me give another example: the decline in the role of local government. Over the last twenty-five years there has been a gradual transition of local government from an independent tier of government, accountable to the local electorate, to an agency of central government. It has happened despite the commitment of the Conservative Party in 1987 to "reform local government finance and strengthen local democracy and accountability,"[16] and despite the commitment of New Labour ten years later to "[m]ore independent but accountable local government"[17] in 1997 and to a reform of local government through decentralization of services in 2001.[18]

On 20 October 2004, Charles Clarke, as Secretary of State for Education, made the new relationship clear in a speech to a National Social Services Conference in Newcastle. He identified a need for a new settlement that would

> be honest about the basis of the relationship between local and central government which will vary from service to service. ... I believe the public expect these services [i.e. education and child protection] to be provided as national services which means that local government role is in effect (and I use this word advisably) active agents for central government in relation to these key services.[19]

There was little or no reaction to this major pronouncement of government policy. It was barely reported. One may agree or disagree with the desirability of the move; but the significance for today's discussion is that it is possible for a major change in the character of the institutions of the state to take place without substantial comment or protest. Discussion in the public sphere is selective. At any one time there is an intense focus on some issues but also a silence on other aspects of public life that may in the long run be more important.

Conclusion

To conclude, the concept of the public sphere is both relevant and real when one discusses the role of the state in modern Britain. Changes in the character of the public sphere can be as important in shaping the workings of government as the other way around, as the growth in the power of the media has shown. Governments are necessarily important contributors in the public sphere, but it is not clear that they are always effective in their contributions, if the test is effecting change and implementing policies rather than just the exercise of ephemeral influence. But the interventions of government may be very significant if they mold perceptions of what the government is doing. If a government creates one perception in the public sphere of what it is doing and silently implements another reality, the dangers for the citizen may be very great. It is always important to pay attention to the silences in the public sphere as well as to the noise.

Notes

1. *Eds.*: Chaired by Lord Hutton and commissioned by the UK Labour government, the Hutton Inquiry (2003–4) investigated the death of David Kelly, an employee of the Ministry of Defence, who was named as the source of several BBC reports claiming that the Labour government had knowingly overemphasized the threat of Iraqi weapons of mass destruction. The inquiry ultimately cleared the government of any involvement in Kelly's death, but—in a move widely seen as highly controversial—strongly criticized the BBC. Following the Hutton Inquiry, Greg Dyke, the Director-General of the BBC, and Gavyn Davis, the BBC's chairman, resigned. The final report of the Hutton Inquiry can be found at http://www.the-hutton-inquiry.org .uk/content/report/index.htm (accessed 2 April 2010).
2. *Eds.*: See the contributions by Christopher Kelty and Georgina Born in this volume.
3. *Eds.*: The Guido Fawkes blog can be found at http://order-order.com (accessed 2 April 2010).
4. *Eds.*: See "Semi-connected: British Politics in Missing Out on the Potential of New Media," *The Economist* 387 (19 April 2008): 67–68, and a list of the top political blogs at http://www.totalpolitics.com/blogs/index.php/2009/09/15/the-top-100-political-blogs (accessed 1 April 2010).
5. *Eds.*: See Colin Crouch, *Post-Democracy* (Cambridge, 2004), and Andreas Dörner, *Politainment: Politik in der medialen Erlebnisgesellschaft* (Frankfurt am Main, 2001).
6. *Eds.*: See *Code of Practice on Consultation* (London, 2008), for the most recent version.
7. Cmnd. 2764 = *The National Plan* (London, 1965). *Eds.*: For an early critical assessment of the National Plan, see K. J. Wigley, "The Development of the National Plan," *Journal of the Royal Statistical Society Series* A 129, no. 1 (1966): 6–25. A concise overview of the assumptions and effects of the National Plan can be found in Alec Cairncross, *The British Economy since 1945*, 2nd ed. (Oxford, 1995), pp. 154–56. On the economic and public policy context of the National Plan, see Geoffrey K. Fry, "Whitehall in the 1950s and 1960s," *Public Policy and Administration* 13, no. 2 (1998): 2–25; Noel Thompson, *Political Economy and the Labour Party* (London, 1996), pp. 179–93; and Jim Tomlinson, *Government and the Enterprise since 1900: The Changing Problem of Efficiency* (Oxford, 1994), pp. 246–74.
8. Cmnd. 2764, para. 15.
9. Cmnd. 7101 = *Energy Policy: A Consultative Document* (London, 1978), para. 14.40.
10. *Eds.*: *1979 Conservative Party General Election Manifesto*, http://www.conservative manifesto.com/1979/1979-conservative-manifesto.shtml (accessed 2 April 2010).

11. *Eds.*: Peter Mandelson and Roger Liddle, *The Blair Revolution: Can New Labour Deliver?* (London, 1996), p. xx.

12. In Peter Mandelson's words: "The challenge is to promote competitiveness and support good companies through building stronger partnerships between government and industry, business and all its stakeholders, managers and employees." *Eds.*: For a contextualizing account of the role of government in such efforts, see Allen Wrisque Cline, "The Modernisation of British Government in Historical Perspective," *Parliamentary Affairs* 61 (2008): 144–59.

13. *Eds.*: See the detailed overview and discussion in Nigel Forman, *Constitutional Change in the UK* (London, 2002), as well as the contributions in Andrew McDonald, ed., *Reinventing Britain: Constitutional Change under New Labour* (Berkeley, CA, 2007).

14. *Eds.*: On the history of Britain's complex relationship to the European Union, see Craig Parsons, "Britain and Europe: A Tale of Two Constitutions," in *Reinventing Britain*, ed. McDonald, pp. 170–92; Stephen Wall, *A Stranger in Europe: Britain and the EU from Thatcher to Blair* (Oxford, 2008); Colin Pilkington, *Britain in the European Union Today*, 2nd ed. (Manchester, 2001); Andrew Gamble, "The European Issue in British Politics," in *Britain For and Against Europe: British Politics and the Question of European Integration*, ed. David Baker and David Seawright (Oxford, 1998), pp. 11–30; and Simon Bulmer, "Britain and European Integration: Of Sovereignty, Slow Adaptation, and Semi-detachment," in *Britain and the European Community: The Politics of Semi-detachment*, ed. Stephen George (Oxford, 1992), pp. 1–29.

15. *Eds.*: See Vernon Bogdanor, *Devolution in the United Kingdom* (Oxford, 2001) and, with regard to the effects of devolution on specific policy areas, the contributions in John Adams and Peter Robinson, eds., *Devolution in Practice: Public Policy Differences within the UK* (London, 2002) and its follow-up volume, John Adams and Katie Schmuecker, eds., *Devolution in Practice 2006* (London, 2005).

16. *Eds.*: *The Next Moves Forward: 1987 Conservative Party general Election Manifesto*, http://www.conservativemanifesto.com/1987/1987-conservative-manifesto.shtml (accessed 1 April 2010).

17. *New Labour Because Britain Deserves Better*, http://www.labour-party.org.uk/manifestos/1997/1997-labour-manifesto.shtml (accessed 1 April 2010).

18. *Ambitions for Britain: 2001 Labour Party General Elections Manifesto*, http://www.labour-party.org.uk/manifestos/2001/2001-labour-manifesto.shtml (accessed 2 April 2010).

19. Charles Clarke, "Communities That Care, Services That Deliver: Secretary of State's National Services Conference Speech," http://www.dcsf.gov.uk/speeches/search_detail.cfm?ID=144 (accessed 2 April 2010).

Chapter 2

PUBLIC OPINION AND THE PUBLIC SPHERE

Gordon Graham

The Emergence of the Public Sphere

A common understanding of the very broad sweep of European political history goes something like this.

In the ancient world, and in many other places until recently, political societies could be divided into two classes—the rulers and the ruled. Of course, for a society of any complexity there was also a "middle" class of administrators, tax collectors, and bureaucrats of one kind or another. But the members of this middle class nonetheless fell on the side of "the ruled," and though the division between ruler and ruled might be porous enough to allow the occasional move from one side to the other, this was always a matter of military success or historical chance. Such occasional shifts in power did not alter the underlying political structure in which whatever rights and entitlements the ruled might from time to time enjoy were bestowed by the authority of the ruler, while the ruler's own entitlements to wealth and power derived from conquest, lineage, or divine appointment.

A number of widely different influences and historical events changed this, among them the spread of Christianity into northern Europe, the invention of printing, the Reformation, and the emergence of industrial production. The change that eventually came about in the relationship of ruler to ruled was the complete reversal that John Locke articulates in his *Second Treatise of Civil Government* (1690; the *First Treatise* having sought to demolish Robert Filmer's defense of the divine right of kings). Rulers were now understood as owing their authority to the ruled. The legitimate use of coercion derived from a "social contract" by which "the people" transferred to "the magistrate" their natural rights to self-defense and retributive punishment so that by means of a single, central authority they could more effectively protect their other natural rights to life, liberty, and property. In Hobbes and Locke "the contract" is a one-off event in the distant past. For Locke, but not for Hobbes, a magistrate could forfeit political authority as a result of abuse or corruption, since citizens were ultimately sovereign and could nullify the contract.

Serious critical difficulties soon surfaced for this historical conception. When was the contract made? How can past agreements bind the present? The consequence was that the historical conception came to be replaced by a rather different "idealized" contract continuously renewed by a recurring democratic mandate, expressed in regular general elections. By means of these, "the people" have the opportunity to reject governments of which they disapprove, and so their failure to do so can be taken to constitute a renewal of a quasi-contractual relation in which the ruler is authorized by the ruled.

It is with this reversal of authority, and especially its democratic dimension (the story continues), that there emerged a different "middle class." The members of this new class did not simply interpret and enforce the decisions of rulers, but were increasingly instrumental in both forming and transmitting the "public opinion" that rulers had to take account of if they were not to lose their mandate at the next election. This new "intelligentsia" was distinct from the "ruling class" because its members did not occupy offices in government or its associated bureaucracy. At the same time, they were not merely the "recipients" of laws enacted and political decisions taken; they had a role in determining what these were. Typically, it came to include campaigners, researchers, journalists, writers, broadcasters, and so on; in short, everyone outside the class of legislators, governors, and bureaucrats whose thoughts and activities were also focused on political affairs.

Something like this is the historical backdrop against which Jürgen Habermas advances his conception of the public sphere—"a domain of our social life in which such a thing as public opinion can be formed."[1] The public sphere is where we find the journalists and activists just referred to, but it is not the exclusive preserve of such people. Any and every citizen can occupy it, including citizens who hold political office, so long as they are dealing "with matters of general interest without being subject to coercion." The crucial difference then is not membership but purpose. Government officials are subject to coercion in the opinions they may and may not express; private individuals are concerned with personal decisions, not matters of general interest. It is the public sphere that bridges the two, thus giving rise to a three-level social or political structure.

> In the first modern constitutions the sections listing basic rights provide an image of the liberal model of the public sphere: they guarantee society as a sphere of private autonomy; opposite stands a public power limited to a few functions; between the two spheres, as it were, stands the domain of private persons who have come together to form a public and who, as citizens of the state, mediate the state with the needs of bourgeois society, in order, as the idea goes, to thus convert political authority to "rational" authority in the medium of the public sphere.[2]

In this essay I am not concerned with the general accuracy or inaccuracy of this very broad historical sketch. My interest lies in the way the three-level conception of social and political life resulting from this narrative—political power and private life mediated by the public sphere—has structured a hugely influential component in contemporary political philosophy. More generally, it has shaped the understanding of rational justification in politics. The exercise of political power is justified when it is deployed in accordance with a political consensus forged within the public sphere. Such a conception is crucial to what we might call "political philosophy of the recommending sort" (a phrase of Ted Honderich's[3]), of which John Rawls's A Theory of Justice (1972) is unquestionably the most influential modern example. Its publication was widely heralded as the revival of political philosophy proper, which Rawls was thought to have rescued from the graveyard of logical positivism and linguistic analysis where only such works as Thomas D. Weldon's Vocabulary of Politics (1953) were allowed. There followed an explosion of philosophical reflection in a similar vein, including a great deal that subsequently fell within the broader classification of "applied philosophy" or "philosophy and public affairs."

As is well-known, Rawls's A Theory of Justice imagines an original position in which deliberating parties determine, behind a veil of ignorance and under conditions of uncertainty, what sort of society they would agree to live in. The resulting two principles, relating respectively to restrictions on individual liberty and the division of resources, provide the fundamental structure of any society that can properly be regarded as just. Of course, Rawls's readers are not themselves behind a veil of ignorance.

Neither are they forming a society. The point of the exercise, rather, is an engagement in practical reason that should enable them to arrive at a rationally grounded view of what justice requires and does not require in their own political context. This is how it has been widely understood. Many philosophers have questioned the foundations of Rawls's reasoning, while others have sought to trace the implications of his principles for the political questions of the day, but both groups share the assumption that the adequacy or inadequacy of his theory is an important matter for political and not just philosophical debate. It is on this assumption that the appealing idea of the political philosopher as a public intellectual relies. Political philosophy of the recommending sort requires a public sphere within which to make its recommendations. Without such a sphere, the relation between political theory and political practice becomes seriously problematic, and a question arises over what the significance of political philosophy might be and whether it has any significance at all (though an argument might be made for thinking that practical relevance is a decidedly modern requirement in political philosophy).

The Basis of Political Warrant: Consensus or Reason?

In his essay entitled "The Public Sphere," Habermas expresses doubts about whether such a thing can survive in mass welfare state democracies:

> The political public sphere in the welfare state is characterized by a singular weakening of its critical functions. Whereas at one time publicness was intended to subject persons or things to the public use of reason and to make political decisions susceptible to revision before the tribunal of public opinion, today it has often enough already been enlisted in the aid of the secret policies of interest groups; in the form of "publicity" it now acquires public prestige for persons or things and renders them capable of acclamation in a climate of nonpublic opinion. The term "public relations" itself indicates how a public sphere that formerly emerged from the structure of society must now be produced circumstantially on a case-by-case basis. The central relationship of the public, political parties and parliament is also affected by this change.[4]

This passage appears to record a sociological change characteristic of recent times. Contemporary society can only have witnessed such a change, though, if the concepts employed to describe it are coherent, and there is good reason to think that they are not. The difficulty is this. The concepts of public opinion and the public sphere are related in such a way that increased emphasis on the first implies a diminished role for the second (in at least one of its aspects). In other words, the *triumph* of public opinion by the extension of political influence to all social groups and economic classes regardless of their level of education and social status implies the *demise* of the public sphere in its role as the place where a political consensus on the questions of the day is forged. Once we have grasped this conflict between public opinion and the public sphere, the need to rethink the role of political philosophy and the concept of the public intellectual becomes evident—and pressing.

To understand the full import of this conceptual tension, it is useful to begin by noting that the public sphere has two functions. The first is its role in mediating between rulers and ruled. It does this by providing a "tribunal" of public opinion at which those who exercise political power are held accountable. Its second function is to be the forum in which public opinion is formed. It serves this function by providing a sphere for the free exchange of information and ideas, and by the promotion and protection of the social institutions that make this possible—the media, the universities, political parties, think tanks, and so on. Taken together, these institutions provide not simply for the expression of political opinion, but for its critical scrutiny.

The public sphere can only perform the first of these functions—holding governments properly accountable—if public opinion is the sort of thing that actually *bestows* justification on political decisions and policies (or denies it to them). There appear to be two ways in which this could work. One possibility is that any political action conforming with or adequately reflecting public opinion is *automatically* justified. This makes the basis of political warrant *consensus*. An alternative possibility is that public opinion is the *rational* standard by which political actions are best judged. This makes the basis of political warrant *reason*. The implications of these two possibilities are importantly different.

Consider the first. If simple conformity with public opinion is sufficient to justify political action, it cannot matter how public opinion is formed, or whether it is "formed" in any meaningful sense at all. Political justification is assured so long as rulers act in accordance with the general opinion of the ruled. If this is the case, however, the second of the functions identified above—the critical, or rational screening of political opinion—becomes otiose. The institutions of the public sphere can be replaced (or more accurately displaced) by opinion polling. If what matters is that rulers truly have the support of the ruled in their use of the coercive power of the state, then *why* they have that support is not of any special relevance.

This displacement of the public sphere in modern mass democracies is different from the one Habermas describes in "The Public Sphere." In that essay, his anxiety is about politicians acting in accordance with the private lobbying of special interest groups—big business, wealthy individuals, powerful professional associations, and the like. Such groups and individuals are often able to manipulate appearances by means of public relations (PR)—the apparatus of advertising campaigns, press offices, publicity stunts, and so forth. The very concept of public relations is one that Habermas looks on with suspicion, and he points to the formal institution of basic rights as one possible way of guarding against the danger this kind of manipulation poses. The fact is, however, that populist politicians who use opinion polls or focus groups to discover what "the people" want so that they can secure reelection are as much reaching over the heads of special interest groups as they are reaching over the world of journalists, researchers, and public intellectuals. If what matters to political justification is the consensus of the governed, such a strategy is entirely legitimate. Furthermore, if public opinion is all that matters, irrespective of the way in which it is formed, the fact that it has been powerfully influenced by the public relations activities of individuals or corporations is irrelevant to its justifying function. The point is exactly parallel to a similar one that might be made about elections under universal suffrage. It is quite widely accepted that advertising campaigns of wealthy candidates composed largely of sound bites and electioneering slogans may well influence the outcome of an election far more than serious investigative journalism or policy reviews, but from the point of view of political legitimacy, all that matters is that the successful candidate commands the majority of votes. This is the ultimate test, regardless of why voters voted as they did.

Increasingly, this is how democracy appears to be conceived in many modern societies, to the point where the amount of money a candidate or party can raise for such purposes is almost taken in itself as an indication of the likelihood of electoral success. But, though there is a common tendency to deplore this condition as a debasement of democracy, it is in fact one realization of the nineteenth-century slogan *vox populi, vox Dei*. Whereas at one time people looked to God as the fount of justice and right, or to a political class something along the lines of Plato's philosopher-kings, in a modern liberal democratic society, there can be no higher authority than the voice of the people. The outcome is a political ideal that inevitably lends ultimate authority to public opinion, however it is formed—the very shift that Alexis de Tocqueville noted in *Democracy in America* (1835–40) from Jeffersonian representation to Jacksonian populism.

This important change in political culture from the world of the eighteenth century is not a result of the *destruction* of the public sphere, but its *transformation*, brought about by the elevation of one of its features, namely, public opinion as the proper court of appeal in politics. The alternative is to emphasize the role of the public sphere in *forming* public opinion. With this alternative, though, a different difficulty arises. Among self-appointed public intellectuals there is always a risk of mistaking the opinions of "the chattering classes" for the opinion of the public as a whole. This is not the central problem here, however. Once our attention turns from merely recording public opinion, in the way that opinion polls (and elections) do, to its formation, a question arises as to how we should conceptualize the process of formation. By what mark or standard is public opinion said to be properly "formed"? One possible criterion is purely procedural, the sort of process to which Habermas seems to allude—a fairly widely held consensus on "matters of general interest" emerging from a context that has permitted the exchange of information and ideas "without being subject to coercion." Such a criterion, however, is entirely consistent with the content of that opinion being contrary to truth and rationality. In short, a political policy, or government, that is in accord with the opinions of citizens may yet be contrary to the best interests of citizens. Falsehoods can be widely believed, and convergent prejudices can hold sway with large numbers of people.

This is true not only of circumstances in which racist and other kinds of sectarian prejudices are widespread. It can also hold of well-intentioned subscription to abstract political ideas. The political history of the twentieth century suggests that a plausible example is the once widely held belief that social justice necessarily implies state ownership of the means of production, a belief that resulted in long years of economic stagnation and political repression. It can also hold for strictly empirical beliefs and hypotheses that take on symbolic meaning. It is commonly held, but could well be false, that the recycling of glass and metal effectively combats global warming (as opposed, say, to slowing the rate of increase). In reality, the complexity of the causal connections between climate change, the use of raw materials, and the energy costs involved in recycling is such that understanding it adequately is a major intellectual task, and hard information is difficult to find, even with the resources of the Internet. Since very few people have this information, we should conclude that recycling and more generally "green" policies and parties are sustained by what they symbolize, not by the empirical verification of the collective actions they recommend.

When the free exchange of information and ideas without political or other forms of coercion results in public support for parties and policies detrimental to the interests of citizens, we are presented with a dilemma. Public opinion tells us to pursue a policy that rationality tells us not to.

Whichever horn of the dilemma we choose, its existence is sufficient to show that the formation of public opinion in the public sphere is not the same as its formation by rational inquiry. The implication is evident; there is no ground for accepting Habermas's claim that "the idea of the public sphere itself" signifies "a rationalization of authority in the medium of public discussions among private persons."[5]

The conclusion seems inescapable. Either being in accord with public opinion legitimizes political action regardless of how that opinion has been formed, or only opinion formed within the public sphere legitimates the exercise of political authority. Since there is a tendency to identify the public sphere with "public reason," this suggests that the second has a rational authority that the first does not. But on reflection this turns out not to be the case. Whether we call extensive exchange of information and free discussion of ideas "public reason" or not, the fact remains that though *consensus* may be better that mere *congruence* for certain purposes, it can just as readily conflict with reason in the normal sense. That is to say, it may rest upon false beliefs or be manifestly imprudent. It may also, we might add, be directly contrary to the rights of a minority of citizens, possibly a large minority.

The conclusion must be that whether we simply sound out public opinion or seek to form it we cannot escape this further implication. Political philosophy of the recommending sort (like the investigations of scientists and economists) can at best be one voice in a conversation. The fact that it is (let us agree) the voice of reason does not give it any special authority in that conversation or any greater influence on the outcome over less reflective voices. If this is the case, why would we continue to pursue its conclusions? If its recommendations must take their chance in the political maelstrom of the media, pressure groups, and popular prejudices, why would anyone engage in political philosophy of the recommending sort?

The Public Sphere as Rational Authority

One objection to this analysis of the public sphere is that the argument on which it rests operates with a dichotomy between reason and public discourse that Habermas himself has thrown into doubt. In other words, it ignores the possibility that "conversation" in the public sphere has (or can be given) a distinctive structure that lends it rational authority. This is of course the key notion behind Habermas's concept of "discourse ethics"—an exchange that sets its sights on the "transcendental-pragmatic justification" of norms in response to skeptical doubts about the possibility of any absolute, objective justification. Habermas lays out a fourfold "programmatic justification of discourse ethics" that includes "an explicit statement of normative content (e.g. in the form of discourse rules)," thereby making the structure of the discourse more than merely procedural.[6] If the public sphere were to have a similar structure, and if Habermas's account of discourse ethics is cogent, then we could say that the public sphere *is* a sphere of public reason, and that the consensus that emerges from it *does* bring with it rational authority.

There are, however, two difficulties facing this move. First, in order for such a structure to hold, citizens could only be admitted to the conversation if they are able and prepared to converse in accordance with the rules of discourse. More precisely, the views expressed by some citizens could legitimately be discounted and disregarded because of failure to accord with these rules. The relevant rule as Habermas (following Robert Alexy) formulates it is, "Every subject with the competence to speak and act is allowed to take part in a discourse," but the other side of this rule is that *only* subjects with the competence to speak and act are allowed to take part in a discourse.[7] Depending upon what the standard of competence is taken to be, this could mean that substantial sections of society are excluded from participation in the public sphere. This is an implication that sets the conception at odds with the expectations of contemporary democratic societies in which exclusion is minimal and confined largely to the mentally incompetent and convicted criminals. If, for instance, a basic knowledge of constitutional structures and current events were required (as it often is for "naturalization," i.e., securing citizenship), empirical research has consistently shown that large numbers of voters would count as incompetent.[8] In short, a public sphere modeled on discourse ethics appears to favor a kind of eighteenth-century republicanism that expressly rejected democracy as we now understand it.

Second, rational discourse in the public sphere is perpetually at risk of being sidelined in the actual course of political and social life, as Habermas expressly acknowledges:

> Like all argumentation, practical discourses resemble islands threatened with inundation in a sea of practice where the pattern of consensual conflict resolution is by no means the dominant one. The means of reaching agreement are repeatedly thrust aside by the instruments of force. Hence, action that is oriented toward ethical principles has to accommodate itself to imperatives that flow not from principles but from strategic necessities.[9]

Habermas describes one interpretation of this problem as "trivial" and appears to think that the only substantial issue is how material conditions are to be put in place that will protect practical discourse from such inundation. But this ignores a more important conflict. Talk of force thrusting aside the means of reaching agreement begs the question, since the use of force can itself be such a means. The issue, then, is why someone should *prefer* discourse to force, if the aim in view is securing agreement and force is much more likely than discourse to secure agreement.

This second point has even stronger application if the discourse in view involves philosophy, because philosophy is notorious for generating *disagreement*. In other disciplines such as history, physics, or the biological sciences, convergence on truth secures consensus, and hypotheses that were once viable cease to be so, and recede into the history of the subject. Philosophy knows no such convergence. There are no philosophical doctrines that cannot come around again. This is why, of all the rational discourses one might choose in order to arrive at an agreed political consensus, philosophy appears the least well suited. Consequently, if the need for agreement is paramount, and if the use of force will secure this while engagement in philosophy will not, there is every reason to prefer force. This (or something very close to it) is the line of argument in Hobbes's *Leviathan* (1651).

In summary, the model of discourse ethics as the structure of the public sphere that will convert it from a sphere of unstructured conversational exchange to a sphere of public reason makes that sphere both antidemocratic and ineffectual. The former flaw we could live with, but the latter we could not. In order to see this, it is worth remembering that the primary role of the concept of discourse ethics is in morality, not politics. Its purpose is to show how, in the absence of demonstrable universal norms, morality need not fall prey to either skepticism or cultural relativism. In the context of moral theory, it is the *possibility*, not the *fact*, of agreement that is crucial. But the role it must have in the public sphere is quite different. The legitimation of political action through consensus can only be accomplished by *actual* agreement. Hypothetical consent is not enough. We are free to declare that those who will not abide by the rules of discourse ethics—racists, for instance—have renounced their entitlement to be considered serious contributors to moral debate. It is quite a different matter to declare that they have no claim to citizenship.

I have here been considering Habermas's concept of "discourse ethics" as a kind of public reason. The "idea of public reason" explicitly invoked under that name is more commonly identified with John Rawls, who devotes a substantial chapter to the subject in *Political Liberalism* (1993), the major sequel to *A Theory of Justice*. Rawls's conception of public reason is closely connected with the liberal quest for political legitimacy. Its purpose is to lay down conditions for participation in public discussion that will make the outcome of such discussion capable of justifying political coercion, and this purpose is unmistakably consonant with the idea of a public sphere.

> Our exercise of political power is proper and hence justifiable only when it is exercised in accordance with a constitution the essentials of which all citizens may reasonably be expected to endorse in the light of principles and ideals acceptable to them as reasonable and rational.[10]

This assertion is importantly different from a very similar one—namely, the view that the exercise of political power is proper and hence justifiable when it is in accordance with a constitution, the essentials of which are reasonable and rational. Between constitutional provisions and what is reasonable and rational, Rawls places endorsement on the part of citizens. This is why some conception of *public* reason is required, and with it some concept of the public sphere—because it is only with the existence of these that there is any basis for the element doing all the justificatory work to show that "all citizens may reasonably be expected to endorse" those provisions. The picture is in sharp contrast to, for instance, a straightforward appeal to natural law or human rights as tests for the validity of constitutional provisions. Rawls, of course, rules out any appeal of this kind to a "comprehensive" moral doctrine, which is why he requires the middle step of hypothetical endorsement arrived at through the medium of public reason. Habermas's framework of thought (as I understand it) allows such moral doctrines to act as the ultimate tests of political authority, but only insofar as they are the outcome of discourse ethics in the public sphere. In the end, though, both contentions amount to pretty much the same, and are thus both subject to the objections I have raised.

Conclusion

The position we have reached is this. A widely held conception thinks of the political structure of modern societies as having three levels (or perhaps comprising three interlocking circles). One level is made up of the ruling class that governs and another of private individuals subject to that government. In between is a mediating public sphere, open to all citizens and constituted by an uncoerced exchange of information and ideas. It is in this public sphere that government is subjected to the tribunal of public opinion. Political actions must pass this test if they are to be exercises in rational authority rather than arbitrarily imposed dictates. The picture is a plausible and influential one, but closer examination reveals that the crucial connection with rationality is impossible to sustain. Either the test is public opinion, in which case it is of no consequence how it is arrived at, or the test is rational scrutiny, in which case the mere opinions of citizens as revealed by opinion polls and the like should be ignored. The additional elements in both Habermas and Rawls that might be called upon to address this difficulty—discourse ethics and public reason—which at first sight offer the possibility of construing the public sphere as itself a sphere of reason, founder on essentially the same dichotomy; either political consensus is what we ought to have in view, in which case coercion might be far more effective at securing it, or it is rational justification, in which case what citizens actually agree about is irrelevant.

If all this is correct, a question arises for "political philosophy of the recommending sort." Its role, and its significance, depends upon some such concept as the public sphere. If the public sphere is fundamentally unstable—threatened by popular democracy on the one side and the authority of reason on the other—there can be no role for political philosophy of the recommending sort, whose ambition precisely is to be a rationally authoritative contributor to debates in that sphere. The most it can be is one more voice in the political cacophony of voices. And given its distinctive character as a mode of thought that typically raises critical questions rather than producing definitive answers in which intellectual opinion converges, it is more likely to intensify the cacophony than generate rational harmony.

What, then, is political philosophy to do? The answer is to content itself with the Hegelian dictum that the owl of Minerva takes its flight at dusk. Philosophical reflection applied to politics is no different than philosophical reflection applied to anything else. It offers a distinctive understanding of the sphere in view—humanity as *zoon politikon*—but it is no more capable of directing that sphere, or of making recommendations within it, than metaphysics is capable of constituting matter or recommending materials. Philosophy, Peter Winch once remarked, can no more tell us what to attach importance to than geometry can tell us where to stand.[11] It would be odd for geometers to have ambitions contrary to this perception, in the way that moral and political philosophers have done. But if they did, it would be equally odd for them to wonder whether there was anything for them to do once they had been persuaded to abandon the positions.

Notes

1. Jürgen Habermas, "The Public Sphere," in *Contemporary Political Philosophy: An Anthology*, ed. Robert E. Goodin and Philip Pettit (Oxford, 1997), p. 105.
2. Ibid.
3. Ted Honderich, *Political Violence* (Ithaca, NY, 1976).

4. Habermas, "The Public Sphere," p. 106.
5. Ibid.
6. Habermas, "Discourse Ethics: Notes on a Program of Philosophical Justification," in *Moral Consciousness and Communicative Action*, trans. Christian Lenhardt and Shierry Weber Nicholsen (Cambridge, MA, 1990), pp. 43-115: 96–97.
7. Ibid., p. 89.
8. See, for instance, Robert Erikson and Kent Tedin, *American Public Opinion: Its Origins, Content, and Impact*, 7th ed. (New York, 2006).
9. Habermas, "Discourse Ethics," p. 106.
10. Rawls, *Political Liberalism*, p. 217.
11. Peter Winch, "Moral Integrity," in *Ethics and Action* (London, 1972), p. 191.

Chapter 3

THE TYRANNY OF MAJORITY OPINION IN THE PUBLIC SPHERE

Gary Wihl

First published in 1962, Habermas's *The Structural Transformation of the Public Sphere* has lost none of its originality.[1] Habermas was the first critical philosopher to introduce a rich concept of the public into the fields of political philosophy, legal theory, discourse analysis, and intellectual history. But have we lost sight of that originality? Or the implications of this early work for a host of current issues, including legal debates over the boundaries of the public versus the private, public opinion as a political tool, or the division of the public into majority and minority voting blocs? In this chapter I would like to restore an appreciation of the novelty of the public as a term of critical theory but also assess some of its limitations in Habermas's original formulations. We are indebted to Habermas for placing the concept of the public sphere at the center of questions about legitimate, rational governance within modern liberal democracies. At the same time, it is fair to say that the intellectual energy unleashed by bringing to light an original formulation of a public sphere exacts a price upon its philosophical sources. Concepts like privacy, public opinion, and tolerance end up as weak features of the modern liberal state in Habermas's account. Even as we respect Habermas's larger effort to draw the limitations and flaws of the liberal state, there may be other ways to reconstruct the value and critical function of these concepts.

Habermas and the Public Sphere

In the first part of this chapter, I would like to examine a portion of Habermas's dialectic, focusing on his discussion of opinion because it leads directly to interesting questions about privacy, tolerance, and the status of minorities. According to Habermas, opinion is both the first articulation of the emergent public and also a very weak category of critical reflection, subject to instability and communicative distortion.[2] It is perfectly fit for dialectical analysis, containing contradictions that lead to the undoing of opinion as a force for critical reflection. My overall aim is to capture Habermas's original insights into the workings of one dimension of the public sphere, centered on the analysis of opinion, and then look beyond Habermas for rather more positive considerations of the meaning of private judgment or majority opinion. I will present a summary of the main arguments from Part IV of *The Structural Transformation of the Public Sphere*, concentrating on the discussions of Alexis de Tocqueville and J. S. Mill.[3] The writings of Tocqueville and Mill are at the crux of the issues about opinion.

How does opinion, in the technical sense of *doxa*, transform into *opinion publique* or *öffentliche Meinung*? The early philosophical sense of uncertainty, revisable judgment, speaks to the open-endedness of the modern public sphere, the inevitable emergence of various degrees of agreement about major political questions, including the status of religious belief, the speed of democratic reform, separation of powers in representative government, and the authoritative claims of the interests of the state. From Thomas Hobbes's account of religious civil war, to John Locke on property, to Jean-Jacques Rousseau on social vice, to Hegel on the historical progress of autonomous identity, opinion is defined as a fluid mixture of privately held beliefs, sanctions, publicity, and collective interests. The public sphere is, by definition, a gradual process of enlightenment, rational debate, and greater social justice. Opinion conveys the steps within that gradual process, associated positively with the emergence of a private zone of judgment, a precursor to critical judgment, or associated negatively with various cultural sanctions, such as the public censure of vice, as in having a bad opinion of someone.[4]

According to Habermas, opinion does not attach itself properly to public opinion as a method of democratic argument and political judgment until we come to writers like Edmund Burke and Rousseau. In Burke's writings on America, public opinion now conveys the important principle of consent with the actions of a representative government; legislation must heed public opinion in order to acquire legitimacy with the governed.[5] Moving beyond private belief and reflection, or moral pressure exercised through civic association, public opinion gradually becomes an integral feature of democratic government; moreover, government, crucially, becomes a matter of public concern, something that is discussed openly among the literati, merchants, and landowners.

Habermas's goal is to sort out the progressive elements of public opinion from the emerging negative ones. Fluidity of opinion is necessary to the deliberative process; but distorted opinion erodes the public sphere. Kant and Hegel represent the great leap forward in attaching a stronger account of moral reflection and historical progress to the formation of public opinion as a vehicle of public reason. Philosophers, as a class of professionals, and a growing domain of civil law add reflective depth to the progression of opinion, which, according to Habermas, becomes public agreement or *das öffentliche Zusammenstimmen*.[6] Public agreement harmonizes with the entire logic of Habermas's argument from the early work on the public sphere, through the theory of communicative action up to his most recent work on law, because this public just is the realization in politics of a form of consciousness. The totalizing perspective is a constant in Habermas's writing, and in *Between Facts and Norms* (1992) he writes:

> [T]he public sphere can best be described as a network for communicating information and points of view ... the streams of communication are, in the process, filtered and synthesized in such a way that they coalesce into bundles of topically specific *public* opinions. Like the lifeworld as a whole, so, too, the public sphere is reproduced through communicative action ... it is tailored to the *general comprehensibility* of everyday communicative practice.[7]

Discordant elements remain despite the totalizing movement toward comprehensibility.

In Hegel, the underlying weakness of opinion, as opposed to knowledge, becomes apparent in the growing contradictions of the modern state. For Hegel, political power drives the articulation of freedom through its stages of progress, but opinion fails to carry the collective expression of a public that Kant projected. Habermas sums up the situation in the following way:

> Hegel took the teeth out of the idea of the public sphere of civil society; for anarchic and antagonistic civil society did not constitute the sphere ... in which autonomous private people related to one another. Thus it did not provide the basis on which a public of private people could translate political into rational authority.[8]

By the time Habermas's discussion reaches Tocqueville and Mill, antagonisms in civil society are too readily accepted as a feature of the democratic state. Tocqueville and Mill are classically liberal in their efforts to define a sphere of private judgment, now the realm of things like religious belief, childrearing practices, or aesthetic taste—all of which should remain outside the purview of the government. They represent a partial turning back to a lighter framework of opinion, one that fills up the public sphere with controversies, a burgeoning periodical press, a host of moral conflicts that stir the pot of congress and parliament but do not lead to greater justice.

Mill's essay on liberty provides a rich discussion of public opinion, tolerance, and persecution, within the framework of an argument about the legitimate use of legislative authority over the individual's right to pursue the religion, occupation, and recreations of his or her choice.[9] But Mill's use of the term opinion does not appear to carry much philosophical weight. It lacks the technical depth of Rousseau's *opinion publique* or Hegel's *öffentliche Meinung*, and so for Habermas it fails to illuminate the substance of rational public deliberation, focused on the ends of reason and justice, which make up the modern public sphere. Mill's extensive interest and commentary on public opinion is rather more of a bibliographical necessity for Habermas: the acknowledgment of a moral thinker who has written on the topic of public opinion, but whose work is largely on the sidelines of the tradition that runs from Hobbes and Locke to Rousseau, Kant, and Hegel. Mill was, of course, directly influenced by Tocqueville and wrote a lengthy review of *Democracy in America* (1835–40), where in fact he responds with keen interest to Tocqueville's analysis of public opinion, best known for the version of public opinion that Tocqueville dubbed the tyranny of the majority in Chapter 15 of the first volume of *Democracy in America*.[10] From the point of view of intellectual history and influence, Habermas is right to treat Tocqueville and Mill as a pair. But are they marginal to the line of inquiry about the public sphere? Habermas is quick to categorize Tocqueville and Mill as liberals, too narrowly focused upon the question of protecting individual freedom from abusive authority. This swift categorization of opinion in Mill's writings obscures the conflict between majority and minority opinion, perhaps the most novel feature of Mill's essay on liberty.

Isaiah Berlin offers a good description of Mill as the reformer and politician brandishing opinion all over the place:

> [Mill] declared that a revolution that would kill all men with an income of more than £500 per annum might improve things … he expressed delight at Palmerston's fall over the Bill that sought to make conspiracy against foreign despots a criminal offense … he denounced the Southern States in the American civil war, or made himself violently unpopular by speaking in the House of Commons … for the rights of women, of workers, or of

colonial peoples, and thereby made himself the most passionate champion in England of the insulted and the oppressed.[11]

But the description of opinion's circulation and sanctions leaves big ideas about the systemic causes of disparities in wealth, in colonialism, in gender inequality out of the equation. Habermas writes:

> Liberals like Tocqueville and Mill, therefore, who favored the process [of public opinion] devalued its consequences. This was because the unreconciled interests ... which flooded the public sphere were represented in a divided public opinion and turned public opinion ... into a coercive force, whereas it had once been supposed to dissolve any kind of coercion into the compulsion of reason.[12]

Tolerance, fallibility, limited government, and protection make up the vocabulary of Mill's writings. Even Berlin concedes that the essay on liberty is not the most original writing we can find in mid-Victorian England.[13] Similarly, Tocqueville is fascinated with the rapidity of free association and party formation in America in the 1830s, but he limits his philosophical discourse to notions of the sovereignty of the people and of civic engagement brought about by the ability to acquire property.

From the moment that public opinion takes on coercive force and loses its philosophical connection with reason, Habermas writes it off as perspectivist epistemology, as a shallow competition of interest, and ultimately as a reactionary force. Too many opinions lead to the blockage of electoral reform. Eventually, privacy—which had emerged as the source of reflective consciousness and deeply held belief—becomes its own distinct sphere in contrast to the public, further weakening the political function of public opinion.

Given Habermas's original reconstruction of Rousseau, Kant, and Hegel as precursors of communicative reason, it is disappointing to see Tocqueville and Mill used as straw men for rather predictable flaws in liberalism. If we look more closely at the literature on Tocqueville and Mill, however, their most striking contribution to public opinion has to do with the emergence of majorities and minorities within the public sphere. When Habermas speaks of the divisions that turn public opinion into a coercive force, he pays no attention to the nature of that division. Compare his remark on coercion, quoted above, to Mill's commentary on Tocqueville:

> The silent sympathy of the majority may support on the scaffold the martyr of one man's tyranny; but, if we would imagine the situation of a victim of the majority itself, we must look to the annals of religious persecution for

a parallel ... In America tyranny will seldom use the instrument of law, because there is, in general, no permanent class to be tyrannized over. The subjects of oppression are casual objects of popular resentment ... Already, in the United States, the spirit of outrage has raised a spirit of resistance to outrage; of moral resistance first ... if that fails, physical resistance will follow. The majority ... will be taught by experience that it cannot enjoy both the advantages of civilized society, and the barbarian liberty of taking men's lives or property at its discretion. Let it once be generally understood that minorities will fight, and majorities will be shy of provoking them.[14]

I quote this passage at length because it points to a discussion of majoritarian politics that does not fit neatly into Habermas's structural schema. Majority opinion is not simply divided; it involves redress and dissent, and it provokes reflection in the mind of the majority about its use of moral coercion. How well do we really understand this so-called divided opinion, and why do Tocqueville and Mill frame it in terms of majorities and minorities rather than harm directed against an individual?

Mill and Majoritarian Politics

Jeremy Waldron has written a remarkable essay that asks us to take seriously Mill's use of the term opinion throughout the essay On Liberty (1859).[15] Waldron goes even further in asserting that On Liberty has been systematically misread as an argument about the limits of criminal law, when in fact its discussions of opinion and coercion reflect the great movements in nineteenth-century social theory[16] from Tocqueville through Marx and Emile Durkheim to Max Weber. Why? Mill obviously shares with Tocqueville an awareness of increasing conformity of opinion, and he follows Tocqueville in his discussion of the coercive potential of opinion with regard to human conduct and morality. Habermas, on the other hand, sees this as a veering away from the critical path that leads from Hegel to Marx: Mill focuses on the liberal protection of the individual from harm instead of pursuing the path to universal reason. But Waldron argues that coercive opinion in Mill's essay is directly related to the effort to rise above mass timidity and collective mediocrity and the blandest platitudes; it is a force that may build moral discourse.[17]

Waldron begins by taking seriously Mill's claim that moral and intellectual positions must be contested in order for them to gain public acceptance. While some opinions may be genuinely coercive, say the colonization of the African continent, others are subject to contestation: voting rights, divorce laws, child labor, the working population's need for a day of rest, the right to a trial by peers, etc. Particularly vexing, however, are those that concern moral issues. Here is the real crux of debate for Waldron:

> Mill's overall case depends on the existence of vigorous argumentative action. So because he thinks some forms of social interaction are coercive, it is incumbent on him to find some way of distinguishing the argumentative from the coercive. But that distinction—all very well when persuasion is being contrasted with the violent means characteristic of the state—is much harder to draw when argument is being contrasted with the imperceptible pressure of public opinion.[18]

In fact, Mill offers us a spectrum of public opinion and a competing model of the public sphere. There is outright coercive opinion, manifested in the interests of the state, where harm to individuals and groups is a real possibility. There is social pressure and conformism, and there is contested opinion, where persuasion and debate have to be sifted out from sheer coercion. Within the last decades of the twentieth century, contested opinion might be seen in debates about abortion rights, discrimination in the form of subtle racism and sexism, the legitimacy of certain genetic therapies, or the degrees of tolerance for the use of alcohol, tobacco, and drugs. Waldron wants to make more room in the public sphere for contested opinion, particularly before it reaches the stage of statist coercive opinion, or legislation, but not where it can be safely tucked away from the public in the form of private opinion. Because coercion is on a scale that includes public persuasion, Waldron sees much greater latitude in Mill for the role of opinion in the modern public sphere.

But there is another feature in Tocqueville and Mill that Waldron treats too lightly in his discussion: the formation of majority and minority opinion. Waldron tests coercive opinion in Mill by applying it to the example of Queensberry's prosecution of Oscar Wilde in the notorious trial for the homosexual corruption of Queensberryy's son. How can Wilde's liberty to live the private life that he desires, his individual liberty, fit with Queensberry's liberty to express the view that Wilde's life is corrupt, unhealthy, and depraved? Moreover, should Wilde be made to suffer, as he clearly did in prison, for leading a depraved life? To solve this moral conundrum, as Waldron calls it, there needs to be some social space, a public sphere, where beliefs about homosexuality can be contested. Only the process of contestation, some common ground between Queensberry and Wilde, will advance our moral understanding of active liberty. Mere tolerance for the individual returns us to a legalistic argument that diminishes the role of public persuasion. Coercion of homosexuals leads back to the tyranny of the majority. Waldron only hints at a solution when he reminds us that Queensberry versus Wilde is of limited public interest, unless we begin to see the contest as greater than the conflicting liberties of two individuals. We must take account of the larger background, the potential for collective action by the public against homosexuals or the danger that Queensberry's attack is the forerunner of a mass response to people like Wilde.[19] Waldron never quite fleshes out this portion of his argument, but I believe it holds the key to our estimation of Mill's contribution to the definition of the public sphere. Mill's arguments about coercive public opinion do in fact belong to a larger framework of justice and reason as defined by John Rawls.

Like Mill, Rawls is frequently pegged as too liberal, a defender of equality and tolerance who fails to account for the complexities of civil society. But Rawls's discussion of majority and minority speech in A *Theory of Justice* (1971) has not received sufficient attention. Rawls describes a built-in imperfection of constitutional democracies, the likelihood that the majority will create laws that infringe upon the liberty and equality of minorities from time to time.[20] A minority may be racially constituted, religious, socioeconomic, immigrant, farm-based, industrial-based, or gender-based. The delicate balance between majoritarian politics and the social ideal of justice may provoke acts of dissent, which test the justness of certain laws by the minority. According to Rawls, acts of dissent may take the form of militancy or civil disobedience; that is, they are public actions that defy the law but also create a public awareness for the fact that the law is harming the minority.[21] Every constitutional democracy, in Rawls's view, should uphold a definition of civil disobedience.

Rawls introduces a novel concept when he proposes a definition of civil disobedience as a collective form of speech, in a broad sense, a mode of address in actions and words. Civil disobedience speech is how the minority addresses the injustice perpetrated by the majority so as to cause the majority to amend legislation. This idea of a particularly collective form of speech stays within the law, but it is not the same thing as free speech or peaceful assembly. He is rather more interested in a genuinely political process on a collective level, the orderly conflict between majority and minority views within the constitutional state. Civil disobedience falls somewhere between Thoreau, the archetype of solitude and withdrawal, and the militant who has moved outside the bounds of law. When civil disobedience reaches the critical mass of a minority opinion it becomes a form of collective speech addressed to the majority. As such, the majority is made to realize that it cannot continue to impose its views on a minority without risking an escalation to social violence. Civil disobedience today refers to the cluster of issues that Tocqueville, Mill, and Waldron name the tyranny of the majority, coercive public opinion, and liberty of speech and thought. The coercive element is not set in strict opposition to reason, and the public sphere is not reduced to legalism and rights talk. Rather, liberals like Mill, Waldron, and Rawls attempt to provide order and deliberative weight to the kinds of moral conflicts that they see at work in the emergence of modern democratic states. Opinion increases in strength as it enters the public sphere, but the question then becomes: how do we dissolve its coercive force in the appropriate way? To treat the status of public opinion largely as false consciousness or ideology may be true in certain cases in which the interests of the state lead to measurable injustices and harms. On the other hand, we are faced with daily public debate about the extent of our privacy, about human reproduction as a form of property, about subtle forms of discrimination, and about religious conflicts within and between states.

Rawls's account of civil disobedience and nearly perfect justice also provides a point of transition for a reexamination of private opinion. Private opinion, like mere tolerance of opinion, is a major weakness of the liberal state that foreshadows the destruction of Habermas's public sphere. Privacy, of course, is a vast field for analysis, and for the purposes of this chapter I shall primarily consider recent controversies embedded within the legal framework of the US constitution.[22] As Raymond Geuss notes, with a strident note of reluctance:

> Much as we might regret it, we are in fact living in a time and at a place in which we do not really have any effective general framework for thinking about politics apart from liberalism, so the main place that a distinction between public and private occupies in such a general scheme is in the context of a defense of the private sphere from encroachment by the public, where that public is construed as the coercive apparatus of government … or the subtle pressure of public opinion.[23]

This is indeed precisely the formulation of coercive opinion that has its roots in Mill. Geuss sees many flaws in the parochialism of liberal politics, in the narrow construal of human agency and collective responsibility, but he takes it as a given that any philosophical consideration of privacy and public opinion must work its way through the legalistic paradigm of individual protections and harms that constitute contemporary discourse about public coercion. My argument goes in a different direction, however, picking up on Waldron and Rawls's insights that we need to think through the relationship between coercion and majority opinion *within* the liberal scheme that we now occupy. Geuss and Habermas, on the other hand, are more interested in rebuilding the public sphere as a vehicle of critical reason. Habermas attempts to step outside the profusion of opinions that circulate through the media and attach truth conditions to communicative actions. Geuss follows John Dewey and suggests that there is no turning back to a monolithic distinction between private and public. Instead, we must recognize multiple publics and steer our course in a highly pluralistic moral world, refusing to overcategorize goods and rights as belonging to one sphere or the other. My own contribution is rather more modest: there is a strain of liberal argument, which is indebted to the legal emphasis on harms and protections, but which introduces an analysis of *majority* opinion into questions about coercion, protection, and harm.

The Right to Privacy: *Roe v. Wade*

In the American version of liberal democracy, privacy is a matter of legal protections, liberties, and unenumerated rights—a cluster of issues that has produced a canon of decisions about contraception, abortion, intimate practices, and human sexuality. The legal terms of the debate about privacy are purposefully narrow and case-specific, but they point to very large questions that concern privacy in relation to a larger public sphere of moral debates and controversies. Morality and law have become intertwined in Supreme Court justices' dissents, in narrow majorities, in the militancy of pro-life groups, and in the big questions about the relationship of the legislative process to judicial activism. It is necessary to work through these issues in the terms that are in play, namely, family values, the rights of the unborn, freedom to choose, and the development of the human fetus. My ultimate goal is to tie the underlying problems connected with privacy back to the larger question of the operation of the public sphere. Just as minority opinion in the public sphere may be reconstructed out of its negative version in Habermas, so too private judgment may be reconstructed out of its apparent problems in relation to the public sphere.

Perhaps it is best to start with the exact issue of fundamental rights in Justice Harry A. Blackmun's opinion for the majority in *Roe v. Wade* in 1973.[24] There were many questions before the Court, including the medical debate about the trimester sequence, the history of the medical community's practice and attitude to abortion, the Hippocratic oath to protect life, and, most of all, the compelling interests of the states in protecting human life, including the so-called rights of the unborn (which have never been recognized in law, as opposed to the criminalization of acts of feticide). While all these issues played into the reasoning of the Court, the constitutional issue that needed to be decided was whether there exists a fundamental right that would secure a women's freedom to obtain an abortion legally within the first trimester of a pregnancy. By a

7:2 majority, the Court stated and upheld the existence of such a right. The right was first articulated by the district court in Texas that ruled in favor of Roe and her coappellants: the fundamental right of single women and married persons to choose whether to have children is protected by the Ninth Amendment through the Fourteenth Amendment. The Ninth Amendment, which concerns unenumerated rights that are retained by the people, made privacy first enter the canon of legal decisions, in the so-called penumbra of rights articulated by Justice William O. Douglas in the earlier case on contraception, *Griswold v. Connecticut*.[25] The Fourteenth Amendment, which primarily concerns due process, offered new constitutional protections for liberty.

Ellen Alderman and Caroline Kennedy offer a neat summary of the legacy of the Fourteenth Amendment in their book *The Right to Privacy* (1995):

> Beginning nearly a hundred years ago the Supreme Courts interpreted liberty as encompassing certain fundamental rights not specifically listed in the Bill of Rights. Giving substance to the term liberty in this way is known as substantive due process. In this view, rights deeply rooted in this Nation's history and traditions and implicit in the concept of ordered liberty such that neither liberty nor justice would exist if they were sacrificed are protected.[26]

That tradition of ordered liberty encompasses the right to decide a child's education, the right to interracial marriage, and the right to use contraceptives. All these rights of privacy and ordered liberty offer constitutional protection against state governments that have attempted to outlaw citizens' decisions to pursue a particular choice with regard to life and death issues. As this tradition of interpretation has evolved and strengthened, it has not at all been clear whether fundamental liberty and privacy belong to a coherent set of beliefs and practices that could be set beside the compelling interests of the state. All that we know for sure within the Court's decision making and its use of precedent is that, at certain times, it has felt the need to step in and offer a fundamental, incontrovertible right to individuals as a protection against certain coercions of a moral nature put forward by state legislatures. The battle between fundamental rights that are protected and the compelling interests of the state is at the heart of the American constitutional experiment, and the tension between these poles, fundamental and compelling, is what brings certain issues to the level of a constitutional matter in the first place.

Having ascertained that a fundamental right was in question in *Roe v. Wade*, the Court could only provide a rather weak description of its substance:

Maternity, or additional offspring, may force upon the woman a distressful life and future. Psychological harm may be imminent. Mental and physical health may be taxed by child care. There is also the distress, for all concerned, associated with the unwanted child, and there is the problem of bringing a child into a family already unable, psychologically and otherwise, to care for it. In other cases, as in this one, the additional difficulties and continuing stigma of unwed motherhood may be involved.[27]

I think it is very important to pause over these words, since they hold the crux of all the debates that have followed and since they influence where we find ourselves today in matters of privacy, particularly as they bear on issues of public concern. On the surface, none of these considerations seem extraordinarily in need of legal protection, though they most definitely demand respect and fairness.

The decision as to whether or not to proceed with a pregnancy certainly imposes terrific psychological burdens, and all of these factors mentioned by the Court could apply as well in the life of a woman who decides to proceed with the pregnancy. The health risks, various kinds of pride and pressure that have become associated with childrearing, etc., cut both ways in the decision. Nevertheless, the Court offered these risks and pressures the category of fundamental protection, the level of protection offered by the Constitution, because the decision is deeply personal and bears upon a whole pattern of life. As Justice Blackmun noted, only personal rights that can be deemed fundamental or implicit in the concept of liberty are included in the guarantee of personal privacy.[28] In 1992, Justice Sandra Day O'Connor affirmed the same principle in her opinion on *Planned Parenthood v. Casey:*

> It is a promise of the Constitution that there is a realm of personal liberty which the government may not enter … At the heart of liberty is the right to define one's own concept of existence, of meaning, of the universe, and of the mystery of human life. Beliefs about these matters could not define the attributes of personhood were they formed under compulsion of the State.[29]

The Court could not permit state legislatures to intrude into matters that could have a profound bearing on the shape of a person's life, although the debate continues to rage over the true profundity of that choice. The Court has backtracked on many issues that would support the decision, including funding, informed participation by parents, guardians and spouses, medical consultation, and the two subsequent trimesters where the balance shifts to the state's compelling interest. Inescapably, the protection and defense of a fundamental right that is not specifically enumerated in the constitution must draw upon those sources and traditions that Alderman and Kennedy cited, such as historically rooted rights and traditions that are "implicit in the concept of ordered liberty."[30]

At this point, I would like to frame rather more starkly the tension within a fundamental right to privacy. Is privacy a zone that places a great burden upon the conscience of an individual? Is the Court affirming protection for a core moment of one's life that could shape a host of attachments, associations, obligations for many years to come? Or is the Court actually carving out a zone of personal choice by treating privacy in isolation from any normative frameworks that would give it substantive purpose, that would justify an order around liberty reflected in a way of life? This is where we reenter larger questions about the function of the public sphere. These questions find radically opposite answers in the writings of Ronald Dworkin and Michael Sandel.

Fundamental or Foundational?

Ronald Dworkin tries to rebuild a strong constitutional right to choose, but he cannot address social conflict on a larger scale, that is, the pressures to legislate morality. He presents a moment of isolated, private judgment that is rich in values and norms, but it cannot be construed as public speech, even under the protections derived from the First Amendment. On the opposite side, Michael Sandel takes on the problem of family law and the legal boundaries of privacy by examining the broader moral condition of society, but he is unable to point to a framework of reason or collective debate that would guide public discussion. In other words, Habermas's initial concerns about the collapse of the public sphere reappear in the polarization of the privacy issue: should we strengthen private judgment and leave matters of childbirth to individuals, or should we return legislative power to the government in the hope of regaining a shared moral framework? To answer this question we have to return to the previous discussion of Mill and Rawls and reconstruct the debate about privacy in terms that could rebuild the public sphere.

In an essay entitled "Unenumerated Rights: Whether and How *Roe* Should be Overruled," published in 1992, Dworkin set out an argument for protecting the right to choose under the First Amendment rather than the Ninth or the Fourteenth Amendments.[31] His argument would find fuller expression in connection with assisted suicide in the book that followed, *Life's Dominion* (1994).[32] There are many technical aspects to his argument that are not relevant to this particular discussion, such as his dismissal of the whole debate as to whether a fetus is a constitutional person. Central to his argument about privacy, however, is an argument about constitutional coherence and integrity, about the nature of rights themselves. If privacy evades a host of distracting questions about the intent of the framers, or the meaning of the Ninth Amendment, it must cohere with the principles that guide the constitution as whole. First and foremost, says Dworkin, is the tradition of religious and personal freedom, which, admittedly, frequently collides with the competing tradition of guarding public moral space.[33] I have already identified this conflict in the background of the protection of a fundamental right. What is new, however, is the deep sense Dworkin attaches to the concept "fundamental": the latter is not equal to the right to obtain an abortion, but refers to a quasi-religious right to follow a belief about the value of life, on the same level that we allow for differences in fundamental beliefs about God. Thus, a woman who must bear a child whose life will be deformed or stunted or impoverished is forced to act in defiance of her own beliefs about what respect for human life means and requires.[34] These decisions are foundational to the rest of one's moral personality, interwoven with other major structural convictions of one's life. This level of belief, he goes on, should be deemed "religious" within the meaning of the First Amendment. In short, the Ninth or Fourteenth Amendments do not offer enough protection for the right to choose. Matters of life and death are too grave by their very nature to be subject to state coercion or moral conformity.

However we may argue with Dworkin over the interpretation of the Constitution, he is making a philosophical argument about the kind of deliberation and reflection that underlies any decision involving life and death. As long as we are fully assured that these decisions are not frivolous, light, or expedient, but actually contain profound tests of belief about matters of the deepest value, they must be protected. In fact, when the community is divided with regard to what the best understanding of the value in question requires, it is all the more reason for the state not to curtail liberty. The moment of choice is beyond secular convictions about morality, and it is beyond competing interests of particular people. Dworkin appreciates Rawls for offering a good account of justice, but one that is not relevant to the level of constitutional protection that applies to the cases of profound belief and conviction.[35]

If we argue that governments may not impose legislation that defines one point of view about the sanctity of life, we have arrived at a much richer definition than Blackmun's about the contents of the fundamental decision. But Dworkin appears to fill in the space of privacy with remarkable burdens and tests. The pregnant woman is pictured as facing a momentous decision about the entire meaning of life, and I suggest there is an element of fantasy in this picture that is being used to uphold a certain kind of argument about the coherence of constitutional interpretation. The value of this fantasy is that it points us to one of the consequences of protecting privacy as a fundamental right. For privacy to be fundamental, it must have substance.

The other direction belongs to Michael Sandel, in his book *Democracy's Discontent* (1996), specifically the chapter on privacy rights and family law in which he presents a counternarrative to Dworkin.[36] Far from having deepened the order of liberty, the Court has confused liberty with a particular philosophy of voluntarism through a sequence of poor decisions about privacy involving marriage, procreation, contraception, and abortion. In permitting greater freedom of choice over these intimate decisions, the Court has effectively created the unencumbered self, the end product of liberal neutralism and proceduralism with respect to moral conflict. Richard Rorty and others have questioned Sandel's sad, metaphysical diagnosis of a republic in decay, and I am largely sympathetic to their criticisms. But the contrast with Dworkin bears some attention and takes us back to the language of Justice Blackmun in *Roe v. Wade*. Is the decision to abort a moment of deep value restructuring in the course of an individual's life? Or is it a moment of low-level choice concerned with a network of values and beliefs found in the coexistence of marriage partners, families, communities, and obligations? In *Griswold v. Connecticut* and *Eisenstadt v. Baird*,[37] two pivotal contraception cases, Sandel finds two innovations: the explicit change was to redescribe the bearers of privacy rights from persons qua participants in the social institution of marriage to persons qua individuals, independent of their roles or attachments.[38] Eisenstadt challenged restrictions on the distribution, not the use, of contraceptives, but in foreshortening the moment of decision over the issue of intrusion, it paved the way for Roe and for a realm of pure autonomy and volunteerism, precisely the opposite of the image projected by Dworkin. Is the fundamental right fundamental? Or philosophically speaking, foundational? Is it a burden of conscience that must be protected as the groundwork of a life pattern, or is it the protection of an unfettered choice that leaves the moral realm of our attachments and beliefs?

Privacy as a Clash between Majority versus Minority Opinion

Parallel to the discussion about the fundamental rights at stake in discussions about privacy runs another strand of argument: the inevitable clash between majority and minority opinion in constitutional democracies and the increasingly plural nature of society. Even Justice Blackmun's decision cites Justice Oliver Wendell Holmes Jr. in his preface, offering this reason for entering the abortion controversy in the first place: the Constitution is made for people of fundamentally different views.[39] So too Dworkin: we are governed not by a list but by an ideal, and controversy is at the heart of our story.[40] But what would privacy look like, and how could it be protected and preserved, by taking into account the controversial values that now surround it? Would it be of lesser value and integrity if it were less fundamentally protected or constitutionally guaranteed?

My suggestion is to liken privacy debates in some ways to debates about conscientious objection and what Rawls terms the nearly just conditions of all constitutional democracies. The clash of values that makes debate about privacy worthwhile cannot be credible if it is framed at the level of fundamental beliefs about life. Rawls takes all the remnants of metaphysics out of these discussions and looks to the operational assumptions that make constitutional democracy work in the face of majority/minority conflict. Privacy becomes an issue, like conscientious objection, when the values of a majority begin to impose too much of a burden on the values of a minority. Minority views about childrearing, conception, intimacy, and abortion are defensible in terms of justice, though perhaps we have reached the point in the dialectic of fear and protection at which we cannot trust sufficiently in Rawls's theory of justice to do the work it was designed to do.

Profound conflicts over religions, family values, and moral standards, the stuff of controversy and plurality in the legal language, will lead to the formation of certain moral majorities who may enact laws that conflict with the opposing minority's values. Rawls is writing before *Roe v. Wade* and privacy is not the issue before him. Rather, as we saw earlier, it is conscientious objection during the Vietnam War. The key point is that Rawls frames the battle between majority and minority opinion as public speech. He does not resort to arguments about fundamental protection of religious belief to save the conscientious objector from imprisonment. On the contrary, he concedes the illegality of the act. Remedies involve what Rawls calls an appeal to public reason, to a basic framework of cooperation and civility that at root maintains a legal regime.

Without a concept of public reason a just society cannot exist. Rawls joins company with Habermas rather than with Dworkin, and he would agree with Sandel that tolerance is not sufficient. Public reason does not need to point to some deep metaphysical concept. But by the same token, mere group identity is not enough to uphold public reason. When deep conflicts emerge, the resolution must appeal to a public sense of reason based on cooperation and reciprocity. Justice rules controversy by public mechanisms that are necessary to social cooperation. By this account, abortion should not be tolerated, nor should it be given metaphysical dimensions of religion, but rather operate as a minority view, shared by a sufficient number of men and women who affirm life choices that may or may not conflict with the majority in a particular state. Part of Rawls's argument involves the test of reversibility. Abortion should not be criminalized by the majority; neither should it be mandated, as in modern China, in the satire of Jonathan Swift, or the catastrophe theory of Thomas Malthus. In a nearly just society, which has all the features described by Blackmun, Dworkin, Sandel, and Kennedy, profound moral conflict requires public resolutions, one way or another. The law is a vehicle for testing public dissent and accommodation, but not a good vehicle for creating private zones of legal protection.

I have described privacy as a fundamental right. In that respect, it offers both a protection and a problem. Does it protect profoundly held beliefs or place undue burdens on women facing agonizing decisions in a host of contingent circumstances? To answer such questions, I propose that we construe conflicts over privacy for what they are; that is, conflicts over the recognition and respect for minorities, gays, impoverished or younger women, or professional, career-centered households that do not prioritize childrearing. These beliefs are not strictly private; at this point, they are very likely minority values, though this too is subject to change. These minorities may provoke moral responses by majorities of voters and legislators.

As Sandel argues, the just battle over identity, or situatedness, does require a public sphere, and we are greatly indebted to Habermas for questioning the status of opinion, and by extension private judgment, perhaps more deeply than any contemporary philosopher. But that is not to say that he gave fair consideration to the work of writers who have preceded him, in particular two of the most original on the topic of public opinion, Tocqueville and Mill. In this chapter, I have turned back to Tocqueville and Mill for their original insights into the formation of majority and minority opinions, categories of public opinion that Habermas treats too lightly. I have followed Rawls's account of minority opinion as a form of public speech: as public speech, the analysis of minority opinion presents new ways to consider the operation of the public sphere in the contemporary liberal state. Debates about privacy can be reconstructed from the perspective of minority opinion, and so reenter debates about the operation of a public sphere in today's liberal democracies. We would not have this discussion, however, without Habermas's pioneering insights into the very concept of a public sphere as a feature of civil society and the modern state.

Notes

1. Habermas, *The Structural Transformation of the Public Sphere*, trans. Thomas Burger and Frederick Lawrence (Cambridge, MA, 1991).
2. Ibid., pp. 89–90.
3. Ibid., pp. 129–40.
4. Ibid., pp. 107–9.
5. Ibid., pp. 94–95.
6. Ibid., p. 117.
7. Habermas, *Between Facts and Norms: Contributions to a Discourse Theory of Law and Democracy*, trans. William Rehg (Cambridge, MA, 1996), p. 360.
8. Habermas, *The Structural Transformation of the Public Sphere*, p. 122.
9. John Stuart Mill, *The Philosophy of John Stuart Mill: Ethical, Political, Religious*, ed. Marshall Cohen (New York, 1961), pp. 185–319.
10. Alexis de Tocqueville, *Democracy in America* (New York, 1945), vol. 1, p. 258.
11. Isaiah Berlin, *Four Essays on Liberty* (New York, 1969), p. 179.
12. Habermas, *The Structural Transformation of the Public Sphere*, p. 133.
13. Berlin, *Four Essays on Liberty*, p. 201.
14. Mill, *The Philosophy of John Stuart Mill*, pp. 152–53.
15. Jeremy Waldron, "Mill as a Critic of Culture and Society," in *On Liberty*, ed. David Bromwich and George Kateb (New Haven, CT, 2003), pp. 224–45.
16. Ibid., p. 225.
17. Ibid., p. 229.
18. Ibid., p. 233.
19. Ibid., p. 237.
20. Rawls, *A Theory of Justice*, pp. 351–55.
21. Ibid., pp. 364–66.
22. One further clarification: in the legal literature, there is a well-known distinction between two different kinds of privacy. On the one hand, privacy is understood in terms of tort law as unwanted attention or as an invasion of the private sphere by surveillance, the media, or by advertisers. This is the so-called old privacy of Samuel D. Warren and Louis D. Brandeis, who coined the phrase "right of privacy" in order to define this tort. See their "The Right to Privacy," *Harvard Law Review* 4 (1890). A second notion of privacy that has been the focus of Supreme Court decisions about contraception and abortion is rather more strictly concerned with fundamental rights. I am concerned only with the latter.
23. Geuss, *Public Goods, Private Goods*, p. 114.
24. *Roe v. Wade*, 410 U.S. 113 (1973).
25. *Griswold v. Connecticut*, 381 U.S. 479 (1965).
26. Ellen Alderman and Caroline Kennedy, *The Right to Privacy* (New York, 1995), p. 55.
27. *Roe v. Wade*, 410 U.S. 113 (1973).
28. Ibid.
29. *Planned Parenthood v. Casey*, 505 U.S. 833 (1992).
30. Alderman and Kenney, *The Right to Privacy*, p. 55.
31. Ronald Dworkin, "Unenumerated Rights: Whether and How *Roe* Should be Overruled," *University of Chicago Law Review* 59, no. 1 (Winter 1992): 381–432.
32. Dworkin, *Life's Dominion*.
33. Dworking, "Unenumerated Rights," 407.

34. Ibid., 412.
35. Ibid., 414.
36. Sandel, *Democracy's Discontent*, pp. 91–119.
37. *Eisenstadt v. Baird*, 405 U.S. 438 (1972).
38. Sandel, *Democracy's Discontent*, p. 46.
39. *Roe v. Wade*, 410 U.S. 113 (1973).
40. Dworkin, "Unenumerated Rights," 394.

Part II

KNOWLEDGE AND THE PUBLIC SPHERE

Chapter 4

EPISTEMIC PUBLICS
On the Trading Zones of Knowledge

Christian J. Emden

R

In 1925, the American journalist Walter Lippmann, one of the founders of the periodical the *New Republic*, made a startling observation: "We must assume that a public is inexpert in its curiosity, intermittent, that it discerns only gross distinctions, is slow to be aroused and quickly diverted; that, since it acts by aligning itself, it personalizes whatever it considers, and is interested only when events have been melodramatized as a con-flict."[1] It is also important to note that Lippmann's characterization of the predicaments of the public sphere in mass democracies, as he presented them in *The Phantom Public* (1925), seems almost the very opposite of what Jürgen Habermas, in *The Structural Transformation of the Public Sphere* (1962), described as the emergence of a "bourgeois public sphere" in the course of the eighteenth century. For Habermas, the public sphere is "the sphere of 'civil society' that as the genuine domain of private autonomy stood opposed to the state."[2] The congruence of public sphere and civil society entails the possibility of rational consensus, or at least informed de-bate, while for Lippmann there is only a "phantom public." Despite these differences, however, Habermas and Lippmann also share much common ground as far as the conditions of democracy and the public in highly industrialized societies are concerned. For Habermas, modern societies in the aftermath of the Enlightenment are marked by what he described as a degeneration of the public sphere. In the eighteenth century, Habermas noted, "the bourgeois public sphere may be conceived above all as the sphere of private people coming together as a public," their interactions being marked by the matrix of "commodity exchange and social labor."[3] The liberal economic market allowed for "the problematization of areas that until then had not been questioned," thus redefining the relationship between state and public.[4] After the eighteenth century, it was, however, precisely the liberal market that, as Habermas argued, began to undercut "rational-critical debate" (*öffentliches Räsonnement*): the conflict of interests that mark the public sphere in industrialized and capitalist societies can only be solved by the intervention of social institutions and the state, which tend to transform the rational "private reflection upon public affairs" into the manipulation, or shaping, of public opinion.[5]

The gross distinctions, emotive arousal, and dramatic presentation of events and things that Lippmann regarded as central to public discourse, of course, also mark the public perception of scientific endeavors, and it is remarkable that neither Lippmann nor Habermas, in their respective investigations into the public sphere, address the forms and functions of scientific knowledge and practice. What I am interested in here is not, however, to outline a grand narrative of how, and why, scientific knowledge and practices have contributed substantially to the formation of publics. This would be far too ambitious. Even if one were to restrict oneself to a specific discipline, historical period, and geographic region, such an undertaking would require an engagement with a broad range of material that would exceed the confines of a simple book chapter.[6] Rather, what I shall attempt to do is to describe a problem, or perhaps a constellation of problems, that centers on the question of how we can examine the complex interface between science and public from a historical perspective, without losing sight of the epistemological dimension that is part of scientific practice. To be sure, the practices that take place within scientific communities, and that shape such communities, have to be examined both from a historical perspective and with regard to the normative import of the claims that are attached to these practices. Any history of science will do well to proceed along both historical and conceptual lines.[7] At the same time, historical perspectives, through their emphasis on practice over theory, are often able to shed much light on the formation of those normative claims that emerge within any given scientific community, or within any given network of agents and institutions. In the "mangle of practice" that characterizes a scientific enterprise, historical shifts are often indicators of changing normative commitments.[8] It is against this background that this chapter favors a more historical approach to describe what I am going to term "epistemic publics." Any account of such "epistemic publics"—that is, publics that come into existence through the exchange of objects, practices, images, and tools between different scientific fields as much as between science and its perception by society at large—will have to take history seriously.

Networks of Publicity

Of course, much has changed since Habermas, in 1962, introduced the notion of a "public sphere," or *Öffentlichkeit*, whose long-standing success is dependent on its somewhat metaphorical quality.[9] This is already the case with regard to the German term *Öffentlichkeit*, which refers, at one and the same time, to both a specific social space and to the openness of debate. Not surprisingly, immediately after Habermas's initial publication the notion of *Öffentlichkeit* was debated rather criticially within the context of political and constitutional theory in Germany.[10] Habermas's most vocal early critic, Niklas Luhmann, for instance, pointed out that no serious sociologist would accept the principles of Habermas's consensus-driven rational-critical debate, since in all complex and highly differentiated societies public discourse is purely functional: public relations, in other words, are always more important than the public sphere.[11] But the conceptual vagueness of *Öffentlichkeit* as a philosophical and political term is perhaps even more obvious in English, where it can be translated as "publicness," "publicity," "public culture," "political culture," "public opinion," or simply as "the condition of being in the public realm," thus leaving open what "the public" actually refers to. It is precisely for this reason that the "public sphere" continues to be a matter of theoretical debate and, since the 1990s, has received considerable attention from social scientists, political theorists, philosophers, and intellectual historians alike. In an almost Whiggish account, Margaret C. Jacob has, for instance, reemphasized the intrinisc value of Habermas's model for the eigtheenth-century setting, while Charles Taylor, from a more comparative perspective, has sought to trace the origins of different European models of public space and the public spheres.[12] Despite this continued interest in Habermas's model, which in the Anglo-American world has been triggered to some extent by the belated translation of Habermas's early work as much as by the crisis of philosophical liberalism in the aftermath of the Cold War, Geoff Ely is certainly right in noting that "the concept has migrated a long way from its original usage."[13] This has led Craig Calhoun to remark that, if the concept is supposed to make much sense, the public sphere should not be seen as identical with civil society.[14]

It is precisely in this respect that it will be worthwhile to conceptually pluralize the public sphere: the notion of "publics" can be of explanatory value, perhaps even of particular explanatory value, if it is used with regard to historical periods, cultural contexts, and intellectual fields that fall outside Habermas's original narrative. Indeed, some of the most interesting reinterpretations have been formulated by social theorists such as Margaret R. Somers, Mustafa Emirbayer, and Mimi Sheller. Somers, for instance, pointed out that concepts like the public sphere need to be regarded as being embedded in specific historically situated narratives of modernity.[15] Outside these narratives, one could argue, the public sphere might not really be a relevant concept. Although this is not Somer's own example, the understanding of the Internet as generating a new public sphere clearly shows the limits of the latter. After much initial enthusiasm about the Internet as a new public sphere in Habermas's sense, and after many fantasies about the latter's radically democratic potential, we can now observe a more critical and perhaps even skeptical approach: projecting the bourgeois public sphere, together with its image of civil society, into a global digital discourse even seems to obscure the problems of democracy and openness.[16] The suggestive homogeneity of the public sphere, thus, seems to underestimate the complexity of the way in which publics emerge in relationship to other publics, continuously reshaping their own agenda and identities. The example that Somers discusses herself is the problem of citizenship.[17] In contrast to both the Anglo-American tradition of liberal civil society and the German discourse about the public sphere, it might be worthwhile to regard central social and constitutional concepts, such as citizenship, not as a "status" we are in posession of, but rather as a "process" that depends on relational and associational patterns among different publics and their respective interests.[18]

Like Somers, Emirbayer and Sheller—in an essay on "Publics in History" (1998) that, like Somers, draws on social systems theory[19]—have rejected static and monolithic notions of the public sphere, instead focusing on what they perceive as "the *complex and reciprocal determinations*" between different publics or *"networks of publicity."*[20] Publics, they argue, need to be seen as "open-ended flows of communication that enable socially distant interlocutors to bridge social-network positions" in order to "formulate collective orientations ... in pursuit of influence over common concerns."[21] Of course, one could simply note that publics generally consist of strangers coming together and willing to exert influence over common concerns—concerns that can undergo dramatic shifts as the boundaries between different publics realign.[22] But what is a crucial insight in this account is the realization that (a) publics are dependent on cultural perception and social imaginaries and (b) publics are embedded in changing historical situations that both trigger and, at least to some extent, even determine their agency.[23] These are the two lessons I would like to draw with regard to the problem of how to understand what it means to make scientific "things" public. Understanding epistemic publics, in other words, needs to take into account the historically variable relationship between different publics and their respective interests as much as the way in which these publics produce, and are themselves the product of, social imaginaries.

Public Science

The relationship between scientific activity and the public outside science has been a central problem within the history and philosophy of science at least since the mid-1980s. Heavily influenced by research on the social function of spatial relationships, Steven Shapin and Thomas F. Gieryn have sought to define the tense relationships between science and nonscience by emphasizing the role public perception, together with the self-perception of scientists, plays in the formation of scientific communities, disciplines, and methods.[24] Shapin has convincingly argued, for instance, that different scientific methods and theoretical frameworks that are present in the same discipline generate different publics, as in the case of seventeenth-century physics at the Royal Society: the audience of Robert Boyle and Robert Hooke is marked by an understanding of scientific enterprise as based on the claims of empirical observation, while for Isaac Newton's audience such empirical claims are replaced by an emphasis on mathematical demonstration.[25] In fact, many of the central claims of Newton's *Principia Mathematica* (1687) cannot be empirically observed, at least not in the late seventeenth century, but require geometric proof.

The constitution of these audiences, or publics, is moreover strictly regulated; in a certain sense these publics are, in fact, private and marked by a relatively clear threshold or boundary between those who have access and those who stand outside. For Habermas, on the other hand, the public sphere, at least until the end of the eighteenth century, consisted primarily of "private people coming together as a public."[26] As such, the public sphere is necessarily characterized by an openness that, for instance, the seventeenth-century "house of experiment" and its public do not really possess. On either side of the divide between inside and outside, the very conditions of knowledge and scientific understanding are fundamentally different.[27] To gain the right of access to a seventeenth-century "house of experiment" requires at the very least a letter of recommendation, while certain groups, such as women, are excluded regardless of their educational status or personal connections—some "laboratories," such as Tycho Brahe's castle on the island of Hven close to Copenhagen, are virtually off-limits even to those who have the necessary expertise.[28] But it is one of the ironies of seventeenth-century natural philosophy that, while the site of experiment remained private, the actual experiments required public testimony, so that the experimental claims could become authoritative statements about natural phenomena.[29] Experiments that were public were almost always demonstrations and were often part of a strategy of persuading a much broader audience that the experimental knowledge demonstrated was in fact sound and trustworthy. Public experiments, in other words, could not fail, but those carried out in the secluded site of the "house of experiment" were allowed to fail, since such failure at least led to new experimental arrangements. Failure in public, however, led to embarrassment.

The paradoxical nature of experimental settings in seventeenth-century natural philosophy, and the importance of public testimony in order to safeguard the authority of the experiment at stake, becomes particularly obvious in an example that is mentioned only in passing by Shapin, but which might be worthwhile to consider in more detail. In 1667, the Royal Society experimented with the transfusion of animal blood into the human circulatory system. The physicians involved were faced with the problem that the human subject needed to be both expendable if the experiment went wrong and sufficiently trustworthy to prepare a self-report in case the experiment was successful, even though there were serious doubts that the experiment could actually succeed.[30] In the event, the experiment proved to be successful—at least in the sense that the human subject, a Cambridge graduate by the name of Arthur Coga, survived—even though the two physicians involved did not gain any valuable knowledge. It is remarkable, however, how the experimental outcome, the transfusion of reportedly 9 or 10 ounces of sheep's blood into a human body, leaves the site of experiment by virtue of a chain of testimonies, published in the Royal Society's *Philosophical Transactions* on 9 December 1667. This chain of testimonies asserts the veracity of the experimental outcome, but at the same time changes the epistemological status of the experiment itself as it moves between different publics, from the house of experiment to first-hand accounts and the pages of the *Philosophical Transactions*. The "EXPERIMENT OF TRANSFUSION ... was perform'd, Novemb. 23. 1667. upon one Mr. Arthur Coga, at Arundel-house, in the presence of many considerable and intelligent persons."[31] Directed by the physicians Richard Lower and Edmund King, the experiment thus proceeded under the observation of a specifically invited public, but the mere witnessing of the event needed to be further enhanced by the suriving human subject,

Arthur Coga, who composed "his own Narrative under his own hand" for the physicians—a smaller public within the public of interested direct observers—while one of the physicians, King, "communicated" the entire event in a letter to the Royal Society, subsequently published in its *Philosophical Transactions* for a public beyond those who were able to observe the experiment itself. Enthused about the success of the experiment, Coga himself, as King noted, asked for the entire affair to be "repeated" within a few days, "but it was thought advisable, to put it off somewhat longer."

Leaving aside the well-being of the human subject, it should be noted that the outcome of the experiment was clouded by uncertainty: exactly how much blood was transferred between the animal and the human subject remained unkown. But despite this deficiency, the experiment clearly shows that the rhetoric of scientific authority, supported by the precise date and the credentials of the two physicians involved, was not alone in safeguarding the veracity of the experiment for the public of the *Philosophical Transactions*.[32] Rather, the experiment was deemed trustworthy because it had been witnessed by those who had access to the experimental site, because Coga himself provided a self-report that, by virtue of his status as a Cambridge graduate, had to be regarded as fairly accurate, and because of King's communication of the experiment.[33] Experiments can end badly, though, and in the same volume of the *Philosophical Transactions* we find a report on a similar experiment of blood transfusion that was carried out in France and culminated in the autopsy of the unfortunate human subject. During the autopsy of the man, who was experimented upon because he had already been sick, suffering from violent fever and a "bilious Diarrhea," no trace of animal blood could be found in the veins or heart, which were both said to be dry. The report itself ends with the note: "All of which this *Author* assures, can be attested both by a dozen persons of great veracity, who were present at this dissection, and confirmed by the *Certificates* given by the Physicians themselves."[34] In both cases, the trustworthiness of the experiments, despite their meager results, relied on a set of interlocking agents and publics coming together; that is, it relied on the dynamic relationships among a number of publics.

The interested London physician, who might consult the *Philosophical Transactions*, has to take on trust what he does not have access to, with limited knowledge about the actual site and context and with no tacit knowledge of the experimental process itself. The tense relation between the publics of science and the translation of scientific activity into publics outside science begins to take shape in the course of the seventeenth century. As such, it is important to note that the boundaries of science and nonscience are historically shifting.[35] They tend to be defined according to the practices and things—real objects as much as their representation in images and books—that circulate between different publics and their interests, but they can also be defined according to the self-interests of specific actors within a given epistemic public. The perception among scientists, for instance, as to whether their work is theoretical or empirical, pure or applied, often seeks to demarcate science from publics that are seen as nonscientific in order to strategically gain access to both authority and resources.[36] The expulsion of competitors, the expansion of one's own disciplinary commitments, and the protection of one's autonomy are closely interlinked and take place against the background of the relationship between science and nonscience. At the same time, scientific practice and the things that are part of it have the curious tendency to move outside the realm of their original context, thus continuously redefining the boundaries between different epistemic publics.

It is safe to say that, among historians of science, there is little debate about the fact that science is embedded in a complex set of social relationships. One does not need to be a radical social constructivist to accept that scientific practices, in one way or another, are also social practices. But it is necessary to avoid taking these social practices at face value: the way in which scientists and engineers—as well as the professional "science writers" that seek to communicate the work of the laboratory to a lay audience—describe how scientific things become public knowledge is often marked by an idealizing rhetoric of openness that underestimates the tensions between different publics. Consider, for instance, an article by Carol L. Rogers, published in 1981. Rogers, at the time an official at the American Association for the Advancement of Science, rightly pointed out that "[s]cientific organizations have a special contribution to make to the understanding of public issues involving science and technology, as well as a special responsibility to do so."[37] But her account of the way in which knowledge becomes public is in many ways removed from the way in which scientific things actually do become public by virtue of their circulation between different epistemic publics and by virtue of the tensions between these epistemic publics. Scientific societies, Rogers continued, simply collect all necessary expertise to resolve a public issue and provide the necessary infrastructure for relevant experts to reach a well-informed and balanced consensus, which is finally passed on in a commonly agreed form to the media, from television shows to popular science books.[38]

The only relationship between science and society, then, is that of public education, and this relationship is ostensibly a one-way street from a sphere of experts to the uneducated public. Of course, Rogers is correct in assuming that a broader understanding of scientific issues is necessary, while her premise of a largely inexpert and disinterested public, echoing the earlier account by Lippmann, is entirely accurate. The question is not, however, whether public education about science is necessary—it undoubtedly is—but whether science really does enter the public imagination in the way described. Only a few years after Rogers's article, the practical enterprise of how to make scientific things public beyond science was increasingly seen as highly problematic: as far as the relationship between "science" and "the public" was concerned, it is extraordinarily difficult to negotiate between scientific evidence and policy preferences, and John Ziman—then the director of the Science Policy Research Group, a British think tank that operated between 1986 and 2003 and that had been set up by the Economic and Social Research Council—concluded that there was in fact little reliable data on the public understanding of science.[39]

The year in which Rogers's article was published also saw the publication of a short bulletin by Michael S. Gottlieb for the Centers for Disease Control and Prevention. Gottlieb observed a cluster of cases of an otherwise fairly rare form of pneumonia, which was suggestive of a much more complex disease that only a few months later, in 1982, was termed acquired immune deficiency syndrome or AIDS.[40] By 1983 a retrovirus was established as the underlying cause of the disease and by 1986—when AIDS was already being debated controversially in the mass media, raising a number of ethical and political concerns—the retrovirus received its common name, HIV.[41] Rogers's 1981 article, in other words, was followed by a scenario that certainly supported her premise about the need for public education, but it also highlighted the limits, at least in the first few years of the public debate on AIDS, of the possibility of successfully directing this debate. Things becoming public and making things public have only a tenuous relationship with the communication of a rational consensus. Not surprisingly, in 1999—with the public debate about AIDS already well established and the equally controversial debate about climate change gaining increasing momentum—Rogers pointed out that making science public also required taking into account "audience needs"; that is, "lack of information" and "lack of context" need to be compensated for by the structure and framing of the "story," enhanced by "visuals."[42] Making things public, in other words, requires what Lippmann all too well understood as the melodramatic representation of issues. One possible conclusion to be drawn from the ideal of "public science," as Frank M. Turner remarked with regard to the British context around 1900, is that it has little to do with the actual motivations of scientific research, but rather seeks to persuade both public and government "that science can perform desired social and economic functions"—even if the cultural authority of science stands in some contrast to the actual practice of science.[43]

Making Things (Almost) Public

The public and, by implication, cultural effects of scientific knowledge constitute a well-traversed field of research, especially as far the British context is concerned: from the rise of Newtonianism to the public displays and institutions of Victorian science, scientific knowledge is always connected to forms of public and cultural authority.[44] Given the role of coffeehouses, salons, and table societies in the eighteenth century, together with the growing print culture, it is not surprising that the dissemination of scientific knowledge should have had a considerable effect on the public, so much so that Habermas's notion of the public sphere was also introduced into the history of eighteenth-century science as a powerful explanatory model.[45] Within this context, however, the notion of a relatively monolithic public sphere also became immediately questionable. Taking into account that the public sphere as an explanatory model is based on the exchange of both goods and information, examining the international exchange of scientific information should provide detailed insights into the effect of scientific knowledge on the emergence of rational-critical public debate, which, according to Habermas's description, had to take place "in principle without regard to all preexisting social and political rank and in accord with universal rules."[46] The results of such examination proved to be disappointing, at least as far as Habermas's public sphere was concerned: despite the institutional growth of scientific authority across Europe and a growing network of scientific correspondents, the international exchange of scientific communication in the later seventeenth century was marked by closed circles and weak ties that stood in sharp contrast to the openness of debate envisaged by Habermas. As David Lux and Harold Cook have shown, the institutionalization of science in the various academies produced quite the opposite of what one might expect, namely, ambiguity about scientific results and a closure of open networks of communication.[47] Secrecy, as Lisa Jardine pointed out, was commonplace among the members of the Royal Society.[48] Indeed, "the idealised picture of information globally available to all as the ... model for the successful transmission and growth of knowledge needs to be qualified."[49]

Jardine's reminder about the specific publicness of science remains relevant today. In an article derived from his work on the history of microphysics during the Cold War, Peter Galison highlighted the ubiquitous secrecy surrounding not only actual research results but even possible research outcomes that, eventually, might have an effect on US national security, as far-fetched as this effect in most cases actually is.[50] In 1995, the US Department of Energy alone estimated its holdings of classified documents, mostly related to nuclear research, to be in the region of 280 million pages.[51] Just taking into account the classified documents produced by university and college professors in the United States, "the classified universe is … in the order of five to ten times larger than the open literature that finds its way to our libraries."[52] Secrecy is a crucial dimension of the circulation of knowledge that impacts the way in which such knowledge relates to different publics. It even seems that, as soon as scientific practices and their agents become institutionalized in academies, societies, research centers, or laboratories, and as soon as scientific research becomes a crucial factor within public debate, secrecy becomes an equally important element, substantially limiting what Habermas regarded as rational-critical debate, even among scientists. As a consequence, the relationship between secrecy and openness has emerged as a central problem for any account of publics.[53]

Already the rapidly changing social environment of the seventeenth and eighteenth centuries was bound to continually revise what it meant to do science and, thus, the relationship between scientific practice and its perception in public. Robert Boyle's air pump and the Leyden jar are particularly famous examples of the fact that the public dissemination of scientific knowledge was less dependent on the actual circulation of detailed knowledge that could be rationally debated and more on the immediacy of public demonstration.[54] Otto von Guericke, levitating a feather over a ball molded from sulfur in 1663, demonstrated the principle of electrical repulsion, a phenomenon that his audience could only describe along the lines of magic.[55] Secrecy was one dimension of the relationship between science and nonscientific publics, but it was such spectacular demonstrations that really did make things public.

The transmission of scientific practice into the public realm also involved the intervention of state authorities, even at a time when, according to Habermas, the relationship between the bourgeois realm of the public sphere and the politics of the state authorites was rather tense. Consider, for instance, the seemingly obscure debate over blunt or pointed lightning rods, which raged between Benjamin Wilson and Benjamin Franklin in the eighteenth century. Launching an appeal to King George III to adopt one or the other had the unintended effect of politicizing a primarily scientific debate that was thus suddenly transformed into a debate about the political authority over science between Britain and its former colony across the Atlantic.[56] Likewise, even internal scientific debate, for instance, about the research direction of microscopy among the medical professors of nineteenth-century Paris, is often directly connected to political configurations: the neurologist Pierre Paul Broca, best known for his research on aphasia and the localization of cerebral functions, argued, for instance, that the frontlines within science did not exclusively relate to professional disagreements about research but to different national models and traditions—a truly French neurologist would proceed differently from a German neurologist.[57]

The effects of secrecy, public demonstrations, and politics on the way in which scientific knowledge is, or is not, embedded in different publics tend to undermine any clear-cut assumptions about "public science." This situation is further complicated by the translation of images from the realm of laboratory notebooks and peer-reviewed scientific publications into the realm of public discourse and even the social imaginary. The cultural authority of medical images is a case in point: Ludmilla Jordanova has shown with regard to the eighteenth century that medical representations and their public reception follow along the lines of wider socially determined gender representations.[58] It might even be possible to argue that, in the course of the eighteenth century, the model for anatomical representation shifted from the male to the female corpse. Such translations between visual evidence and the public imagination, and thus also the social imaginary, seem to accelerate, for obvious technological reasons, in the course of the nineteenth century. On the one hand, changing technologies of representation, especially photography and film, change the cultural perception of scientific knowledge and practice.[59] Peter Galison and Lorraine Daston have rightly argued that the production of scientific objectivity is, to a considerable extent, dependent on the methods of standardized technical visualization that exemplifies the cultural authority of scientific knowledge: scientific objectivity becomes a moral standard that is dependent on the standardization of images and on ways of seeing things.[60] Furthermore, and as the example of nineteenth-century Germany clearly shows, the popularization of science through institutional networks, public education, popular science books, and amateur societies renegotiates the boundaries between the expert publics and lay publics, which are often embedded in much wider political interests.[61]

At times, as in the case of Wilhelm Conrad Röntgen's X-rays, the translation from the laboratory to the public is almost immediate.[62] On 22 November 1895, Röntgen produced the first proper X-ray image, depicting his wife's hand after twenty minutes of radiation; in early 1896 he published his well-known paper "Eine neue Art von Strahlen," and a few months later the first cartoons appeared in *Life* magazine.[63] The public dissemination of X-ray imagery and its enormous effect on the public imagination, which can also be traced in Thomas Mann's novel *Der Zauberberg* (1924), is not an isolated case.[64] Consider, for instance, PET scans. While the technological conditions for positron emission tomography emerged with the development of biological tracer techniques during the 1940s, the first commercial PET scanners became available only in 1979.[65] Four years later the visual representation of different brain states (normal-depressed-schizophrenic) had already become such a popular image that, for instance, a whole article was devoted to the topic in the July 1983 edition of *Vogue* magazine.[66]

The cultural authority of scientific knowledge, promised visually in the medical field by X-rays, fMRI, and PET scans, undoubtedly has a direct impact on the formation of medical models and representations among publics that are, by and large, entirely unrelated to the technology's site of origin. How, then, is it possible to trace and reconstruct the effects of scientific practices within publics outside the research laboratory, if their sites of origin are different from their sites of use, and if the cultural meaning of scientific things, or "epistemic things," as Hans-Jörg Rheinberger noted, is fundamentally different from their epistemological or material status in the laboratory? Mapping techniques, for instance, are always spectacular—quite in contrast to the dissolution of the human body into complex statistical curves or the scattering of cloud chamber events into computerized algorithms.[67] As such, they are also always easily adapted within different cultural and social settings. The cultural authority of science, and its relationship to publics outside science, in other words, does not need to be based on rational-critical debate; an appeal to the spectacular is sufficient. The peculiar logic of scientific images exacerbates the problem of how to account for, and how to examine, the role of scientific practice within the formation of publics.[68]

The Standardization of Things

Objectivity, Theodore M. Porter argued, "implies the subordination of personal interests and prejudices to public standards."[69] These standards, and the process of standardization, are of crucial importance to the way in which the things generated in a research laboratory or in a field study leave their site of origin. Numbers, needless to say, play a crucial role in this context precisely because they are able to "defy disciplinary and even cultural boundaries."[70] But the seemingly universal translatability of complex figures, numerical tables, and statistical outcomes necessarily erases the initial interpretive work that has gone into compiling such numbers. This interpretive work is, in more ways than one, of a local character, and, as Joseph Rouse reminds us, scientific knowledge "is extended outside the laboratory not by generalization into universal laws instantiable elsewhere, but by the adaptation of locally situated practices to new local contexts."[71] Rouse is careful to emphasize that scientific practices are nevertheless normative—it is just that this normativity is the product of our interaction with natural things, so that any distinction between a "meaningful 'social world' and an anormative 'natural world'" is at least questionable.[72] Scientific practices are normative, and can therefore be valid beyond their site of origin, because they are reproducible and because the concepts they generate are at the same time "part of the material configuration of the world."[73] On this account, phenomena, instruments, and human agents are so closely intertwined that they travel together once they leave one laboratory and move into a different one. It is only "the creation of a phenomenon" that is a "highly localized activity," and the question is how such a localized activity is able to become "reliable and authoritative knowledge about the world."[74]

One answer to this question, of course, has been suggested by Thomas S. Kuhn. Observing that "a paradigm developed for one set of phenomena" can be rather "ambiguous in its application to other closely related ones," he suggested that experimental testing can resolve such ambiguities, at least "within a single normal-scientific tradition."[75] As a consequence, paradigms "relate by resemblance and modeling to one or another part of the scientific corpus which the community in question already recognized as among its established achievements," thus standardizing scientific knowledge and, in effect, generating claims to objectivity.[76] The effects of tacit knowledge, of accepted methods, and of social control stabilize paradigms and disciplines.[77] The outcome of this process is, in the words of Ludwik Fleck, the establishment of a particular "thought collective" with a specific "thought style."[78] In nineteenth-century German physiology, for instance, we can observe that instruments and the phenomena they generate are packaged with each other and tied to a specific research site, say the University of Königsberg, but the techniques and methods are highly mobile and are transferred easily both to other research institutes, say Heidelberg, and to different fields, such as research on optics and electricity.[79]

Although he is often credited as a founding father of social constructivism in the history of science, Kuhn mainly focuses on developments within science and largely refrains from discussing in more detail possible external factors that exert influence on the formation of what he describes as a "disciplinary matrix."[80] But a more ethnographic approach that gained traction after Kuhn has highlighted precisely the disunity of the sciences and the heterogeneous outlook of scientific practice.[81] Although the epistemological framework employed in this context is not without problems, the general direction of constructivism has at least highlighted the fundamental question as to how external factors do indeed play a crucial role in the formation of what Kuhn regarded as scientific paradigms.[82] Given the complexity of the relationship between the evidence of experimental results and their social context, historians of science, at least since the late 1980s and even more so since the mid-1990s, have thus sought to realign internal and external factors in the development of specific disciplines by seeking to explain the historically dynamic social and political contexts of scientific practice.[83]

It would be interesting, however, to reverse this perspective and focus on the way in which the things that emerge in the context of scientific practice begin to shape the political imagination and cultural self-description of publics that are more detached from the scientific field in question. One way of taking such a reversed perspective into account was suggested by Bruno Latour during the 1980s—a solution that still holds much sway over contemporary work in the area of science studies. Drawing on Gaston Bachelard's concept of "phenomenotechniques," Latour argued that the reality of scientific phenomena is inherently linked to the material techniques and instruments that brought them into existence.[84] Observing the work of biologists at the Salk Institute in La Jolla, California, he noted that these techniques and instruments are forgotten once the phenomenon in question, say a specific hormone or protein, is actually materially present, for instance, in a photographic inscription. Following up on this initial account several years later, Latour began to draw wider lessons from his earlier observations with regard to the standardization of scientific phenomena: the phenomena created in a specific experimental setting begin to "define reality" by combining "human and non-human resources" and by generating networks that undermine any strict distinction between science and nonscience, between the original site of experiment and the public world outside.[85] For Latour, this process is entirely dependent on instrumentation, that is, on nonhuman factors: "Facts and machines are like trains, electricity, packages of computer bytes or frozen vegetables: they can go everywhere as long as the track along which they travel is not interrupted in the slightest. … Metrology is the name of this gigantic enterprise to make of the outside world a world inside which facts and machines can survive."[86] Latour's most famous example is perhaps the standardization of time, which has been a central concern among historians of science over the last twenty years or so: "Time is not universal; every day it is made slightly more so by the extension of an international network that ties together, through visible and invisible linkages, each of all the reference clocks of the world and then organises secondary and tertiary chains of references all the way to this rather imprecise watch I have on my wrist."[87]

Leaving aside the epistemological problems of Latour's account about the way in which the phenomena and things of scientific activity become public, it is quite remarkable that the networks of metrology are almost exclusively the product of nonhuman agents. For Latour and others, the success of metrology is based on "material collectives."[88] The international standardization of electrical units in the late nineteenth century, for instance, is therefore described as "an internationally distributed collective of instuments, electrical apparatuses, resistors, and batteries."[89] This tells us little, however, about the actual impact of this material collective on the formation of specific epistemic publics, on the self-perception of these publics, or about their political interests—aspects that come to the fore, for instance, in the close links between the emergence of the metric system and the French Revolution or between the standardization of time, the modern telegraph, and political administration in the nineteenth century.[90] Latour, in short, has no room for epistemic publics: the social unravels into a series of anonymous networks.[91] In contrast, Jan Golinski rightly suggested that the standards Latour speaks of "are only reproducible because of ... those responsible for circulating and sustaining the equipment, materials, and skills needed to reproduce them at many different sites."[92] What happens when the things generated by scientific activity leave their original context is a fundamental change in their meaning and cultural value. This is where we encounter the full complexity of epistemic publics.

From Trading Zones to Epistemic Publics

It is interesting to note that, while the history of science has turned toward the political for several decades, intellectual historians have only relatively recently begun to consider the broad spectrum of theoretical issues relevant to the field of science studies broadly conceived.[93] Readdressing the political implications of the formation of epistemic publics, however, also means accounting for the fact that, as Steven Shapin noted on more than one occasion, scientific knowledge needs to be understood as the product of a continuous negotiation between ideas, procedures, phenomena, instruments, and human agents, which always relate, for instance, the laboratory to a specific audience as well as to a wider public.[94] Understanding that "the shape and success of the sciences" depend on the way in which "scientific communities" are linked to "allies, audiences, publics, consumers and reproducers," underlines that scientific practice is always already embedded in different publics and thus forms of political exchange.[95] Understanding that experimental knowledge circulates between different publics might also lead to an understanding of the way in which the boundaries between the public and the private are constantly redrawn. Of course, as we have seen, the sciences have internal publics: specialist institutions, textbooks, the repetition and verification of experimental outcomes, demonstrations to expert audiences, and the dissemination of tacit knowledge fall into this category. The question, then, is not: how does science become public? It is: how do its instruments, techniques, images, and phenomena of scientific practice gain a presence that shapes the social imaginary of epistemic publics in a way that is not always entirely obvious? Understanding epistemic publics in a way that takes into account both conceptual and historical issues has to be guided by the fact that the trade in scientific things cannot be reduced to an exchange between "science" and "the public." Such an opposition, if at all, can only be of heuristic value. Instead, we will do well to recognize what I have initially quoted as "networks of publicity," that is, the web of relationships and travel routes between different epistemic publics.

In a detailed study on the material culture of microphysics from the late nineteenth century to the present, Galison has suggested a model that seeks to describe how scientists working in different experimental and cultural traditions are able to collaborate: "trading zones."[96] For Galison, such trading zones are the "social, material, and intellectual mortar binding together the disunified traditions of experimenting, theorizing, and instrument building."[97] But while Galison is mainly interested in the collaboration between different physical research laboratories, it seems that this concept can also be used quite efficiently to outline the relationship between scientific knowledge and its practices, on the one hand, and its public perception beyond the realm of the laboratory, on the other. Taking into account that publics are embedded in each other, as I have noted with regard to the example of blood transfusion in seventeenth-century England, they are also embedded in changing historical constellations. In order to investigate, then, the way in which such epistemic publics are conceptually as well as historically interrelated, we will have to consider the way in which *actors* move between different publics, the *practices* such actors are involved in, the *instruments* and *images* that migrate between different publics, and finally the way in which scientific practices do not simply represent nature but rather *intervene in, or interact with, the material world*. It seems that Rouse was quite right when he pointed out that knowledge "is always shaped by the goods, practices, and projects whose allocation and pursuit are at issue, and by the institutions and social networks that are organized around those pursuits." The "boundaries and configurations" of specific disciplines "are continually challenged and partially reconstructed, as epistemic alignments shift."[98] But what counts for expert disciplines also counts for the way in which the practices and representations of these disciplines shape nonexpert publics in almost imperceptible ways. Knowledge, then, is indeed always already embedded in a network of publics and their respective interests. But the crucial point is that such epistemic publics are always determined by their respective historical settings and conditions. The trading zones of knowledge are always historical. As such, they will neither be stable, nor will they be simple.

Notes

For critical comments and suggestions I am grateful to Steven Crowell, Jan Golinski, Ludmilla Jordanova, David Midgley, and John H. Zammito, as well as audiences at the University of Cambridge, the University of Leeds, Trinity College Dublin, and Rice University.

1. Lippmann, *The Phantom Public* (New Brunswick, N.J., 1993), pp. 54–55.
2. Habermas, *The Structural Transformation of the Public Sphere*, trans. Thomas Burger and Frederick Lawrence (Cambridge, MA, 1989), p. 12.
3. Ibid., p. 27.
4. Ibid., p. 36. See also Michael McKeon, "Parsing Habermas' 'Bourgeois Public Sphere,'" *Criticism* 46 (2004): 274.
5. Habermas, *The Structural Transformation of the Public Sphere*, pp. 28, 88, and 94.
6. For a particularly interesting example, see Jan Golinski, *Science as Public Culture: Chemistry and Enlightenment in Britain, 1760-1820* (Cambridge, 1992).
7. For an excellent example of such an approach, see Peter Galison, *Image and Logic.: A Material Culture of Microphysics* (Chicago, 1997).
8. Andrew Pickering, *The Mangle of Practice: Timage, Agency, and Science* (Chicago, 1995).
9. On the metaphorical quality of *Öffentlichkeit*, see also McKeon, "Parsing Habermas' 'Bourgeois Public Sphere,'" 275–76.
10. See the account in Peter Uwe Hohendahl, "Critical Theory, Public Sphere and Culture: Jürgen Habermas and His Critics," *New German Critique* 16 (1979): 89–118.
11. Niklas Luhmann, "Öffentliche Meinung," *Politische Vierteljahresschrift* 11 (1970): 2–28. See also Hohendahl, "Critical Theory, Public Sphere and Culture," 99–102, and Thomas McCarthy, "Complexity and Democracy, or the Seducements of Systems Theory," *New German Critique* 35 (1985): 27–55.
12. Jacob, "The Mental Landscape of the Public Sphere," 95–113, and Charles Taylor, "Modes of Civil Society," *Public Culture* 3 (1990): 95–118. For a balanced review of Habermas's public sphere thesis with regard to the eighteenth-century context, see LaVopa, "Conceiving a Public," 79–116.
13. Geoff Ely, "Politics, Culture, and the Public Sphere," *Positions* 10 (2002): 223. Ely has set off Habermas's more "proceduralist *Öffentlichkeit*" from less consensus-driven and more antagonistic "publics" that he sees as having emerged in the 1960s and 1970s.
14. Craig Calhoun, "Civil Society and the Public Sphere," *Public Culture* 5 (1993): 267–80.

15. Margaret R. Somers, *Genealogies of Citizenship: Markets, Statelessness, and the Right to Have Rights* (Cambridge, 2008), pp. 171–209.
16. For the enthusiastic reception, see Douglas Kellner, "Globalization from Below? Toward a Radical Democratic Technopolitics," *Angelaki* 4 (1999): 101–13, and Lincoln Dahlberg, "Cyberspace and the Public Sphere: Exploring the Democratic Potential of the Net," *Convergence* 4 (1998): 70–84. For a more skeptical point of view, see Hubertus Buchstein, "Bytes that Bite: The Internet and Deliberative Democracy," *Constellations* 4 (1997): 248–63, and Jodi Dean's "Cybersalons and Civil Society: Rethinking the Public Sphere in Transnational Technoculture," *Public Culture* 13 (2001): 243–65, and "Why the Net is Not a Public Sphere," *Constellations* 10 (2003): 95–112. See also the contributions in Mark J. Lacy and Peter Wilkin, eds., *Global Publics in the Information Age* (Manchester, 2005).
17. Margaret R. Somers, "Narrating and Naturalizing Civil Society and Citizenship Theory: The Place of Political Culture and the Public Sphere," *Sociological Theory* 13 (1995): 229–74.
18. Margaret R. Somers, "Citizenship and the Place of the Public Sphere: Law, Community, and Political Culture in the Transition to Democracy," *American Sociological Review* 58 (1993): 587–620.
19. Mustafa Emirbayer and Jeff Goodwin, "Network Analysis, Culture, and the Problem of Agency," *American Journal of Sociology* 99 (1994): 1411–54.
20. Mustafa Emirbayer and Mimi Sheller, "Publics in History," *Theory and Society* 27 (1998): 727 and 747–61.
21. Ibid., 738.
22. On the public as an association of "strangers," see Warner, "Publics and Counterpublics," 55–57, who refers back to Georg Simmel's notion of the "stranger." See Georg Simmel, *Soziologie: Untersuchungen über die Formen der Vergesellschaftung*, in *Gesamtausgabe*, ed. Otthein Rammstedt, vol. 11 (Frankfurt am Main, 1992), pp. 764–71.
23. Emirbayer and Sheller, "Publics in History," 740–41 and 761.
24. See Steven Shapin's "Science and the Public," in *Companion to the History of Modern Science*, ed. R. C. Olby, G. N. Cantor, J. R. R. Christie, and M. J. S. Hodge (London, 1989), pp. 990–1007, and *A Social History of Truth: Civility and Science in Seventeenth-Century England* (Chicago, 1994), as well as Thomas F. Gieryn's "Boundaries of Science," in *Handbook of Science and Technology Studies*, ed. Sheila Jasanoff, Gerald E. Markle, James C. Peterson, and Trevor J. Pinch (Thousand Oaks, CA, 1994), pp. 393–443, and *Cultural Boundaries of Science: Credibility on the Line* (Chicago, 1999). For a general overview, see Jan Golinski, "The Theory of Practice and the Practice of Theory: Sociological Approaches in the History of Science," *Isis* 81 (1990): 492–505.
25. Steven Shapin, "'The Mind Is its Own Place': Science and Solitude in Seventeenth-Century England," *Science in Context* 4 (1990): 206.
26. Habermas, *The Structural Transformation of the Public Sphere*, p. 12.
27. Steven Shapin, "The House of Experiment in Seventeenth-Century England," *Isis* 79 (1988): 374.
28. Ibid., 388–89; see also Paula Findlen, "Masculine Prerogatives: Gender, Space, and Knowledge in the Early Modern Museum," in *The Architecture of Science*, ed. Peter Galison and Emily Thompson (Cambridge, MA, 1999), pp. 29–57; and Owen Hannaway, "Laboratory Design and the Aim of Science: Andreas Libavius versus Tycho Brahe," *Isis* 77 (1986): 585–610.
29. Shapin, "The House of Experiment in Seventeenth-Century England," 377–78.

30. Ibid., 376. For the respective correspondence concerning this experiment, see A. Rupert Hall and Marie Boas Hall, eds., *The Correspondence of Henry Oldenburg* (Madison, WI, 1965–86), vol. 3, pp. 611 and 616–17, and vol. 4, pp. xx–xxi, 6, 59, and 77.

31. "An Account of the Experiment of Transfusion, practised upon a Man in London," *Philosophical Transactions of the Royal Society of London* 30 (9 December 1667): 557 and 559.

32. On the uses and functions of rhetoric in science, see, in general, Alan G. Gross, *The Rhetoric of Science* (Cambridge, MA, 1990).

33. On observation and reporting as factors in the establishment of scientific authority during the seventeenth century, see especially Steven Shapin and Simon Schaffer, *Leviathan and the Air-Pump: Hobbes, Boyle, and the Experimental Life* (Princeton, NJ, 1985), pp. 22–78, and Peter Dear, "Narratives, Anecdotes, and Experiments: Turning Experience into Science in the Seventeenth Century," in *The Literary Structure of Scientific Argument: Historical Studies*, ed. Peter Dear (Philadelphia, 1991), pp. 135–63.

34. "A Relation of Some Trials of the same Operation, lately made in France," *Philosophical Transactions of the Royal Society of London* 30 (9 December 1667): 564.

35. Shapin and Schaffer, *Leviathan and the Air-Pump*, p. 342. At least to some extent, this will have something to do with the dynamics of scientific interests. The latter undergo drastic changes as scientists are unable to fulfill their research obligations in the face of resistance from the phenomena and in the face of social constraints. See Pickering, *The Mangle of Practice*, pp. 63–67 and 208–12.

36. Gieryn, *Cultural Boundaries of Science*, pp. 15–17, and Thomas F. Gieryn, "Boundary-Work and the Demarcation of Science from Non-Science: Strains and Interests in Professional Ideologies of Scientists," *American Sociological Review* 48 (1983): 791–92.

37. Carol L. Rogers, "Science Information for the Public: The Role of Scientific Societies," *Science, Technology, and Human Values* 6 (1981): 36.

38. Ibid., 36–38.

39. Marc J. Roberts, Stephen R. Thomas, and Michael J. Dowling, "Mapping Scientific Disputes that Affect Public Policymaking," *Science, Technology, and Human Values* 8 (1984): 112–22, and John Ziman, "Public Understanding of Science," *Science, Technology, and Human Values* 16 (1991): 99–105.

40. "Epidemiologic Notes and Reports: Pneumocystis Pneumonia—Los Angeles," *Morbidity and Mortality Weekly Report* 30, no. 21 (1981): 1–3; "Update on Acquired Immune Deficiency Syndrome (AIDS)—United States," *Morbidity and Mortality Weekly Report* 31, no. 37 (1982): 507–8 and 513–14; and J. L. Marx, "New Disease Baffles Medical Community," *Science* 217 (1982): 618–21.

41. F. Barré-Sinoussi et al., "Isolation of a T-lymphotropic Retrovirus from a Patient at Risk for Acquired Immune Deficiency Syndrome (AIDS)," *Science* 220 (1983): 868–71, and J. Coffin et al., "What to Call the AIDS Virus?" *Nature* 321 (1983): 10.

42. Carol L. Rogers, "The Importance of Understanding Audiences," in *Communicating Uncertainty: Media Coverage of New and Controversial Science*, ed. Sharon M. Friedman, Sharon Dunwoody, and Carol L. Rogers (Mahwah, NJ, 1999), pp. 179 and 188–95. See also the contributions in Sharon M. Friedman, Sharon Dunwoody, and Carol L. Rogers, eds., *Scientists and Journalists: Reporting Science as News* (New York, 1986).

43. Frank M. Turner, "Public Science in Britain, 1880–1919," *Isis* 71 (1980): 590 and 607.

44. See, for instance, Jan Golinski's *British Weather and the Climate of Enlightenment* (Chicago, 2007) and *Science as Public Culture*, as well as Larry Stewart, *The Rise of Public Science: Rhetoric, Technology, and Natural Philosophy in Newtonian Britain, 1660–1750* (Cambridge, 1992).

45. Thomas H. Broman, "The Habermasian Public Sphere and Eighteenth-Century Historiography: A New Look at 'Science in the Enlightenment,'" *History of Science* 36 (1998): 123–49, and Jacob, "The Mental Landscape of the Public Sphere," 105–6. Without reference to Habermas, but making a similar point about the publicness of eighteenth-century science, see Thomas L. Hankins, *Science and the Enlightenment* (Cambridge, 1985), pp. 7–10.

46. Habermas, *The Structural Transformation of the Public Sphere*, p. 54.

47. David S. Lux and Harold J. Cook, "Closed Circles or Open Networks? Communicating at a Distance during the Scientific Revolution," *History of Science* 36 (1998): 179–211.

48. Lisa Jardine, *Ingenious Pursuits: Building the Scientific Revolution* (London, 1999), pp. 325–31.

49. Ibid., p. 317.

50. Peter Galison, "Removing Knowledge," *Critical Inquiry* 31 (2004): 229–43.

51. Ibid., 233.

52. Ibid., 231.

53. Agnes S. Ku, "Boundary Politics in the Public Sphere: Openness, Secrecy, and Leak," *Sociological Theory* 16 (1998): 172–92.

54. Shapin and Schaffer, *Leviathan and the Air Pump*, pp. 22–79, and Hankins, *Science and the Enlightenment*, pp. 67–72.

55. Charles Bazerman, "Forums of Validation and Forms of Knowledge: The Magical Rhetoric of Otto von Guericke's Sulfur Globe," *Configurations* 1 (1993): 201–27.

56. Trent A. Mitchell, "The Politics of Experiment in the Eighteenth Century: The Pursuit of Audience and the Manipulation of Consensus in the Debate over Lightning Rods," *Eighteenth-Century Studies* 31 (1998): 307–31.

57. Ann F. La Berge, "Debate as Scientific Practice in Nineteenth-Century France: The Controversy over the Microscope," *Perspectives on Science* 12 (2004): 437–38.

58. Ludmilla Jordanova, *Images of Gender in Science and Medicine between the Eighteenth and Twentieth Centuries* (New York, 1989).

59. Bernd Stiegler, *Philologie des Auges: Die photographische Entdeckung der Welt im 19. Jahrhundert* (Munich, 2001), pp. 17–141; Lisa Cartwright, *Screening the Body: Tracing Medicine's Visual Culture* (Minneapolis, 1995); and Jonathan Crary, *Techniques of the Observer: On Vision and Modernity in the Nineteenth Century* (Cambridge, MA, 1990).

60. Lorraine Daston and Peter Galison, *Objectivity* (New York, 2007), pp. 17–53, and Olaf Breidbach, *Bilder des Wissens: Zur Kulturgeschichte der wissenschaftlichen Wahrnehmung* (Munich, 2005).

61. Andreas W. Daum, *Wissenschaftspopularisierung im 19. Jahrhundert: Bürgerliche Kultur, naturwissenschaftliche Bildung und die deutsche Öffentlichkeit, 1848–1914* (Munich, 1998); Pierangelo Schiera, *Laboratorium der bürgerlichen Welt: Deutsche Wissenschaft im 19. Jahrhundert* (Frankfurt am Main, 1992); and Timothy Lenoir, *Politik im Tempel der Wissenschaft: Forschung und Machtausübung im deutschen Kaiserreich*, trans. Horst Brühmann (Frankfurt am Main, 1992).

62. Stiegler, *Philologie des Auges*, pp. 136–41.

63. Wilhelm Conrad Röntgen, "Ueber eine neue Art von Strahlen (Vorläufige Mittheilung)," *Sitzungsberichte der physik.-med. Gesellschaft zu Würzburg* (1895): 132–41, and

"Ueber eine neue Art von Strahlen (II. Mittheilung)," *Sitzungsberichte der physik.-med. Gesellschaft zu Würzburg* (1896): 11–19. See the account in *Annalen der Physik* 64 (1898): 1–37, and his "Weitere Betrachtungen über die Eigenschaften der X-Strahlen," *Sitzungsberichte der Königlich Preussischen Akademie der Wissenschaften zu Berlin* (1897): 576–92. An English translation of the first two papers is available as "On a New Kind of Rays," *Science* new series 3 (1896): 227–31, and "A New Form of Rays," *Science* new series 3 (1896): 726–29.

64. Thomas Mann, *The Magic Mountain*, trans. H. T. Lowe-Porter (London, 1996), pp. 211–19.

65. Joseph Dumit, *Picturing Personhood: Brain Scans and Biomedical Identity* (Princeton, NJ, 2004), p. 30. For a history of PET scanning, see Dumit, *Picturing Personhood*, pp. 27–31, and Bettyann Holtzmann Kevles, *Naked to the Bone: Medical Imaging in the Twentieth Century* (New Brunswick, NJ, 1997), pp. 201–27.

66. On the popular imagery of medical techniques and representations, see Dumit, *Picturing Personhood*, pp. 139–69, as well as Barbara Maria Stafford's "Medical Ethics as Postmodern Aesthetics," in *Good Looking: Essays on the Virtue of Images* (Cambridge, MA, 1996), pp.130–44, and *Body Criticism: Imaging the Unseen in Enlightenment Art and Medicine* (Cambridge, MA, 1991).

67. Compare, for instance, Anne Beaulieu, "Images Are Not the (Only) Truth: Brain Mapping, Visual Knowledge, and Iconoclasm," *Science, Technology, and Human Values* 27 (2002): 53–86; Peter Galison, "Images Scatter into Data, Data Gather into Images," and Hans-Jörg Rheinberger, "Auto-Radio-Graphics," both in *Iconoclash: Beyond the Image Wars in Science, Religion, and Art*, ed. Bruno Latour and Peter Weibel (Cambridge, MA, 2002), pp. 300–23 and 516–19, respectively; Michael Hagner, "Hirnbilder: Cerebrale Repräsentationen im 19. und 20. Jahrhundert," in *Der Entzug der Bilder: Visuelle Realitäten*, ed. Michael Wetzel and Herta Wolf (Munich, 1994), pp. 145–60; and Soraya de Chadarevian, "'Die Methode der Kurven' in der Physiologie zwischen 1850 und 1900," in *Die Experimentalisierung des Lebens: Experimentalsysteme in den biologischen Wissenschaften 1850/1950*, ed. Hans-Jörg Rheinberger and Michael Hagner (Berlin, 1993), pp. 28–49.

68. On the complex logic of scientific images, see Christian J. Emden, "Scanned Brains, Dyed Bacteria, and Magnified Flies: On Scientific Images and Things," in *Image-Scapes: Studies in Intermediality*, ed. Christian J. Emden and Gabriele Rippl (Oxford, 2010), pp. 67–94, and Jan Golinski, *Making Natural Knowledge: Constructivism and the History of Science* (Cambridge, 1998), pp. 145–61.

69. Theodore M. Porter, *Trust in Numbers: The Pursuit of Objectivity in Science and Public Life* (Princeton, NJ, 1995), p. 74.

70. Ibid., p. 86.

71. Joseph Rouse, *Knowledge and Power: Toward a Political Philosophy of Science* (Ithaca, NY, 1987), p. 125.

72. Rouse, *How Scientific Practices Matter*, pp. 12–13.

73. Ibid., pp. 286–87.

74. Joseph Rouse, *Engaging Science: How to Understand Its Practices Philosophically* (Ithaca, NY, 1996), pp. 184 and 259.

75. Thomas S. Kuhn, *The Structure of Scientific Revolutions*, 3rd ed. (Chicago, 1996), pp. 29 and 45.

76. Ibid., p. 46.

77. Kathryn M. Olesko, "Tacit Knowledge and School Formation," *Osiris* 2nd series 8 (1993): 16–29.

78. Ludwik Fleck, *Genesis and Devlopment of a Scientific Fact*, trans. Thaddeus J. Trenn and Robert K. Merton (Chicago, 1975).

79. Timothy Lenoir, "Models and Instruments in the Development of Electrophysiology, 1845–1912," *Historical Studies in the Physical and Biological Sciences* 17 (1986): 1–54.

80. On the formation of disciplines, see Rudolf Stichweh, "The Sociology of Scientific Disciplines: On the Genesis and Stability of the Disciplinary Structure of Modern Science," *Science in Context* 5 (1992): 3–15. On Kuhn as the founding-father of constructivism, see Golinski, *Making Natural Knowledge*, pp. 13–27.

81. Bruno Latour and Steve Woolgar, *Laboratory Life: The Construction of Scientific Facts*, 2nd ed. (Princeton, NJ, 1986), pp. 235–61; Michael Lynch, *Art and Artefact in a Laboratory Science* (London, 1985); and Karin Knorr-Cetina, *Epistemic Cultures: How the Sciences Make Knowledge* (Cambridge, MA, 1999), pp. 1–25.

82. In their postscript to the second edition of *Laboratory Life*, pp. 273–86, Latour and Woolgar sought to replace the emphasis on the social by a new emphasis on the ethnographic, thus rejecting the description of their work as social constructivist. From a different and more philosophically oriented direction, Ian Hacking has also somewhat modified his position. Compare his *Representing and Intervening* (Cambridge, 1983) to *The Social Construction of What?* (Cambridge, MA, 1999).

83. Golinski, *Making Natural Knowledge*, pp. 43–46, and Galison, *Image and Logic*, pp. 46–63; see also Dominique Pestre, "Pour une histoire sociale et culturelle des sciences: Nouvelles définitions, nouveaux objets, nouvelle practiques," *Annales* 50 (1995): 487–522.

84. Latour and Woolgar, *Laboratory Life*, pp. 63–69, and Gaston Bachelard, *Le Rationalisme appliqué*, 3rd ed. (Paris, 1998), pp. 2–3. For detailed epistemological accounts of Bachelard's phenomenotechnique, see Hans-Jörg Rheinberger, "Gaston Bachelard and the Notion of 'Phenomenotechnique,'" *Perspectives on Science* 13 (2005): 313–28; Teresa Castelao-Lawless, "Phenomenotechnique in Historical Perspective: Its Origins and Implications for Philosophy of Science," *Philosophy of Science* 62 (1995): 44–59; and Stephen W. Gaukroger, "Bachelard and the Problem of Epistemological Analysis," *Studies in the History and Philosophy of Science* 7 (1976): 189–244.

85. Latour, *Science in Action*, pp. 93, 144, and 158–59.

86. Ibid., p. 250–51.

87. Ibid., p. 251. For historical accounts of the standardization of time, see Peter Galison, *Einstein's Clocks, Poincaré's Maps: Empires of Time* (New York, 2004), pp. 84–218, and David S. Landes, *Revolution in Time: Clocks and the Making of the Modern World* (Cambridge, MA, 1983). For a discussion of the effects of this standardization as a central characteristic of modernity, see Stephen Kern, *The Culture of Time and Space, 1880–1918*, 2nd ed. (Cambridge, MA, 2003), pp. 10–35, and Götz Großklaus, *Medien-Zeit, Medien-Raum: Zum Wandel der Wahrnehmung in der Moderne* (Frankfurt am Main, 1987).

88. Joseph O'Connell, "Metrology: The Creation of Universality by the Circulation of Particulars," *Social Studies of Science* 23 (1993): 130.

89. Ibid., p. 137.

90. On the first example, see Ken Alder, "A Revolution to Measure: The Political Economy of the Metric System in France," in *The Values of Precision*, ed. M. Norton Wise (Princeton, NJ, 1995), pp. 39–71, and J. L. Heilbron, "The Measure of Enlightenment," in *The Quantifying Spirit in the Eighteenth Century*, ed. Tore Frängsmyr, J. L. Heilbron, and Robin E. Rider (Berkeley, CA, 1990), pp. 207–42. On the second example, see Christian J. Emden, "Epistemische Konstellationen, 1800–1900: Ner-

ven, Telegrafen und die Netzwerke des Wissens," in *Netzwerke: Eine Kulturtechnik der Moderne*, ed. Jürgen Barkhoff, Hartmut Böhme, and Jeanne Riou (Cologne, 2004), pp. 148–52; Iwan Rhys Morus, "'The Nervous System of Britain': Space, Time and the Electric Telegraph in the Victorian Age," *British Journal for the History of Science* 33 (2000): 455–75; and Daniel R. Haedrick, *The Tentacles of Progress: Technology Transfer in the Age of Imperialism, 1850–1940* (Oxford, 1988), pp. 97–142.

91. Bruno Latour, *Reassembling the Social: An Introduction to Actor-Network-Theory* (Oxford, 2005), pp. 159–246.

92. Golinski, *Making Natural Knowledge*, p. 177.

93. Consider, for instance, the different approaches in, on the one hand, Quentin Skinner, *Reason and Rhetoric in the Philosophy of Hobbes* (Cambridge, 1996), and on the other, Shapin and Schaffer, *Leviathan and the Air Pump*, pp. 283–331, and Shapin, *A Social History of Truth*, pp. 3–125.

94. Shapin, *A Social History of Truth*, pp. 3–41.

95. Roger Cooter and Stephen Punfrey, "Separate Spheres and Public Spaces: Reflections on the History of Science Popularization and Science in Popular Culture," *History of Science* 32 (1994): 240.

96. Galison, *Image and Logic*, pp. 803–44.

97. Ibid., p. 803.

98. Joseph Rouse, "Beyond Epistemic Sovereignty," in *The Disunity of Science: Boundaries, Contexts, and Power*, ed. Peter Galison and David J. Strump (Stanford, CA, 1996): 413 and 416.

Chapter 5

THE PUBLIC IN PUBLIC HEALTH

Anne Hardy

The concept of public health first emerged in the early decades of the nineteenth century.[1] In Britain, which by 1900 was widely acknowledged as a pioneer and leader in the field, this new concept came as a response to the rapid growth of urban populations, increasing squalor of urban environments, and rising levels of infectious disease and human misery. In earlier centuries, health was a matter for private families and individuals. The people's health became a matter for state concern and intervention only in times of extreme epidemic emergency, notably in outbreaks of bubonic plague. Public health, however, as conceptualized from around 1840, rested on the notion of *population* health, of health for the public. Intrinsic to this formulation was a further implication: that this was health publically provided—health managed and provided by the state.[2] On both counts, public health could be expected to override private interests but might be assumed to have derived from political consensus about what public health entailed—an assumption that runs through older historiography. The twin colossi of Edwin Chadwick, civil servant, disciple of Jeremy Bentham, and supposed architect of the British model of public health, and cholera bestride traditional accounts of the emergence of public health.[3] Pandemic cholera, marching out of India, struck Europe for the first time in the early 1830s. It arrived in Britain in November 1831, and raged throughout the summer and autumn of 1832.

Fifty-two thousand people lost their lives to the disease.[4] While deficiencies in, and the often complete absence of, death registration for most European countries other than England and Sweden during this period make it impossible to guess how many lost their lives to cholera in this first pandemic, there can be no doubt that they numbered in the hundreds of thousands. The disease began spreading out of India along pilgrimage and trade routes in 1826, and reached Moscow in 1830. It spread across northern Europe throughout 1831; at midsummer it was in the Baltic flax port of Riga; by October in Hamburg. Once in Hamburg, the shipping lanes to England's east coast were open; and by early 1832 cholera had also reached France.[5]

The impact of these deaths, and the financial consequences for the state of bereaved families thrown into poverty as a result, are popularly supposed to have opened Chadwick's eyes to the economic costs of disease in the context of Poor Law reform. It was Chadwick who engineered the great Sanitary Report of 1842, which brought these issues into the public domain.[6] The report and subsequent investigations led to the passing of the first Public Health Act in 1848. And it was Chadwick, acting on the theory that the vapors given off by rotting organic matter caused disease, who fashioned the environmentalist character of sanitary reform, in the state regulation for drains and sewers, the removal of nuisances, and the provision of clean water supplies.[7]

These earliest manifestations of the English public health movement occurred in the very years that Habermas pinpointed as the transforming phase of the public sphere. The First Reform Bill, he noted, transformed Parliament into "the very organ of public opinion."[8] In the 1840s, the Chartist movement in England and the 1848 revolts on the Continent "thoroughly altered the outward appearance of the public sphere."[9] No longer could consensus rule—the possibility of "friend-or-foe relations" had come into existence. Under this model, the 1848 Public Health Act could be seen as one of the last pieces of legislation to embody "the reasonable consensus of publicly debating private persons."[10] Although public health reform had widespread popular support in 1847–48, with more than 630 petitions to Parliament in favor of legislation and fewer than 50 explicitly opposed, consensus was nonetheless very far from the case, as recent revisionist historians have demonstrated.[11] Unlike the German model of liberalism, which, especially during the nineteenth century, emphasized the interests and responsibilities of the state over those of "private persons" in regard to public welfare, English liberalism was more individualistic in orientation. Habermas may not have fully appreciated the extent to which notions of public and social justice outside the institutions of the state were discussed and debated, and the extent to which freedom of the individual, and individual responsibility for managing the affairs of life, was accepted in England.[12] Christopher Hamlin, for example, has shown that the Chadwickian model of reform emerged triumphant over a very different approach to problems of poverty and disease—an approach that focused on the problem of poverty and social injustice, rather than on that of the disease, which Chadwick argued underpinned the poverty.[13] Moreover, the very provisions of the Public Health Act suggest that Parliament was well aware that it was not being guided by public opinion in implementing public health reform. The act was essentially adoptive—local authorities were *empowered*, not required, to comply with its provisions, unless they had death rates of over twenty-three per thousand of their populations.[14] In this, the 1848 Public Health Act set a pattern for the future implementation of reforming health legislation in Britain. As late as the 1960s, when government was responding to the debacle of the thalidomide tragedy, participation in the regulatory mechanisms was initially voluntary on the part of the drug companies. Mandatory participation came a few years later.[15] While the twentieth century saw the state develop relations with private corporate bodies, in the nineteenth century the strong tradition of English local government inhibited the state from introducing radical administrative reforms that were nonnegotiable locally—at least in the first instance.[16] The intertwining of state and society in nineteenth-century England was arguably a much slower, and more negotiated, process than Habermas suggested.

Health, in fact, was one area in which consensus was in abeyance almost from the moment that the possibilities of population health began to emerge. In matters of the individual body the imposition of state regulation would always be a highly contentious matter in England. The English passion for liberty, noted by Montesquieu as early as 1729, was arguably at its most passionate with respect to the individual right to control bodily well-being.[17] Moreover, in the well-established tradition of humoral medicine, each individual body possessed its own distinctive character, its own unique constitutional balance of bile, blood, and phlegm. In an understanding of this individuality lay the key to health and the management of illness.[18] In 1758, for example, one—admittedly American—father wrote of his frail son's preparation for inoculation against smallpox, that it must necessarily differ from that practiced among country people, "who are generally of strong robust constitution."[19] Humoral theories persisted in popular understandings of the body, health, and illness into the nineteenth century, reinforcing ideas of personal liberty and autonomy with respect to medical interventions, at least until new forms of medical knowledge had established themselves.[20] The English Friendly society members studied by James Riley, for example, frequently contested medical opinion in the mid-nineteenth century, but by its end had come to accept the doctor's verdict and defer to his judgment.[21] Acceptance of medical expertise was not, however, accompanied by a parallel or unquestioning acceptance of the state's right to impose medical or health-related interventions on the individual citizen, or, indeed, on that citizen's environment.

The history of English attempts to control smallpox illustrates not only potential for dissension within the bourgeois public sphere, but also the ability of dissentient groups to defeat the extending reach of bureaucracy. Smallpox, now again in the news as a potential bioterrorist weapon, is one of the most unpleasant diseases known to man. It is a disease of great antiquity, and during its long history humans have struggled to protect themselves against its more virulent forms. Folk practices such as smearing smallpox matter from mild cases on the skin, or carrying pox scabs in the palm of the hand, in the hope of contracting a similarly mild case are documented in Britain from the seventeenth century at least.[22] In China, the practice of variolation or inoculation, inserting smallpox matter from a mild case under the skin, was developed early and the practice spread with trade out of China as far as Turkey by the early eighteenth century. It was here that Lady Mary Wortley Montagu, wife of the English ambassador to Constantinople, came across it, and introduced it in England in 1720. The English Crown arranged for a trial of the new technique on a group of condemned prisoners, who were promised release and pardon if they survived, but otherwise took no action to promote the operation.[23] The prisoners survived, were pardoned and released, and the scene was set for the technique of inoculation to be adopted by private families and individuals. During the course of the eighteenth century, variolation came to be widely practiced among all social classes, and indeed developed into something of an industry for apothecaries and self-styled inoculators alike.[24] Because the inoculated individual develops a case of (with luck mild) smallpox and he or she is infectious, elaborate rituals developed around the operation, at least for the better-to-do. These involved medically supervised preparation, specially designated "inoculation houses" for isolating patients, and, of course, medical supervision of the course of the disease. The pros and cons of inoculation were widely debated in the bourgeois public sphere,[25] but the decision to inoculate remained a personal, private matter.

This situation changed at the end of the eighteenth century. In 1796, the English general practitioner Edward Jenner developed the technique known as vaccination, based on the observation that local people infected with cow pox were immune to smallpox. Vaccination carried no risk of developing the more severe infection. Within a very short space of time, inoculation versus vaccination became a highly contentious issue. Arguably, a sense of "public health"—of the wider social responsibilities involved in personal health decisions—emerged among the bourgeoisie at this period specifically in response to the inoculation/vaccination issue. Thus, in April 1810, for example, the Reverend William Holland, a Somerset parson, recorded in his diary:

> I went to Doddington, very few at Church as there is an inoculation for Small Pox which shuts up Mr Farthing and one or two families more. But now that the Cow Pox is so much approved of, and so much safer, I do not think it right in Mr Bennet (apothecary) recommending inoculation ... which is infectious and if one family begins it obliges others to adopt the same measures whether they approve it or not.[26]

The operation of the public sphere of debate around the issue of vaccination and variolation is very apparent in England in the years between 1796 and circa 1830. The subject generated a vast pamphlet literature, as the proponents of the rival techniques sought to out-argue each other. Satirical comment flourished. Jenner himself entered into an enormous correspondence with interested individuals—more than six hundred such letters from him still survive; Jenner wryly described himself as "vaccination clerk to the world."[27] There was no consensus here, nor was it possible. Tradition, vested interests, religion, folk beliefs, political culture, and science were all embroiled. To a large degree, natural smallpox and variolation are one and the same thing, and issues of individual choice and public responsibility could coexist. The advent of vaccination, in offering a real choice of avoidance, disrupted that consensus. For devout Anglicans, for example, smallpox was an act of God, and vaccination a deliberate flouting of divine will. For a great many people, the injection of a substance derived from animals into the human body was profoundly unnatural and disturbing.[28] And as European states began to implement measures of compulsory vaccination for their populations, so the English debate became more politically edged. Smallpox was a destroyer of human capital, with a death rate of between 30 and 50 percent, and it not only killed but maimed. Scarring, blindness, and internal damage, notably to the respiratory system, were common sequelae. Smallpox also inhibited fertility—the demographic evidence suggests that women scarred by smallpox married on average a decade later than women who had escaped.[29] From the nation-state's point of view, vaccination was an undoubted public good: it preserved manpower, and the power of the state.[30] In England, however, the state's attitude toward compulsion was from the beginning tempered by the prevailing political culture—by the recognition of the power of the ideal of personal liberty. Again, Germany's failure to develop a serious notion of personal liberty throughout the nineteenth century may have clouded Habermas's vision of English reality. The smallpox vaccination story demonstrates that individual liberty was a potent factor in English politics. Already in June 1808, for example, we find the then foreign secretary, George Canning, declaring before the House of Commons that although he considered the discovery of vaccination to be of the very greatest importance, he "could not figure any circumstances whatever that could induce him to follow up the most favorable report of its infallibility which might be brought forward, with any measure of a compulsory nature."[31]

For these reasons, compulsory smallpox vaccination was a long time coming in England. Only in 1853 was it required for infants under the age of one, and for twenty years the law was patchily observed. In 1867, the government passed the "Cat and Mouse Act," which enabled the serial prosecution of parents who defaulted on their responsibility to vaccinate. And in 1871, under the shadow of the most serious epidemic of the century, a new network of vaccination inspectors was established to enforce the law. The result was the immediate formation of a number of antivaccination groups, both middle class and working class, who mounted an escalating and vociferous opposition to the law over the next thirty years with measures that involved not only collective action, but also repeated and persistent individual acts of defiance.[32] In 1890, the government appointed a Royal Commission to review the whole situation, and within a few years, the vaccination policy was in tatters. In the face of the doubt in the policy that the commission signaled, many local authorities simply stopped trying to enforce the law.[33] Modified to allow conscientious objection in 1898, the law on compulsion was finally abandoned in 1907. The failure of the vaccination acts clearly demonstrates that in matters of health public pressure could influence government, and indeed continues to do so. Into the twenty-first century, no other form of immunization, whatever its public health utility, has been made compulsory for the English people. Where Habermas argues for the public sphere as an arena for conferring legitimacy on government action, we can see here that both public opinion, and the concerted individual actions of private individuals affected—or antagonized—by government provision, can undermine that legitimacy. Other English examples that might be instanced here are the overturning of the Contagious Diseases Acts, which sought to regulate the activities of prostitutes in garrison towns in the 1860s, and Parliament's acceptance of scientific arguments in favor of animal experiments and its concomitant failure to bow to antivivisectionist pressure for their abolition in the 1870s and 1880s. By contrast, the principal countries of continental Europe continued to pursue regulationist policies against prostitutes for most of the century, while animal experimentation never raised the level of public concern in Europe that it did in England.[34]

In terms of public health, the case of vaccination demonstrates that there was not one public but many, even before the concept of "public health" had been formulated. Chadwick's public health did not deal in the human body, however; it was aimed at creating a sanitary environment within which human bodies would be free of the specter of disease. Nonetheless, central government was not directly involved in organizing this transformation of the human environment. The government made the law, but administrative power was devolved to the local authorities. These authorities were, however, not just public bodies; they were elected by local taxpayers from among their own number. They had no tradition of allegiance to central government; indeed, they traditionally resented its authority. Their membership was a socially eclectic mix—doctors, lawyers, ministers, property owners, butchers, bakers, and candlestick makers, even the occasional aristocrat. As individuals, these men had no strong allegiance to central government, but were accustomed to critiquing it from a local perspective. They formed their own opinions and operated in constant dialogue with their local community. The local sanitary state was not distinct from civil society, but closely integrated with it—in the words of Steve Sturdy, the boundaries were blurred and permeable.[35] Even designated health officials employed by local government operated in the wider community—medical officers of health were also surgeons or general practitioners, sanitary inspectors had been schoolteachers or butchers or policemen. Local government bodies provided a focus around which a wide public of householders, shopkeepers, tenants, and other private citizens could and did articulate their needs and interests.[36]

Contrary to Habermas's assumption, the interpenetration of state and society at this level did not stifle critical reflection and debate. The local records show that these citizens could and did engage in discussion with and intense lobbying of local government on a wide range of public health issues, from the siting of mortuaries, public lavatories, and infectious disease hospitals to the keeping of domestic animals.[37] Application of the law on nuisances, for example, was subjected to a range of modifications in practice. Passed in 1855, it gave the local authorities powers to curb environmental practices that were deemed "a nuisance or injury to health." How this was constituted varied, however.[38] As one medical officer noted in 1855: "In this 19th century there are still some, not without education, who believe foulness both healthy and fattening."[39] The local authority officials might use the law against nuisances that they themselves identified. Once in court, however, they might find their case dismissed by a magistrate with very different views—in the 1880s, for example, we find the medical officer for Birmingham complaining that he could not take action against the widespread local habit of keeping quantities of domestic rabbits and fowls in working class houses, since it was argued by those in authority both that these effected moral improvement and that they constituted an essential part of the working class economy.[40] On the other hand, the law might be invoked when individual citizens or communities appealed to the authority against, for example, the keeping of pigs by a neighbor. On occasions, the local community even took action against the local authority. The London district of Newington, south of the Thames, maintained a depot where it accumulated household refuse and street sweepings in large quantities. Always noisome, and deeply offensive in hot weather, the depot also contributed to a vast intensification of the urban fly population in its immediate vicinity. During the 1890s, a decade notorious for its share of blazing summers, local discontent with the depot mounted. Letters of protest to the authority led to public meetings, petitions, and a local press campaign. Eventually the Vestry was forced to make arrangements for the regular and speedy transfer of "dust" out of the parish by rail.[41] Similar vigorous local opposition was roused by the prospect of having an isolation hospital erected locally.[42] In such cases, local opposition, although with common cause, tended to be diverse and heterogeneous rather than the more monolithic entity conceived by Habermas. Fears of infection, fears for property values, the consciousness of nuisance, and local pride were among a multiplicity of factors influencing concerted action. As Steve Sturdy notes, "such movements do not depend for their impact solely on rational debate, or even on more emotive forms of discourse."[43]

Public participation in the construction and interpretation of public health was very much a part of the Victorian local government scene. It was also a two-way process—local officials sought to guide public opinion on sanitary issues. Public education formed a significant strand of the activities of local health officers from the beginning, thus contributing to the creation and shaping of public opinion. Medical officers organized public lectures and published thousands of tracts, leaflets, and pamphlets on health and sanitary subjects—tracts with titles such as *How People Hasten Death* and *The Black Hole in Our Own Bedrooms*.[44] From the 1870s onward such efforts were increasingly supplemented by the activities of voluntary organizations, like the Sanitary Institute, the Ladies Sanitary Association, and even the "Bible women."[45] The message of public health was put across not just by the state through legislation, but also by the independent voluntary participation of local officials and private citizens, many of whom, by the 1880s, were women.

If this vigorous and critical English public involvement in local public health issues was subdued with the completion of the sanitary state, that is to say, as issues of environmental nuisance were resolved, it never quite disappeared. Even though central government began to bypass local government after 1900 to work with private corporations and an increasingly privatized voluntary sector in providing health insurance, social services, and medical care, these publics did not entirely transform into passive consumers.[46] Public health issues continued to engage many and various publics, which continued and still continue to form and to engage in collective social and political action by bringing direct pressure to bear on governments, and by asserting their individual rights as consumers. From the 1890s into the 1940s, for example, women's groups campaigned for family allowances for women, on the grounds that only then could the health of children be properly supported.[47] In the 1960s, many local communities fought vigorously against the introduction of fluoridated water supplies.[48] The recent controversy over the MMR vaccine has seen parents asserting their right to opt for single immunizations instead of the combined vaccine, while individual protesters still seek to challenge official restrictions on access to forms of treatment, or the right to die, through the courts. As Steve Sturdy notes, "we impoverish our understanding of the public and its function if we confine ourselves to thinking solely in terms of discourse, and thereby neglect the role of institutionalized action in the constitution of the public sphere."[49] Collective action by petition to Parliament or through the courts, protests via the media or on the streets, by pressure group or public demonstration or private action, was and is an intrinsic and continuing English approach to critiquing the actions and policies of central and local government. The very term public health, which was displaced in the mid-1970s by the term "community health," has again returned to administrative favor. Public health, with its connotations of state provision and state interest, was never a monolithic state enterprise in Britain. There was no decay of a once unified public sphere of rational discussion and opinion formation: the individuality of the human body, personal assessments of health and well-being, and the evaluation of particular risks to community and individual have always divided opinion on health issues. Throughout its career, public health has engaged multiple publics that, as communities and individuals, have sought to fashion and adapt public health's methods and messages to accommodate their own perceptions of what constitutes healthy environments and healthy practices.

Notes

I am grateful to Hal Cook, Marguerite Dupree, and Michael Neve for helping to clarify my thinking on this topic, and to Christian J. Emden for constructive criticism of an earlier draft.

1. The relationship between public health and the public sphere has been strangely neglected in the historiography of medicine. A distinguished exception is the volume of essays edited by Steve Sturdy, *Medicine, Health and the Public Sphere in Britain, 1600–2000* (London, 2002). The essays in Part III of this volume, "The State and the Public Sphere," especially those by Deborah Brunton, Christopher Hamlin, and Logie Barrow, are particularly relevant to the present chapter. I have, however, not sought to engage with these historiographically, and indeed have read them with glancing eye in the interests of achieving my own reading of the topic. For another recent contribution to this area, see Tom Crook, "Sanitary Inspection in the Public Sphere in Late Victorian and Edwardian Britain: A Case Study in Liberal Governance," *Social History* 32 (2007): 369–93.

2. For this background, see Anthony S. Wohl, *Endangered Lives: Public Health in Victorian Britain* (London, 1984); Dorothy Porter, *Health, Civilisation and the State: A History of Public Health from Ancient to Modern Times* (London, 1999); and Christopher Hamlin and Sally Sheard, "Revolutions in Public Health: 1848, and 1998?" *British Medical Journal* 317 (1998): 592–96.

3. See, for example, Samuel E. Finer, *The Life and Times of Sir Edwin Chadwick* (London, 1952), and Richard A. Lewis, *Edwin Chadwick and the Public Health Movement, 1832–48* (London, 1952).

4. R. J. Morris, *Cholera, 1832: The Social Response to an Epidemic* (London, 1976).

5. Ibid., pp. 22–23.

6. The background to the report was rather more complicated than popular myth allows. See Michael W. Flinn, ed., *Report on the Sanitary Condition of the Labouring Population of Great Britain by Edwin Chadwick* (Edinburgh, UK, 1965); Margaret Pelling, *Cholera, Fever and English Medicine* (Oxford, 1978); and Christopher Hamlin, *Public Health and Social Justice in the Age of Chadwick* (Cambridge, 1998).

7. Hamlin and Sheard, "Revolutions in Public Health."

8. Habermas, *The Structural Transformation of the Public Sphere*, p. 62.

9. Ibid., p. 131.

10. Ibid., p. 132.

11. On these petitions see James G. Hanley, "The Public's Reaction to Public Health: Petitions Submitted to Parliament, 1847–1848," *Social History of Medicine* 15 (2002): 393–94.

12. See also Ole Peter Grell and Andrew Cunningham, "Health Care and Poor Relief in 18th- and 19th- Century Northern Europe," in *Health Care and Poor Relief in 18th- and 19th-Century Northern Europe*, ed. Ole Peter Grell and Andrew Cunningham (Aldershot, 2002), p. 4.

13. Hamlin, *Public Health and Social Justice*.

14. Hamlin and Sheard, "Revolutions in Public Health," 587.

15. D. Gould, "Can We Handle Modern Drugs?" *New Scientist* 62 (1974): 460–71.

16. On the English local government tradition, see Derek Fraser, *Power and Authority in the Victorian City* (Oxford, 1979).

17. Cited in Alan Macfarlane, *The Origins of English Individualism: The Family, Property and Social Transition* (Oxford, 1978), pp. 168–69.

18. Andrew Wear, *Knowledge and Practice in English Medicine, 1550–1680* (Cambridge, 2000), pp. 37–40.
19. Sara Stidstone Gronin, "Imagining Inoculation: Smallpox, the Body and Social Relations of Healing in the Eighteenth Century," *Bulletin of the History of Medicine* 80 (2006): 254–58.
20. N. Jewson, "The Disappearance of the Sick-man from Medical Cosmology, 1770–1870," *Sociology* 10 (1976): 225–44.
21. James C Riley, *Sick Not Dead: The Health of British Workingmen during the Mortality Decline* (Baltimore, 1997), pp. 270–71. Riley puts an economic interpretation on this behavioral shift, but the evidence for the increasing professional authority of medicine in the period makes it permissible to offer this as a contributory or parallel factor influencing the shift.
22. Maisie May, "Inoculating the Urban Poor in the Eighteenth Century," *British Journal for the History of Science* 30 (1997): 293.
23. Isobel Grundy, *Lady Mary Wortley Montagu* (Oxford, 1999), pp. 209–22.
24. Peter Razzell, *The Conquest of Smallpox: The Impact of Inoculation on Smallpox Mortality in Eighteenth-Century Britain* (Firle, 1977).
25. Andrea Rusnock, *Vital Accounts: Quantifying Health and Population in Eighteenth-Century England and France* (Cambridge, 2002), chap. 2 and 3.
26. Jack Ayres, ed., *Paupers and Pig Killers: The Diary of William Holland, a Somerset Parson, 1799–1818* (Gloucester, 1984), pp. 280–81.
27. Genevieve Miller, ed., *Letters of Edward Jenner* (Baltimore, 1983), pp. xix and xxii.
28. Roy M. McLeod, "Law, Medicine and Public Opinion: The Resistance to Compulsory Health Legislation, 1870–1907," *Public Law* (Summer/Autumn, 1967): 108–13.
29. Peter Sköld, *The Two Faces of Smallpox: A Disease and Its Prevention in Eighteenth- and Nineteenth-Century Sweden* (Umeå, 1996), pp. 210–20.
30. Peter Baldwin, *Contagion and the State in Europe 1830–1930* (Cambridge, 1999), pp. 245–46.
31. *Hansard Parliamentary Debates* xi (9 June 1808), col. 844.
32. Ann Beck, "Issues in the Anti-vaccination Movement in England," *Medical History* 4 (1960): 310–321; McLeod, "Law, Medicine and Public Opinion"; Roy and Dorothy Porter, "The Politics of Prevention: Antivaccinationism and Public Health in Nineteenth-Century England," *Medical History* 32 (1988): 231–52; Logie Barrow, "In the Beginning was the Lymph: The Hollowing of Stational Vaccination in England and Wales 1840–98," in Sturdy, *Medicine, Health and the Public Sphere in Britain*, pp. 205–23; Nadja Durbach, *Bodily Matters: The Anti-vaccination Movement in England 1853–1907* (Durham, NC, 2005). See also Baldwin, *Contagion and the State in Europe*, chap. 4.
33. Anne Hardy, *The Epidemic Streets: Infectious Disease and the Rise of Preventive Medicine* (Oxford, 1993), pp. 126–28.
34. On the regulation of prostitutes, see Roger Davidson and Lesley Hall, "Introduction," in *Sex, Sin and Suffering: Venereal Disease and European Society since 1870*, ed. Roger Davidson and Lesley Hall (London, 2001), pp. 1–14, for an excellent overview, as well as individual essays. See also Baldwin, *Contagion and the State*, chap. 5. On antivivisection, see Nicolaas A. Rupke, ed., *Antivivisection in Historical Perspective* (London, 1990); and Mark N. Ozer, "The British Vivisection Controversy," *Bulletin of the History of Medicine* 40 (1960): 158–67.
35. Sturdy, "Introduction," in Sturdy, *Medicine, Health and the Public Sphere in Britain*, pp. 12–13. See also Deborah Brunton, "Policy, Powers and Practice: The Public Re-

sponse to Public Health in the Scottish City," in Sturdy, *Medicine, Health and the Public Sphere in Britain*, pp. 171–88.

36. Brunton, "Policy, Powers and Practice," p. 182.
37. Ibid., pp. 171–88.
38. Christopher Hamlin, "Public Sphere to Public Health: The Transformation of 'Nuisance,'" in Sturdy, *Medicine, Health and the Public Sphere in Britain*, pp. 189–204.
39. *Medical Officer's Half-Yearly Report*, St George-the-Martyr (London), July 1856, p. 14.
40. Anne Hardy, "Pioneers in the Victorian Provinces: Veterinarians and Public Health and the Urban Animal Economy," *Urban History* 29 (2002): 387.
41. *St Mary Newington, Vestry Minutes*, 1892–1900.
42. Hardy, *The Epidemic Streets*, p. 139.
43. Sturdy, "Introduction," p. 20.
44. Hardy, *The Epidemic Streets*, pp. 275–77.
45. See Frank Prochaska's "Body and Soul: Bible Nurses and the Poor in Victorian London," *Historical Research* 60 (1987): 336–48, and "A Mother's Country: Mothers' Meetings and Family Welfare in Britain, 1850–1950," *History* 74 (1989): 379–99.
46. Sturdy, "Introduction," pp. 19–20.
47. Jane Lewis, *The Politics of Motherhood: Child and Maternal Welfare in England 1900-1939* (London, 1980), pp. 165–89.
48. Charles Webster, *The Health Services since the War, II: Government and Health Care—the British National Health Service, 1958–1979* (London, 1996), pp. 131–33 and 661–65.
49. Sturdy, "Introduction," p. 20.

Chapter 6

GEEKS AND RECURSIVE PUBLICS
How the Internet and Free Software Make Things Public

Christopher Kelty

Since about 1997, I have been living with geeks online and off. I have been drawn from Boston to Bangalore to Berlin to Houston to Palo Alto, from conferences and workshops to launch parties, pubs, and Internet Relay Chats (IRCs). Along the way a question has emerged: What binds "geeks" together? Why do they all seem to speak the same language, share the same ideas, and collaborate on building the same kinds of technologies? This essay presents a theory of "recursive publics" as a way to answer these questions.[1] A recursive public is a public that is constituted by a shared concern for maintaining the means of association through which they come together as a public. Geeks find affinity with one another because they share an abiding moral imagination of the technical infrastructure, the Internet, that has allowed them to develop and maintain this affinity in the first place. In the following, I elaborate the concept of recursive public (which is not a term used by geeks) in relation to theories of ideology, publics, and public spheres and social imaginaries. Much of this theory was developed through ethnographic participant observation at, among other sites, a Boston-based health care technology start-up between 1997 and 2003, participation with new media academics and activists in Berlin in 1999–2001, and participation with a group of largely Bangalore-based information technology (IT) professionals on and offline.

I use the phrase "moral and technical order" to signal both technology—principally software, hardware, networks, and protocols—and the imagination of the proper order of collective political and commercial action, that is, of how economy and society should be ordered collectively. Recursive publics are just as concerned with the moral order of markets as they are with that of commons; they are not anticommercial or antigovernment. They exist independent of, and as a check on, constituted forms of power, which include markets and corporations. Unlike other concepts of a public or of a public sphere, "recursive public" captures the fact that geeks' principal mode of associating and acting is through the medium of the Internet, and it is through this medium that a recursive public can come into being in the first place. The Internet is not itself a public sphere, a public, or a recursive public, but a complex, heterogeneous infrastructure that constitutes and constrains geeks' everyday practical commitments, their ability to "become public" or to compose a common world. As such, their participation qua recursive publics structures their identity as creative and autonomous individuals. The fact that the geeks described here have been brought together by mailing lists and e-mail, bulletin board services and websites, books and modems, air travel and academia, and cross-talking and cross-posting in ways that were not possible before the Internet is at the core of their own reasoning about why they associate with each other. They are the builders and imaginers of this space, and the space is what allows them to build and imagine it.

Recursive Publics

Recursion (or "recursive") is a mathematical concept, one which is a standard feature of any education in computer programming. The definition from the *Oxford English Dictionary* reads: "2. a. Involving or being a repeated procedure such that the required result at each step except the last is given in terms of the result(s) of the next step, until after a finite number of steps a terminus is reached with an outright evaluation of the result." It should be distinguished from simple iteration or repetition. Recursion is always subject to a limit and is more like a process of repeated deferral, until the last step in the process, at which point all the deferred steps are calculated and the result given. Recursion is powerful in programming because it allows for the definition of procedures in terms of themselves—something that seems at first counterintuitive.[2]

In the present essay a recursive public is one whose existence (which consists solely in address through discourse) is only possible through discursive and technical reference to the means of creating this public. Recursiveness is always contingent on a limit that determines the depth of a recursive procedure. So, for instance, a free software project may depend on some other kind of software or operating system, which may in turn depend on particular open protocols or a particular process, which in turn depend on certain kinds of hardware that implement them. The "depth" of recursion is determined by the openness necessary for the project itself. James Boyle has also noted the recursive nature, in particular, of free software: "What's more, and this is a truly fascinating twist, when the production process does need more centralized coordination, some governance that guides how the sticky modular bits are put together, it is at least theoretically possible that we can come up with the control system *in exactly the same way*. In this sense, distributed production is potentially recursive."[3]

The concept of "recursive publics" is, then, used for two reasons: first, to signal that this kind of public includes the activities of making, maintaining, and modifying software and networks, as well as the more conventional discourse that is thereby enabled; and second, to suggest the recursive "depth" of the public, the series of technical and legal layers— from applications to protocols to the physical infrastructures of waves and wires—that are the subject of this making, maintaining, and modifying. The first of these characteristics is evident in the fact that geeks use technology as a kind of argument for a specific kind of order: they argue *about* technology, but they also argue *through* it. They express ideas, but they also express *infrastructures* through which ideals can be expressed (and circulated) in new ways. The second of these characteristics—regarding layers—is reflected in the ability of geeks to immediately see connections between, for example, Napster (a user application) and TCP/IP (a network protocol) and to draw out implications for both of them. By connecting these layers, Napster comes to represent the Internet in miniature. The question of where these layers stop (hardware? laws and regulations? physical constants?) circumscribes the limits of the imagination of technical and moral order shared by geeks. Above all, "recursive public" is a concept—not a thing. It is intended to make distinctions, allow comparison, highlight salient features, and relate two diverse kinds of things (the Internet and free software) in a particular historical context of changing relations of power and knowledge.

Geeks and Their Internets

What distinguishes geeks? Some are entrepreneurs and some are idealists, and some are a paradoxical combination. They are certainly obsessed with technology, but especially with the Internet, and they clearly distinguish themselves from others who are obsessed with technology of just any sort. Not all geeks are the same, but they all seem to have a certain affinity. Where do their sympathies lie? Who are they *with*? Who do they recognize as being like them? What might draw them together with other geeks if not a corporation, a nation, a language, or a cause? What binds these two geeks to any others?

The term *geek* is meant to be inclusive and to index the problematic of a recursive public. Other terms may be equally useful, but perhaps semantically overdetermined, most notably *hacker*, which, regardless of its definitional range, tends to connote someone subversive and/or criminal and to exclude geek-sympathetic entrepreneurs, lawyers, and activists.[4] *Geek* is meant to signal, like the *public* in "recursive public," that geeks stand outside power, at least in some aspects, and that they are not capitalists or technocrats, even if they start businesses or work in government or industry. *Geek* is meant to signal a mode of thinking and working, not an identity; it is a mode or quality that allows people to find each other, for reasons other than the fact that they share an office, a degree, a language, or a nation.

Until the mid-1990s, *hacker, geek,* and *computer nerd* designated a very specific type: programmers and lurkers on relatively underground networks, usually college students, computer scientists, and "amateurs" or "hobbyists." A classic mock self-diagnostic called the Geek Code, by Robert Hayden, accurately and humorously detailed the various ways in which one could be a geek in 1996—UNIX/Linux skills, love/hate of *Star Trek*, particular eating and clothing habits—but as Hayden himself points out, the geeks of the early 1990s exist no longer. The elite subcultural, relatively homogenous group it once was has been overrun: "The Internet of 1996 was still a wild untamed virgin paradise of geeks and eggheads unpopulated by script kiddies, and the denizens of AOL. When things changed, I seriously lost my way. I mean, all the 'geek' that was the Internet was gone and replaced by Xfiles buzzwords and politicians passing laws about a technology they refused to comprehend."[5]

For the purists like Hayden, geeks were there first, and they understood something, lived in a way, that simply cannot be comprehended by "script kiddies" (i.e., teenagers who perform the hacking equivalent of spray painting or cow tipping), crackers, or AOL users, all of whom are despised by Hayden-style geeks as unskilled users who parade around the Internet as if they own it. While certainly elitist, Hayden captures the distinction between those who are legitimately allowed to call themselves geeks (or hackers) and those who aren't, a distinction that is often formulated recursively, of course: "You are a hacker when another hacker calls you a hacker."

However, since the explosive growth of the Internet, *geek* has become more common a designation, and my use of the term thus suggests a role that is larger than programmer/hacker, but not as large as "all Internet users." Despite Hayden's frustration, geeks are still bound together as an elite and can be easily distinguished from "AOL users." Some of the people I discuss would not call themselves geeks, and some would. Not all are engineers or programmers: I have met businessmen, lawyers, activists, bloggers, gastroenterologists, anthropologists, lesbians, schizophrenics, scientists, poets, people suffering from malaria, sea captains, drug dealers, and people who keep lemurs, many of whom refer to themselves as geeks, some of the time.[6] There are also lawyers, politicians, sociologists, and economists who may not refer to themselves as geeks, but who care about the Internet just as other geeks do. By contrast, "users" of the Internet, even those who use it eighteen out of twenty-four hours in a day to ship goods and play games, are not necessarily geeks by this characterization.

Operating Systems and Social Systems

In 1999, I moved to Berlin, Germany, where I very quickly met up with a community of geeks. Quite often, upon arriving, I found myself having conversations (in halting German that quickly converted to English) about the GNU General Public License, the Debian Linux Distribution, open standards in net radio, and a variety of things that, despite my limited German, still seemed extremely familiar: Internet standards and open systems and licensing issues and namespaces and patent law and so on. These were not businesspeople, not a start-up company in Boston, where I had been until then. Before long, I had met Volker Grassmuck, founding member of Mikro (an occasional and hybrid media/activist/art organization) and organizer of the successful "Wizards of OS" conference, held earlier in the year, which had the very intriguing subtitle "Operating Systems and Social Systems." In the following months I met a huge number of people who seemed, uncharacteristically for artists and activists, strangely obsessed with configuring their Linux distributions or hacking the http protocol or attending German Parliament hearings on copyright reform. The political lives of these folks have indeed mixed up operating systems and social systems in ways that are more than metaphorical.

If intuition can lead one from geek to geek, from start-up in Boston to nightclub in Berlin, and across countries, languages, and professional orientations, it can only be due to a shared set of ideas of how things fit together in the world. These ideas might be "cultural" in the traditional sense of finding expression among a community of people who share backgrounds, homes, nations, languages, idioms, norms, or an ethnos, or other designators of belonging and copresence. But because the Internet—like colonialism, satellite broadcasting, and air travel, among other things—crosses all these lines with abandon, that shared idea of order is better understood as part of a public, or public sphere, a vast republic of letters and media and ideas circulating in and through our thoughts and papers and letters and conversations, at a planetary scope and scale.

"Public sphere" is an odd kind of thing, however. It is at once a concept—intended to make sense of a space that is not the here and now, but one made up of writings, ideas, and discussions—and a set of ideas that people have about themselves and their own participation in such a space. I must be able to imagine myself speaking and being spoken to in such a space and to imagine a great number of other people also doing so according to unwritten rules we share. I do not need a complete theory, and I do not need to call it a public sphere, but I must somehow share an idea of order with all those other people who also imagine themselves participating in and subjecting themselves to that order. In fact, if the public sphere exists as more than just a theory, then it has no other basis than just such a shared imagination of order, an imagination that provides a guide against which to make judgments and a map for changing or achieving that order. Without such a shared imagination, a public sphere is otherwise nothing more than a cacophony of voices and information, nothing more than a stream of data, structured and formatted by and for machines, whether paper or electronic.

Charles Taylor, building on the work of Jürgen Habermas and Michael Warner, suggests that the public sphere (both idea and thing) that emerged in the eighteenth century was created through practices of communication and association that reflected a moral order in which the public stands outside power and guides or checks its operation through shared discourse and enlightened discussion. Contrary to the experience of bodies coming together into a common space (Taylor calls them "topical spaces," such as conversation, ritual, assembly), the crucial component is that the public sphere "transcends such topical spaces. We might say that it knits a plurality of spaces into one larger space of non-assembly. The same public discussion is deemed to pass through our debate today, and someone else's earnest conversation tomorrow, and the newspaper interview Thursday and so on. ... The public sphere that emerges in the eighteenth century is a meta-topical common space."[7]

Because of this, Taylor refers to his version of a public as a "social imaginary," a way of capturing a phenomenon that wavers between having concrete existence "out there" and imagined rational existence "in here." There are a handful of other such imagined spaces—the economy, the self-governing people, civil society—and in Taylor's philosophical history they are related to each other through the "ideas of moral and social order" that have developed in the West and around the world.[8]

Taylor's social imaginary is intended to do something specific: to resist the "spectre of idealism," the distinction between ideas and practices, between "ideologies" and the so-called material world as "rival causal agents." Taylor suggests, "Because human practices are the kind of thing that makes sense, certain ideas are internal to them; one cannot distinguish the two in order to ask the question: Which causes which?"[9] Even if materialist explanations of cause are satisfying, as they often are, Taylor argues that they are so "at the cost of being implausible as a universal principle," and he offers instead an analysis of the rise of the modern imaginaries of moral order.[10]

The concept of recursive public, like that of Taylor's public sphere, is understood here as a kind of social imaginary. The primary reason is to bypass the dichotomy between ideas and material practice. Because the creation of software, networks, and legal documents are precisely the kinds of activities that trouble this distinction—they are at once ideas and things that have material effects in the world, both expressive and performative—it is extremely difficult to identify the properly material materiality (source code? computer chips? semiconductor manufacturing plants?). This is the first of the reasons why a recursive public is to be distinguished from the classic formulae of the public sphere, that is, because it requires a kind of imagination that includes the writing and publishing and speaking and arguing we are familiar with, as well as the making of new kinds of software infrastructures for the circulation, archiving, movement, and modifiability of our enunciations.

The concept of a social imaginary also avoids the conundrums created by the concept of "ideology" and its distinction from material practice. Ideology in its technical usage has been slowly and surely overwhelmed by its pejorative meaning: "The ideological is never one's own position; it is always the stance of someone else, always *their* ideology."[11] If one were to attempt an explanation of any particular ideology in nonpejorative terms, there is seemingly nothing that might rescue the explanation from itself becoming ideological.

The problem is an old one. Clifford Geertz noted it in "Ideology as a Cultural System" (1964), as did Karl Mannheim before him in *Ideol-*

ogy and Utopia (1929): it is the difficulty of employing a non-evaluative concept of ideology.[12] Of all the versions of struggle over the concept of a scientific or objective sociology, it is the claim of exploring ideology objectively that most rankles. As Geertz put it:

> Men do not care to have beliefs to which they attach great moral signifi-
> cance examined dispassionately, no matter for how pure a purpose; and if
> they are themselves highly ideologized, they may find it simply impossible
> to believe that a disinterested approach to critical matters of social and
> political conviction can be other than a scholastic sham.[13]

Mannheim offered one response: a version of epistemological relativism in which the analysis of ideology included the ideological position of
the analyst. Geertz offered another: a science of "symbolic action" based
on Kenneth Burke's work and drawing on a host of philosophers and literary critics.[14] Neither the concept of ideology nor the methods of cultural
anthropology have been the same since. "Ideology" has become one of
the most widely deployed (some might say, most diffuse) tools of critique,
where critique is understood as the analysis of cultural patterns given in
language and symbolic structures for the purposes of bringing to light systems of hegemony, domination, authority, resistance, and/or misrecogni-
tion. However, the practices of critique are just as (if not more) likely to
be turned on critical scholars themselves, to show how the processes of
analysis, hidden assumptions, latent functions of the university, or other
unrecognized features of the material, nonideological real world cause the
analyst to fall into an ideological trap.

The concept of ideology takes a turn toward "social imaginary" in Paul
Ricœur's *Lectures on Ideology and Utopia* (1986), where he proposes ideological and utopian thought as two components of "social and cultural
imagination." Ricœur's overview divides approaches to the concept of
ideology into three basic types—the distorting, the integrating, and the
legitimating—according to how actors deal with reality through (symbolic) imagination. Does the imagination distort reality, integrate it, or
legitimate it vis-à-vis the state? Ricœur defends the second, Geertzian
flavor: ideologies integrate the symbolic structure of the world into a
meaningful whole, and "only because the structure of social life is already
symbolic can it be distorted."[15]

For Ricœur, the very substance of life begins in the interpretation of
reality, and therefore ideologies (as well as utopias, and perhaps conspira-
cies) could well be treated as systems that integrate those interpretations
into the meaningful wholes of political life. Ricœur's analysis of the integration of reality through social imagination, however, does not explicitly
address how imagination functions: What exactly is the nature of this

symbolic action or interpretation, or imagination? Can one know it from the outside, and does it resist the distinction between ideology and material practice? Both Ricœur and Geertz harbor hope that ideology can be made scientific, that the integration of reality through symbolic action requires only the development of concepts adequate to the job.

Reenter Charles Taylor. In *Modern Social Imaginaries* (2004), the concept of social imaginary is distinctive in that it attempts to capture the specific integrative imaginations of modern moral and social order. Taylor stresses that they are *imaginations*—not necessarily theories—of modern moral and social order:

> By social imaginary, I mean something much broader and deeper than the intellectual schemes people may entertain when they think about social reality in a disengaged mode. I am thinking rather, of the ways in which people imagine their social existence, how they fit together with others, how things go on between them and their fellows, the expectations that are normally met, and the deeper normative notions and images that underlie these expectations.[16]

Social imaginaries develop historically and result in both new institutions and new subjectivities; the concepts of public, market, and civil society (among others) are located in the imaginative faculties of actors who recognize the shared, common existence of these ideas, even if they differ on the details, and the practices of those actors reflect a commitment to working out these shared concepts.

Social imaginaries are an extension of "background" in the philosophical sense: "a wider grasp of our whole predicament."[17] The example Taylor uses is that of marching in a demonstration; the action is in our imaginative repertoire and has a meaning that cannot be reduced to the local context: "We know how to assemble, pick up banners and march. ... [W]e understand the ritual. ... [T]he immediate sense of what we are doing, getting the message to our government and our fellow citizens that the cuts must stop, say, makes sense in a wider context, in which we see ourselves standing in a continuing relation with others, in which it is appropriate to address them in this manner," but we also stand "internationally" and "in history" against a background of stories, images, legends, symbols, and theories. "The background that makes sense of any given act is wide and deep. It doesn't include everything in our world, but the relevant sense-giving features can't be circumscribed. ... [It] draws on our whole world, that is, our sense of our whole predicament in time and space, among others and in history."[18]

The social imaginary does not simply consist of the norms that structure our actions; it is also a sense of what makes norms achievable or "realizable," as Taylor says. This is the idea of a "moral order," one that we expect to exist, and if it is absent, one that provides a plan for achieving it. For Taylor, there is such a thing as a "modern idea of order," which includes, among other things, ideas of what it means to be an individual, ideas of how individual passions and desires are related to collective association, and, most importantly, ideas about living in time together (he stresses a radically secular conception of time, secular in a sense that means more than simply "outside religion"). He by no means insists that this is the only such definition of modernity (the door is wide open to understanding alternative modernities), but that the modern idea of moral order is one that dominates and structures a very wide array of institutions and individuals around the world.

The "modern idea of moral order" is a good place to return to the question of geeks and their recursive publics. Are the ideas of order shared by geeks different from those Taylor outlines? Do geeks possess a distinctive social imaginary or do they (despite their planetary dispersal) participate in this common modern idea of moral order? Do the stories and narratives, the tools and technologies, the theories and imaginations they follow and build on have something distinctive about them?

The affinity of geeks for each other is processed through and by ideas of order that are both moral *and* technical—ideas of order that do indeed mix up "operating systems and social systems." These systems include the technical means (the infrastructure) through which geeks meet, assemble, collaborate, and plan, as well as how they talk and think about those activities. The infrastructure—the Internet—allows for a remarkably wide and diverse array of people to encounter and engage with each other. That is to say, the idea of order shared by geeks is shared because they are geeks, because they "get it," because the Internet's structure and software have taken a particular form through which geeks come to understand the moral order that gives the fabric of their political lives warp and weft.

Internet Silk Road

In March of 2000, I moved to Bangalore, India, where I met Udhay Shankar. Udhay "collects interesting people," and it was primarily through his zest for collecting that I met all the people I did. I met cosmopolitan activists and elite lawyers and venture capitalists and engineers and cousins and brothers and sisters of engineers. I met advertising executives and airline flight attendants and consultants in Bombay. I met journalists and gastroenterologists, computer science professors and musicians, and one mother of a robot scientist in Bangalore. Among them were Muslims, Hindus, Jains, Jews, Parsis, and Christians, but most of them considered themselves more secular and scientific than religious. Many were self-educated, or, like their US counterparts, had dropped out of university at some point, but continued to teach themselves about computers and networks. Some were graduates or employees of the Indian Institute of Science in Bangalore, an institution that was among the most important for Indian geeks (as Stanford University is to Silicon Valley, many would say).

While I was in Bangalore, I was invited to join a mailing list run by Udhay called *Silk-list*, an irregular, unmoderated list devoted to "intelligent conversation." The list has no particular focus: long, meandering conversations about Indian politics, religion, economics, and history erupt regularly; topics range from food to science fiction to movie reviews to discussions on Kashmir, Harry Potter, the singularity, or nanotechnology. Udhay started *Silk-list* in 1997 with Bharath Chari and Ram Sundaram, and the recipients have included hundreds of people around the world, some very well-known ones, programmers, lawyers, a Bombay advertising executive, science fiction authors, entrepreneurs, one member of a health care start-up, at least two transhumanists, one (diagnosed) schizophrenic, and myself. Active participants usually numbered about ten to fifteen, while many more lurked in the background.

Silk-list is public in many senses of the word. Practically speaking, one need not be invited to join, and the material that passes through the list is publicly archived and can be found easily on the Internet. Udhay does his best to encourage everyone to speak and to participate, and to discourage forms of discourse that he thinks might silence participants into lurking. *Silk-list* is not a government, corporate, or nongovernmental list, but is constituted only through the activity of geeks finding each other and speaking to each other on this list (which can happen in all manner of ways: through work, through school, through conferences, through fame, through random association, etc.). Recall Taylor's distinction between a topical and a metatopical space. *Silk-list* is not a conventionally topical space: at no point do all of its members meet face-to-face (though there are regular meet-ups in cities around the world), and they are not all online at the same time (though the volume and tempo of messages often reflect who is online "speaking" to each other at any given moment). It is a topical space, however, if one considers it from the perspective of the machine: the list of names on the mailing list are all assembled together in a database, or in a file, on the server that manages the mailing list. It is a stretch to call this an "assembly," however, because it assembles only the avatars of the mailing list readers, many of whom probably ignore or delete most of the messages.

Silk-list is certainly, on the other hand, a "metatopical" public. It "knits together" a variety of topical spaces: my discussion with friends in Houston, and other members' discussions with people around the world, as well as the sources of multiple discussions like newspaper and magazine articles, films, events, and so on that are reported and discussed online. But *Silk-list* is not "The" public—it is far from being the only forum in which the public sphere is knitted together. Many, many such lists exist.

In *Publics and Counterpublics* (2003), Michael Warner offers a further distinction. "The" public is a social imaginary, one operative in the terms laid out by Taylor: as a kind of vision of order evidenced through stories, images, narratives, and so on that constitute the imagination of what it means to be part of the public, and plans necessary to create that public, if necessary. Warner distinguishes, however, between a concrete, embodied audience, like that at a play, a demonstration, or a riot (a topical public in Taylor's terms), and an audience brought into being by discourse and its circulation, an audience that is not metatopical so much as it is a public that is concrete in a different way; it is concrete not in the face-to-face temporality of the speech act, but in the sense of calling a public into being through an address that has a different temporality. It is a public that is concrete in a media-specific manner: it depends on the structures of creation, circulation, use, performance, and reuse of particular kinds of discourse, particular objects or instances of discourse.

Warner's distinction has a number of implications. The first, as Warner is careful to note, is that the existence of particular media is not sufficient for a public to come into existence. Just because a book is printed does not mean that a public exists; it requires also that the public take corresponding action, that is, that they read it. To be part of a particular public is to choose to pay attention to those who choose to address those who choose to pay attention ... and so on. Or as Warner puts it: "The circularity is essential to the phenomenon. A public might be real and efficacious, but its reality lies in just this reflexivity by which an addressable object is conjured into being in order to enable the very discourse that gives it existence."[19]

This "autotelic" feature of a public is crucial if one is to understand the *function* of a public as standing outside of power. It simply cannot be organized by the state, by a corporation, or by any other social totality if it is to have the legitimacy of an independently functioning public. As Warner notes:

> A public organizes itself independently of state institutions, law, formal frameworks of citizenship, or preexisting institutions such as the church. If it were not possible to think of the public as organized independently of

the state or other frameworks, the public could not be sovereign with respect to the state. ... Speaking, writing, and thinking involve us—actively and immediately—in a public, and thus in the being of the sovereign.[20]

Warner's description makes no claim that any public or even "the public" actually takes this form in the present: it is a description of a social imaginary or a "faith" that allows individuals to make sense of their actions according to a modern idea of social order. As Warner, and Jürgen Habermas before him, suggests, the existence of such autonomous publics—and certainly the idea of "public opinion"—does not always conform to this idea of order. Often such publics turn out to have been controlled all along by states, corporations, capitalism, and other forms of social totality that determine the nature of discourse in insidious ways. A public whose participants have no faith that it is autotelic and autonomous is little more than a charade meant to assuage opposition to authority, to transform political power and equality into the negotiation between unequal parties.

Is *Silk-list* a public? More important, is it a sovereign one? Warner's distinction between different media-specific forms of assembly is crucial to answering this question. If one wants to know whether a mailing list on the Internet is more or less likely to be a sovereign public than a book-reading public or the nightly news–hearing one, then one needs to approach it from the specificity of the form of discourse. This specificity not only includes whether the form is text or video and audio, or whether the text is ASCII or Unicode, or the video PAL or NTSC, but it also includes the means of creation, circulation, and reuse of that discourse as well.

For example, consider the differences between a book published in a conventional fashion, by a conventional, corporate press, distributed to bookstores or via Amazon.com, and a book published by an Internet start-up that makes an electronic copy freely available with a copyleft license, yet charges (a lower than usual price) for a print-on-demand hard copy. Both books might easily enter the metatopical space of "the public": discussed in homes, schools, on mailing lists, glowingly reviewed or pilloried, perhaps having effects on corporate behavior, state, or public policy. The former, however, is highly constrained in terms of who will author such a book, how it will be distributed, marketed, edited, and revised, and so on. Copyright law will restrict what readers can do with it, including how they might read it or subsequently circulate it or make derivative use of it. However, a traditionally published book is also enriched by its association with a reputable corporation: it is treated more or less immediately as authoritative, perhaps as meeting some standard of accuracy, precision, or even truth, and its quality is measured primarily by sales.

The on-demand, Internet-mediated book, by contrast, will have a much different temporality of circulation: it might languish in obscurity due to lack of marketing or reputable authority, or it might get mentioned somewhere like the *New York Times* and suddenly become a sensation. For such a book, copyright law (in the form of a copyleft license) might allow a much wider range of uses and reuses, but it will restrict certain forms of commercialization of the text. The two publics might therefore end up looking quite different, overlapping, to be sure, but varying in terms of their control and the terms of admittance. What is at stake is the power of one or the other such public to appear as an independent and sovereign entity—free from suspect constraints and control—whose function is to argue with other constituted forms of power.

The conventionally published book may well satisfy all the criteria of being a public, at least in the colloquial sense of making a set of ideas and a discourse widely available and expecting to influence, or receive a response from, constituted forms of sovereign power. However, it is only the latter "on demand" scheme for publishing that satisfies the criteria of being a *recursive* public. The differences in this example offer a crude indication of why the Internet is so crucially important to geeks, so important that it draws them together, in its defense, as an infrastructure that enables the creation of publics that are thought to be autonomous, independent, and autotelic. Geeks share an idea of moral and technical order when it comes to the Internet; not only this, but they also share a commitment to maintaining that order because it is what allows them to associate as a recursive public in the first place. They discover, or rediscover, through their association, the power and possibility of occupying the position of independent public—one not controlled by states, corporations, or other organizations, but open (they claim) through and through—and develop a desire to defend it from encroachment, destruction, or refeudalization (to use Habermas's term for the fragmentation of the public sphere).

The recursive public is thus not only the book and the discourse around the book. It is not even "content" expanded to include all kinds of media. It is also the technical structure of the Internet as well: its software, its protocols and standards, its applications and software, its legal status and the licenses and regulations that govern it. This captures both of the reasons why recursive publics are distinctive: (1) they include not only the discourses of a public, but the ability to make, maintain, and manipulate the infrastructures of those discourses as well; and (2) they are "layered" and include both discourses and infrastructures, to a specific technical extent (i.e., not all the way down). The meaning of which layers are important develops more or less immediately from direct engagement with the medium.

These two aspects of the recursive public also relate to a concern about the fragmentation or refeudalization of the public sphere: *there is only one Internet*. Its singularity is not technically determined or by any means necessary, but it is what makes the Internet so valuable to geeks. It is a contest, the goal of which is to maintain the Internet as an infrastructure for autonomous and autotelic publics to emerge as part of "the public," understood as part of an imaginary of moral and technical order: operating systems and social systems.

Conclusion: Recursive Public

I started this essay by asking what draws geeks together: What constitutes the chain that binds geeks in the American IT industry to hipsters in Berlin and to entrepreneurs and programmers in Bangalore? What constitutes their affinity if it is not any of the conventional candidates like culture, nation, corporation, or language? A colloquial answer might be that it is simply the Internet that brings them together: cyberspace, virtual communities, online culture. But this does not answer the question of why. Because they can? Because community is good? If mere association is the goal, why not AOL or a vast private network provided by Microsoft?

My answer, by contrast, is that geeks' affinity with one another is structured by shared moral and technical understandings of order. They are a public, an independent public that has the ability to build, maintain, and modify itself, that is not restricted to the activities of speaking, writing, arguing, or protesting. Recursive publics form through their experience with the Internet precisely because the Internet is the kind of thing they can inhabit and transform. Two things make recursive publics distinctive: the ability to include the practice of creating this infrastructure as part of the activity of being public or contesting control; and the ability to "recurse" through the layers of that infrastructure, maintaining its publicness at each level without making it into an unchanging, static, unmodifiable thing.

The affinity constituted by a recursive public, through the medium of the Internet, creates geeks who understand clearly what association through the Internet means. This affinity structures their imagination of what the Internet is and enables: creation, distribution, modification of knowledge, music, science, software. The infrastructure—*this-infrastructure-here*, the Internet—must be understood as part of this imaginary (in addition to being a pulsating tangle of computers, wires, waves, and electrons).

The Internet is not the only medium for such association. A corporation, for example, is also based on a shared imaginary of the economy, of how markets, exchanges, and business cycles are supposed to work; it is the creation of a concrete set of relations and practices, one that is generally inflexible—even in this age of so-called flexible capitalism—because it requires a commitment of time, humans, and capital. Even in fast capitalism one needs to rent office space, buy toilet paper, install payroll software, and so on.

Software and networks can be equally concrete—connecting people, capital, and other resources over time and thus creating an infrastructure—but they are arguably more flexible, more changeable, and more reprogrammable—than a corporation, a sewage system, or a stock exchange. The Internet, in particular, represents a radicalization of this flexibility: not only can one create an application, such as Napster, that takes clever advantage of the layers (protocols, routers, and routes) of the Internet, but one can actually rewrite the layers themselves, rendering possible a new class of Napsters. The difficulty of doing so increases with ever-deeper layers, but the possibility is not (yet) arbitrarily restricted by any organization, person, law, or government. Affinity—membership in a recursive public—depends on adopting the moral and technical imaginations of this kind of order.

Most geeks are urgently concerned with the Internet and its continual maintenance as the technical and moral infrastructure of this kind of public order. The urgency (which stretches from debates about Napster, to those about intellectual property, to those about "net neutrality") is linked to a moral idea of order in which there is a shared imaginary of "the public," and not only a vast multiplicity of competing publics. It is an urgency linked directly to the fact that the Internet provides geeks with a platform, an environment, an infrastructure through which they not only associate but create, and do so in a manner that is widely felt to be autonomous, autotelic, and independent of at least the most conventional forms of power: states and corporations—independent enough, in fact, that both states and corporations can make widespread use of this infrastructure (can become geeks themselves) without necessarily endangering its independence.

Notes

1. Extracted and abridged from my book *Two Bits: The Cultural Significance of Free Software* (Durham, NC, 2008), with the kind permission of Duke University Press.
2. For an example of recursion, see Harold Abelson and Gerald J. Sussman, *The Structure and Interpretation of Computer Programs* (Cambridge, MA, 1985), p. 30.

3. James Boyle, "The Second Enclosure Movement and the Construction of the Public Domain," *Law and Contemporary Problems* 66 (2003): 46. See also James Boyle, "Mertonianism Unbound? Imagining Free, Decentralized Access to Most Cultural and Scientific Material," in *Understanding Knowledge as a Common: From Theory to Practice*, ed. Charlotte Hess and Elinor Ostrom (Cambridge, MA, 2006), pp. 123–44. Available at http://www.james-boyle.com/mertonianism.pdf.

4. For the canonical story, see Steven Levy, *Hackers: Heroes of the Computer Revolution* (New York, 1984). *Hack* referred to (and still does) a clever use of technology, usually unintended by the maker, to achieve some task in an elegant manner. The term has been successfully redefined by the mass media to refer to computer users who break into and commit criminal acts on corporate or government or personal computers connected to a network. Many self-identified hackers insist that the criminal element be referred to as *crackers*. See, in particular, the entries on "Hackers," "Geeks," and "Crackers" in *The Jargon File*, available at http://www.catb.org/~esr/jargon/, also published as Eric S. Raymond, ed., *The New Hackers' Dictionary*, 3rd ed. (Cambridge, MA, 1996). On the subject of definitions and the cultural and ethical characteristics of hackers, see Gabriella E. Coleman, "The Social Construction of Freedom: Hackers, Ethics and the Liberal Tradition," (PhD dissertation, University of Chicago, n.d.), chap. 2.

5. See *The Geek Code*, available at http://www.geekcode.com/.

6. Geeks are also identified often by the playfulness and agility with which they manipulate these labels and characterizations. See Michael M. J. Fischer, "Worlding Cyberspace," in *Critical Anthropology Now*, ed. George Marcus (Santa Fe, NM, 1999), pp. 245–304, for an example.

7. Taylor, *Modern Social Imaginaries*, p. 86.

8. On the subject of imagined communities and the role of information technologies in imagined networks, see Sarah Green, Penny Harvey, and Hannah Knox, "Scales of Place and Networks: An Ethnography of the Imperative to Connect through Information and Communication Technologies," *Current Anthropology* 46 (2005): 805–26.

9. Taylor, *Modern Social Imaginaries*, p. 32.

10. Ibid., pp. 33–48.

11. Paul Ricœur, *Lectures on Ideology and Utopia*, ed. George H. Taylor (New York, 1986), p. 2.

12. Clifford Geertz, "Ideology as a Cultural System," in *The Interpretation of Cultures* (New York, 1973), pp. 193–233, and Karl Mannheim, *Ideology and Utopia: An Introduction to the Sociology of Knowledge*, trans. Louis Wirth and Edward Shils (New York, 1985).

13. Geertz, "Ideology as a Cultural System," p. 195.

14. Ibid., pp. 208–13.

15. Ricœur, *Lectures on Ideology and Utopia*, p. 10.

16. Taylor, *Modern Social Imaginaries*, p. 23.

17. Ibid., p. 25.

18. Ibid., pp. 26–8.

19. Michael Warner, "Publics and Counterpublics," *Public Culture* (14): 51.

20. Ibid., 51–52. See also Warner, *Publics and Counterpublics* (New York, 2003), p. 69.

Part III

DEMOCRACY, PHILOSOPHY, AND GLOBAL PUBLICS

Chapter 7

MEDIATING THE PUBLIC SPHERE
Digitization, Pluralism, and Communicative Democracy

Georgina Born

Introduction

When media theory has addressed the democratic potential of the mass media, it has turned to Jürgen Habermas's concept of the public sphere, which entails reflection on the relations between democratic politics, communication, and the media.[1] For Habermas the public sphere is a forum in which contending viewpoints come together and, through processes of rational and critical deliberation and debate, scrutinize the workings of public and private powers, forging a consensual public opinion. In his analysis, as in contemporary media scholarship, the media play a formative role in diffusing diverse opinions and bringing them into dialogue. In his proceduralist account of deliberative democracy, Habermas conceives of a two-level model in which the informal networks of opinion formation of the public sphere and the formal deliberations of political institutions are portrayed as complementary democratic mechanisms.[2] Reformulations of the public sphere idea and of the media's role in deliberative democracy have become central to scholarly analysis of mass media today. In these debates, one historical institutional form of mass media has often been taken to be an imperfect embodiment of the public sphere ideal: public service broadcasting (PSB).[3] In its structural independence from government, the state, and corporate commercial interests, and its capacity to foster collective critical reflection on such powers, its function as a mediator of relatively free and open communication, and its creation of a "general public" served by mass channels,[4] PSB establishes a field of communicative relationships that approximates and yet updates the Habermasian model. Of all public broadcasting systems, it is Britain's that is commonly seen as exemplary. The BBC was the first and remains the foremost public service broadcaster worldwide; but British PSB is wider than the BBC and exists as an ecology that encompasses also three commercially funded broadcasters regulated for public service principles.[5]

In this essay, with a focus on Britain, I pursue recent attempts to rethink the nature and scope of public service broadcasting and to justify its existence anew. It is uncontroversial that the original conditions—social, cultural, political, economic, and technological—that fostered the birth of PSB and sustained it over decades have undergone such radical transformation that the concept and practice of PSB demand to be reconceived.[6] One critical trigger for such a rethinking is the transition to digital media, a change signaled by the common move to substitute for PSB the phrase "public service communication." Digitization fosters a series of technological, economic, and cultural shifts with enormous repercussions, auguring unprecedented competition and audience fragmentation and intensified commercialization of media systems, changes that in turn are seen by some writers to accelerate the demise of PSB.[7]

But this transition is itself intimately related to wider social and cultural changes. In the words of recent commentators: "The decay in the old idea of 'public service broadcasting' has gone hand in hand with the decay in the old idea of a [national] culture."[8] On the one hand, contemporary societies have witnessed the growth of a heightened and institutionalized individualism;[9] on the other hand, European democracies aspire to a mature cosmopolitanism encapsulated in the notion of a "community of communities."[10] As Ulrich Beck puts it, "Europe today has been cosmopolitanised from within … [It] is if anything in the vanguard of this process."[11] The moral settlement of the nation-state is affected by both transnational migration and internal restructuring; as a consequence, cosmopolitan ideas of citizenship now coexist with new nationalisms and fundamentalisms. In such conditions the social fabric no longer comprises—if it ever did—a cohesive, unified culture built on shared norms, values, and traditions. Instead, it has become pluralistic and culturally heterogeneous to an unprecedented degree—a situation of which, in the age of the "war on terror," we need hardly be reminded. PSB has since its inception taken a formative part in both maintaining and reshaping the boundaries that define the national community. It has done so in four ways: by its power to orchestrate through its representations the processes of inclusion and exclusion that define that community, arbitrating between "community from above" and "community from below";[12] by its articulation, particularly in the era of PSB monopolies, of the substantive contents and boundaries of the nation's cultural life; by both fomenting civil society and by its existence as a central institution of civil society; and by its orchestration of "the dialectic between internal and external definitions,"[13] its authoritative role in playing the nation back both to itself and to the world outside.

If the collective identities that underpin nationhood are subject to continuous processes of recomposition—sometimes under an illusion of timeless continuity, sometimes, as at present, explicitly in flux—then PSB's task of mediating nationhood has become infinitely more complex in the twenty-first century. This is not only due to the challenge of responding to the realities of multiethnic, multicultural, and multifaith societies, and to changing political orders beyond the nation-state, but also because of the changing contours of imaginary identification wrought by transnational media as they cut across and reconfigure national media spaces. Where PSBs formerly positioned themselves in response to the limited competition of national media systems, they now face a deterritorialized media landscape of "global media flows and contra-flows" traversing the boundaries of the nation-state, issuing from and circulating within a wide range of Western, non-Western, and regional hubs and spaces.[14] Such transnational flows of communication respond to accelerating international migration and the diasporic dispersal of populations.[15] Thus, for young British Asians in the UK, South Asian–based satellite television channels such as Zee TV proffer an alternative "imagined community," a fantasized identification with an idealized homeland eased by the experiential gap between their actual lives and the realities of the societies depicted. Such identification can stoke their alienation and disconnect them from their immediate locale, compounding the fracturing of Britain's social fabric.[16]

In Britain the changing social landscape was registered in the 2003 Communications Act. This act updated the Reithian concept of PSB, which for decades underpinned the BBC and Britain's broadcasting regulation, by stipulating both that television should respond to and stimulate the diversity of cultural activity in Britain, and that it should reflect the lives and concerns of different communities and cultural traditions within the UK.[17] In a similar vein, the government's 2006 White Paper on the BBC in the digital age genuflects to the cosmopolitan present when it lists among the BBC's core purposes "[m]aking us aware of different cultures and alternative viewpoints through content that reflects the lives of other people and other communities within the UK."[18] As though acknowledging the recent concern with the potentially divisive tensions between social integration and diversity,[19] the White Paper adds to those purposes "[r]eflecting and strengthening our cultural identity through original programming at local, regional and national levels, on occasion bringing audiences together for shared experiences."[20] Yet for all the pious principles, in the words of a senior media executive, "[m]ulticultural Britain continues to be one of the most under-reported areas of British life."[21] Meanwhile, in its survey of contemporary race relations, the Parekh Report concluded that Britain's mainstream media continue to proffer negative, simplistic, or stereotyped representations of ethnic minorities, when they are not simply rendered invisible, linking this state of affairs to the perpetuation by media organizations of discriminatory employment and access practices.[22] The realities of social and cultural difference and diversity, then, pose challenges to the media—in terms both of output and of employment equity—on a scale to which they have only begun to respond, challenges compounded by commercial restructuring and by digital technologies.

My intention in this essay is to sketch the contours of current discussions of digitization and public service communication, and to weigh them against the challenge posed by multiethnic and multifaith Britain. I make three overall arguments. First, I point to the uncritical way that the American experience of digital transition is held up in contemporary debates about digital communications as a universal model for other territories, ignoring the entirely distinctive media regimes, social and political contexts and histories that prevail in different national spaces. This engenders a political fatalism that forecloses principled debate on the shape of future national media systems, discouraging the political will and imagination that will be required in order to use digitization for progressive public ends. Second, I argue that the discussions have lacked a sufficiently informed, nuanced, and imaginative account of the public service power of digital media. In illustration I outline the BBC's early activities in new media, showing how they exceed the current debates. Third, I argue that attempts to reconceive public service communication for the digital age have been weakened by the absence of a grounding in political philosophy, in particular by lack of attention to established debates concerned with reframing democratic theory in terms of the "democratic politics of difference"[23] that arise in conditions of cultural pluralism and social inequality. I survey aspects of these philosophical debates and draw out central principles. Finally, on the basis of these arguments, I outline some structural proposals that elaborate on the elective affinity between digital media and the politics of difference, proposals with practical implications for how public service communication can utilize digital media radically to enhance and enrich the former mass communication paradigm of PSB.

Digitization and Public Service Broadcasting

Policy Discourses

In what follows I take stock of both policy and academic debates on the future of public service broadcasting in light of digitization. After more than a decade of policy initiatives on digitization it is striking that for all the talk of convergence, they have been limited to a focus exclusively on either the Internet or the advent of digital television (DTV). In both directions the same themes repeatedly occur; indeed, there is something of a conceptual lockdown in the way digitization is framed. Two thematic clusters can be discerned.

First, an economistic discourse has held sway, one that is remarkably continuous with the Peacock Report of 1986 and that has been dominant in policy thinking in the last decade.[24] The tenor of this discourse is well analyzed by Steven Barnett and Patrick Barwise, as it was by Andrew Graham and Gavin Davies, and their criticisms of its assumptions and arguments need no recapitulation here.[25] Instead, I want to focus on its characteristic preoccupations. Prominent are a linked set of concerns with competition, market failure, and the legitimate scope and limits of public intervention via PSB, as well as with the role of digital media in boosting the UK's prosperity and competitiveness. "We aim to make the UK a world leader in digital excellence ... If the UK is to thrive in the future, to succeed in competitive markets and enjoy better and better services, all of us need to be ... living and working in a digital world."[26] A key issue is whether market and technological changes imply that PSB should be confined to market failure provisions in which it supplies only those services or content that commercial actors tend to undersupply—a debate that has elicited hawkish criticisms of the BBC's entry into digital markets;[27] or, in the more extreme position, whether they imply that public funding should be phased out entirely in favor of subscription funding for PSBs such as the BBC.[28] If the core danger identified in this discourse, in the words of a leading representative of Ofcom, the British media and telecommunications superregulator, is that of "pre-empting the market,"[29] the benefits of digitization are portrayed repeatedly in terms of growing consumer choice and interactivity. "Consumers [are enjoying] a gradual but historic act of liberation: the transfer of power into their hands to choose, to select, to schedule and to create, as a result of converging markets and services, powered by the flexibility of digital technology."[30] Or again, in the 2005 Green Paper on the future of the BBC: "The increase in channels means more choice ... Digital technology is likely to provide exciting new opportunities for audiences, who need no longer be so passive ... [It] may signal the end of broadcasting as we know it, allowing people to watch and listen to whatever they want whenever they want to."[31]

The second thematic cluster in policy writing concerns political and social matters, specifically the role of digitization in combating the "digital divide" and mitigating social exclusion, and the development of e-government—the delivery of government and public services online. In government thinking the two are intimately connected, as they are to DTV policies. A core government "vision" is that, since "the market alone will never deliver a fully digital Britain,"[32] DTV can be "a means to provide all citizens with access to e-government services," with the "expectation that DTV can help to overcome the digital divide ... DTV can reach those groups who do not have a PC or have difficulties using one. [It] has the potential to deliver much greater participation in the information society—with the attendant social and economic benefits."[33] DTV is conceived instrumentally as a means of achieving universal digital access, and the Green Paper directs the BBC to add to its purposes "[b]uilding digital Britain." The government's strongest message on digitization and PSB therefore amounts to the BBC taking "a leading role in the process of digital switchover ... [thereby] helping to bring the benefits of digital services to all households."[34] Such an intimate yoking of the BBC to what has been a controversial policy appears to be considered unproblematic. In reality it threatens to compromise the BBC's independence by rendering it a proxy for government.[35] A similar point is made by another commentator when querying the potential elision of e-government directives with the BBC's digital strategies for political reengagement: "There is a fine line between promoting political [interaction] and delivering government information."[36]

If the Communications Act and the Green and White Papers put the creation of a digital Britain high on the agenda, then, they have done so in restricted terms, at the expense of imaginative thinking about digitization's potential political, cultural, and social benefits and PSB's role in realizing them. There are, however, signs of an incipient shift in the dominant terms of policy debate; it is palpable in the gap between two publications on digitization from 2003 and 2005 from the leading New Labour think tank, the Institute for Public Policy Research (IPPR). The first dwells on competition-driven issues: whether market failure justifies

PSB activities in online markets and whether public subsidy is merited in discussion fora and search functions, in passing posing the protection of "public service values" against the promotion of innovation.[37] The 2005 paper, in contrast, evidences a different framing. Cautioning that despite the UK's enviable ICT infrastructure, "[w]e haven't developed the skills or imagination to use it effectively,"[38] it proposes that government must face the complex realities that lie beyond simple universal access, such as psychological and cultural barriers to digital take-up and low morale among public sector staff faced with the digitization of services.[39] It continues that digital networks enable "new types of politics" and can support "communities in a way never seen before [through] local and neighbourhood level communication … But why only appeal to place-based digital initiatives? Civic- and interest-based online activities" should also be encouraged. It goes on: "Government will squash intermediary type activities if it endorses them too heavily, or replicates them, but it can offer tacit endorsement by supporting them with grants." Moreover, the BBC should become a key agent "in the development of a 'multi-tiered public realm,'" encouraging grassroots "social enterprises" and the local generation of content.[40] A subsequent Cabinet Office report echoes this endorsement of the importance of public intervention, specifically by an innovative BBC: "The role of the BBC will be critical in broadband delivery. The BBC has the resources to experiment in ways that the commercial market cannot and to provide support … for the nascent broadband content sector. The Graf report into the BBC's online activity set out measures to … mitigate any crowding out effect of the BBC in the marketplace."[41] Critical of narrow policy discourse, the recent IPPR document nudges impatiently at its limits, etching out a larger conceptual space.

Academic Perspectives on Digitization and Public Service Broadcasting

The later IPPR paper undoubtedly owes a debt to academic writings on PSB and digitization, which have taken thinking further. Academic studies also focus on either the Internet or the future of television. Theoretically, they employ Habermasian ideas to assess digital media in terms of their potential for enhancing or inhibiting public sphere processes. Just as a key source of contention in relation to Habermas has been the relative status, both normative and empirical, of universal or plural conceptions of the public sphere,[42] so scholars writing on PSB and digitization tend to divide between those emphasizing the democratic benefits of media that afford a universal public address and those advocating media systems that enable a pluralistic address among multiple, competing publics or "counter-publics."[43] It is this "either-or" logic of debate that I want to highlight.

Those writing on the public sphere potential of the Internet rightly start from its characteristics of networked interactivity, unbounded spatialization, and transcendence of place, and thus its propensity to remove barriers to communicative and political participation, features that afford new, virtual, and translocal forms of social identification and political mobilization. In a period of globalization and increased migration, the communicative spaces proffered by the Internet and other transnational media, unlike old media systems, are no longer aligned with the geopolitical boundaries and structures of the nation-state. The Internet may be "particularly conducive for alternative social movements, fringe parties and ... transnational advocacy networks seeking to organize and mobilize dispersed groups for collective action."[44] Many political uses of the Internet therefore appear to fall outside the political mainstream, reflecting contemporary redefinitions of the political and the Internet's capacity to catalyze new political objects and associations.[45]

Against this background, two writers offer opposed visions of the Internet's public sphere potential. Stephen Coleman, adopting a national-political frame in his concern with Britain's "crisis of public [political] participation," sees the Internet as a critical vehicle for reinvigorating democracy through its affordance of interactive channels for political mobilization, governmental accountability, and policy consultation and debate.[46] An advocate of direct representation via the Internet—of the technology's potential to augment politicians' accessibility[47]—Coleman's vision is of an "online civic commons" hosted by the BBC that would "inspire and facilitate public participation in [government]."[48] It would be charged with eliciting public deliberation on problems facing and proposals made by public bodies—local authorities, government departments, or Parliament—which would then be expected formally to react to whatever emerges from the public debate. Coleman therefore portrays the "online commons" as a bridge linking informal and formal aspects of a unified, national public sphere.

In contrast, John Keane rejects the view that public service media have ever been a bulwark of the public sphere. PSB is in decay, he says, suffering from "self-commercialisation" and a long-term crisis of legitimacy. He chides the "perilous strategy of [tying] the fortunes of the public sphere ideal to [this] ailing institution,"[49] arguing that "the ideal of a unified public sphere and its corresponding vision of a territorially-bounded republic of citizens ... are obsolete."[50] Instead, he outlines three tiers of mediated public spheres of different spatial scale—micro-, meso-, and macropublic spheres—in which new political forms are facilitated by and articulated with various media. For Keane, micropublic spheres link new social movements to new media; mesopublic spheres represent the normal business of national politics mediated by the national press and broadcasting; and macropublic spheres are the dual outgrowth both of the escalating power of global commercial media and of the Internet.[51] On this basis he advocates a pluralistic, nonfoundational account of democratic public life, stating that "public controversies about power can and should unfold by means of a variety of modes of communication ... A healthy democratic regime is one in which various types of public spheres are thriving."[52] Keane slides unsteadily between media-defined and politically defined public sphere processes. His contention that "the long-term fiscal squeeze [on PSBs rules] out any sustained involvement ... in the [digital] revolution"[53] has proven in the British case to be wrong. He fails, moreover, to give a convincing analysis of new forms of the political. As Damien Tambini has argued regarding the civic networking movement, the central problem of political participation with digital media may not be access to information or voting, "but the very problem of political organization in a period of globalisation ... Whether new media networks can actually be constitutive of interest and identity groups ... is an open question."[54] The existence of networked media does not, then, resolve the question of the formation of political will.

Academic debate on multichannel and digital television exhibits a remarkably similar logic: writers either advocate the PSB model, in which television is seen as promulgating a unified public sphere, or they welcome the likely demise of PSB, linking it to the rise of digital and narrowcast media that allow for the articulation of new identities and politics and the growth of plural public spheres. Consider the arguments of Paddy Scannell and John Hartley. Scannell develops his case around a series of binary terms. Broadcasting is equated with the free dissemination of a universal public good and the creation of a "general public," an inclusive public sphere—that is, with mass democracy, which "grants formal political equality to all and is (like justice) blind to difference."[55] Against this he poses narrowcast and digital media, which he aligns with commercialization, an individualistic consumer address, the personalization of experience, and which offer "technologies of self-expression." Equating the survival of PSB with broadcasting per se, Scannell warns that it "remains an indispensable guarantor of open, democratic forms of public life," and that the expansion of digital media, if accompanied by the attenuation of broadcasting, may have "catastrophic consequences for ... democracy."[56] Hartley, in contrast, writing on the Australian experience, celebrates the development of "post-broadcast" forms of television, which he links to audiences organized around choice, affinity, and decentralized media production, and in particular to the "trail-blazing" indigenous media sector that, over decades, and with increasing intensity, has engaged in narrating aboriginal experience and an alternative account of nationhood. Postbroadcast media are here equated with the creation of an indigenous public sphere.[57]

Limitations of the Early Debates

While productively insisting on the varied topological properties of media technologies, often evoked through spatial metaphors, the academic debates share certain striking features with the policy discourse. In three ways, in both their policy and academic incarnations, the early debates are limited in their assessment of the potential evolution of PSB with digitization.

First, in both policy and the academy, there is a tendency to project monolithic models of digital transition that ignore both the different media ecologies that pertain in different national contexts, with their distinctive regulatory and funding regimes, and the particular social and political environments in which they operate.[58] There are exceptions: if Keane's account of mediated pluralism is uninformed by the sociological realities outlined at the start of this essay, Hartley makes productive reference to social changes and political developments as they interrelate with transformations in the Australian media. But a notable manifestation of this tendency occurred in British debates over DTV, which have been marred by the assumption that the American model of transition to a multichannel environment is a universal one. Both the media industry and media policy have been drawn to forecasts that appear to reduce uncertainty by conceiving of the American transition as providing a template for the evolution of British markets. Yet, recent research portrays clearly divergent patterns in the United States and the UK. American audiences have fragmented "almost beyond recognition," to the extent that in 2005 the main US networks accounted for only 17.3% of all time spent watching television.[59] By contrast, British television does not appear to be undergoing a similar transition. In 2007, 65% of viewing was still taken by the main five networks; in Freeview homes, those taking the BBC's free-to-air digital terrestrial platform, the figure was 68%.[60] Forecasts of extreme fragmentation along US lines, then, may be exaggerated,[61] and the eventual balance struck between mass and niche networks in the UK may be quite different from that in the United States. We should resist the temptation to project the American condition as though it was inevitable, and be more attuned to national media ecologies, their propensities and possibilities. The need to avoid conceiving of the United States as a universal model is all the more urgent given that market forecasts are *performa-*

tive. They do not reflect a pregiven reality; rather, they become the basis for key actors' strategies, in this way powerfully influencing the way new media markets are framed by these actors. In an unstoppable teleology, forecasts can bring about the "reality" they purport merely to reflect.[62]

My second point is that the debates have been inhibited in their appreciation of the variety of new media experiences proffered by digitization that have the potential to be developed for public service ends: in short, they have not attended to the complexity of what is actually going on in digital media. Focused exclusively on underdeveloped notions of "interactivity" and "choice" in relation to the Internet or DTV, the debates have not yet delivered tools for analyzing the new possibilities offered by digitization. Writers have neglected the importance of emerging cross-media content and services, as well as the need to develop an understanding of entirely new kinds of nonlinear content; they have ignored too the continuing significance of linear content, albeit delivered in new ways and on new digital platforms.

To convey the much greater scope and complexity of these possibilities, it is instructive to examine the BBC's early digital activities. The BBC sees itself as operating at different scales—international, national, regional, and local—and at each scale, its digital services now enhance what is offered. Critical is the way new media extend the range and variety of the BBC's mode of address to its publics, inviting participation and response. To exemplify, I want to sketch five contrasting initiatives, each utilizing digital to innovative ends. The first two offer new ways of experiencing content; the remaining three are large-scale interactive experiments in which the BBC has attempted to create, or has used content to animate, public media spaces.

The first initiative is the use of cross-platform links to populate a thematic event. In 2003, for example, the BBC staged an Asylum Day, in which standard linear factual and fictional programs on television and radio were linked to online activities and archives, sources of information on charities and NGOs, advice, and heated debate. On the website, moving personal testimonies of current and past asylum seekers and migrants—online video diaries—sat side by side with pro- and antiasylum polemics. A later thematic event, marked by programming across all the BBC's platforms, was Black History Month.

A second initiative is the use of interactivity to enhance linear broadcast forms. One such experiment was Radio 4's drama *The Dark House*, which was linked to a website where listeners could opt for alternative narratives and follow the story through the experiences and inner thoughts of any one of the three main characters, effecting an innovative, polyphonic narrative.

A third initiative forms part of the BBC's response to the crisis in political communication and the widespread disengagement from formal politics in the UK. In a departure from centralized, Westminster-based political journalism, and responding to the new modes of political connection engendered by the Internet, a website called iCan was launched in 2003 in the mold of a bulletin board and virtual meeting place for extraparliamentary issue-based and activist politics. iCan's aim was to animate new political communities and assist campaigning by offering resources such as links to local government, information on pressure groups, NGOs, and members of parliament, and the means to create links to like-minded activist individuals and groups. Early activities were local in orientation: one pilot scheme involved links with local radio and television in Bristol, Sheffield, and other cities; another, in Lincolnshire, developed in cooperation with the local authority, voluntary and community groups, and targeted disabled people. In 2005 the website was extensively redesigned, and traffic was modest.[63] Yet in its conception, iCan offered a facilitative online space for political self-representation, self-organization, and empowerment, with the aim of reinvigorating the political culture.

The fourth initiative was the BBC's development in Hull through a public-private partnership and regional and city agencies of a broadband-based, local radio–backed pilot for a wired city. Named BBC Hull Interactive, the BBC invested £25 million over five years in the project. It offered unprecedented levels of interactivity and opportunities for local production of content, a dedicated local television news service, a center providing free ICT skills and multimedia training, and the delivery of broadband learning packages for schools and home-based adult education. The project acted also as a test site where the BBC could try out and gauge responses to a range of new media services, such as a navigation tool that enabled the legitimate downloading of and interaction with audiovisual content from a variety of sources. Underlying Hull Interactive was a "micro-community-building" philosophy aimed at enabling users to create their own content, trading technical quality for highly localized, peer-to-peer activities.

The fifth initiative was the Creative Archive (CA), announced by the BBC in 2003, although delayed in its development by government and Ofcom interventions.[64] Building on Lawrence Lessig's notion of a creative commons,[65] and responding to the opportunities offered by Web 2.0 and to the burgeoning of user-generated content, the CA was intended to make available free content from the BBC's extensive audiovisual and music archives, as well as other publicly owned content, for noncommercial creative reuse or "repurposing." By 2005, the CA project had led to the formation of a partnership of public cultural bodies, including the British Film Institute, Channel 4, and the Open University, committed to making their content available for download under the terms of the Creative Archive Licence: a single, shared-user licence scheme for the downloading of moving images, audio, and stills. Inevitably, the CA fuelled ongoing fierce debates over the future optimum shape of intellectual property rights in digital media. Noting the synergies between the CA and the broader "creative economy" and "knowledge economy" policy agenda, Richard Paterson argues that "ownership of the rights to exploit—now vested in those who have the idea rather than those who provide the capital to fix the idea in a commodity—a programme—now take primacy; at the same time ... public sector organisations have seized the initiative to liberate a broader creativity among the public."[66]

In sum, the BBC has pursued the opportunities afforded by digital media at several complementary levels: platforms (with the Freeview digital terrestrial television platform), networks (with its four digital television and five digital radio networks), and old (linear) and new (nonlinear, cross-platform, and interactive) content. It demonstrates an awareness of the need to plan subtly the complementarity between services, essential in an age of convergence, as well as of the public service synergies that can be achieved, enabling innovation to occur between different platforms. In this way the BBC is forging the architecture of a free-to-air, public service digital media system. Its inspiration has been to see that in digital media it should work across all of these fronts and at different levels in transforming its activities and audience address, and to use digital to try to answer major challenges posed by the coevolving political and media ecology: the need to raise political consciousness and respond to new political forms, to rejuvenate civic cultures, to encourage participation, and to innovate in content. In all these senses it is making inventive inroads into the reinvention of PSB demanded by digitization. Yet, to return to the big picture, both academic and policy writings have yet to rise to the task of assessing this complex landscape of new media activities, whether developed by the BBC or elsewhere.

My third and final observation on the limits of current debates, and the primary thrust of my essay, is that they have not paid sufficient attention to the profound social and cultural changes associated with pluralism and their implications for contemporary media; at the same time, they have balked at the challenge of founding ideas for reform on new normative rationales. They lack, that is, a sustained attempt to ground reflection on the evolution of PSB in digital conditions in recent currents in democratic theory, specifically in the concerted attempts to provide a normative account of the changing nature of democracy and its discursive and communicative subsystems in multicultural and stratified societies. It is to this that I now turn.

Democracy, Diversity, and Communication

Faced with the upheavals associated with pluralism, a generation of contemporary political philosophers have retheorized democracy in the light of diversity and difference. My contention is that productive principles can be found in their work that can translate into new normative thinking about the democratic functions of public service communication.[67] As a preliminary I should make clear that the writers I draw upon come from diverse and in some instances contending philosophical currents; but for my purposes this is less important than the commonalities I discern. A second preliminary is to insist that addressing pluralism as a sociological reality does not imply an acceptance of essentialist approaches to multiculturalism that reify ethnic identities and minority cultures as static, bounded, and homogeneous. Rather, following recent anthropological studies, culture should be understood as dynamic, fluid, and differentiated, fuelled by intercultural contacts that generate multiple new hybridities.[68] With this as a starting point, it is nonetheless economical to use shorthand terms like "minority groups" and "minorities" in what follows, as do some of the writers that I discuss.

A first principle centers on self-representation and "presence." Anne Phillips addresses the challenge issued to democratic practice by marginalized groups. Rather than conceive of diversity in the liberal terms of diversity of belief and opinion, or the "politics of ideas," she advocates the "politics of presence"—the necessity of ensuring the presence within the political process of those most dispossessed from it: "Political exclusion is increasingly viewed ... in terms that can be met only by political presence."[69] Similarly, James Tully insists that disadvantaged groups must be empowered to present their case in their own voice in order for effective dialogue to occur.[70] Onora O'Neill, reflecting on the communicative ideals called forth by democratic pluralism, proposes the cultivation of a diversity of voices and the protection of "positions and voices that are in danger of being silenced or marginalised." She stresses the need for "practices of toleration that sustain the presuppositions of public communication, in forms from which nobody is excluded."[71] Taken together, these ideas imply for public service communication that it is not enough to represent a diversity of viewpoints or cultures in terms of content produced, without attending to diversity and inclusion at the level of practice. It points to the need for access to the means of self-representation and self-expression in media production on the part of minority and disadvantaged groups.

A second principle is dialogue. Many theorists of democratic pluralism emphasize the role of communication in engendering dialogue and combating social exclusion. Seyla Benhabib, in an influential account of deliberative democracy, elaborates a communicative ethics centered on the cultivation of a "reciprocity of perspectives" through the provisional adoption by diverse groups of a worldview that may entail a revision of their own, so yielding the "experience of developing commonality." In this account, self- and social transformation require a "politics of complex cultural dialogue" based on public reasoning and exchange.[72] Tully, on the other hand, draws on the experience of aboriginal groups and feminist insights to argue forcefully that "culture is an irreducible and constitutive aspect of politics." He calls for a postimperial citizenship of dialogue and mutual cultural recognition, in which equality entails equity but not uniformity. In this condition, "one's own identity as a citizen is inseparable from a shared history with other citizens who are irreducibly different ... The loss or assimilation of any of the other cultures is experienced as an impoverishment of one's own identity."[73]

A third principle concerns modes of speech, expressive idiom or "voice." Criticizing liberal theorists' rationalist bias and "purified" models of political debate, Bhikhu Parekh argues that

> political deliberation is ... culturally embedded, [and] is never wholly cerebral or based on arguments alone ... The development of a multiculturally constituted common [public realm] requires [a welcoming of] new conceptual languages, modes of deliberation, forms of speech and political sensibilities, [creating conditions] in which their creative interplay could over time lead to a ... broadbased political culture [and a] richer moral culture.[74]

The theme is addressed also by Nancy Fraser, who writes that the historical bourgeois public sphere was

> governed by protocols of style and decorum that were themselves markers of status inequality [which] functioned informally to marginalize women and members of the plebian classes and to prevent them participating as peers ... Deliberation can serve as a mask for domination.[75]

"Universal" public spheres are therefore "not spaces of zero-degree culture," but "accommodate some expressive modes and not others." For Fraser, it follows that public life in multicultural societies cannot consist solely in a single public sphere, since "that would effectively privilege the expressive norms of one cultural group over others."[76]

A fourth principle follows from the concern with idiom or voice: the dialogical mechanisms of democratic pluralism should not be confined to reason and cognition. Support for this proposition is found in writers that address identity and experience in the context of pluralism. Martha Nussbaum makes the case that emotion is a basic component of ethical reasoning. She contends that a compassionate citizenry depends on cultural forms, by engaging the emotions, to extend its capacity for empathy and, therefore, reason; such processes are essential, she avers, for the well-being and the development of the political culture.[77] From another perspective, Moira Gatens and Genevieve Lloyd affirm the critical role of affect and imagination in social identity formation, and the place of the "social imaginary" in negotiations between diverse groups. "Identities are determined ... through processes of emotional and imaginative identification with others, based on relations of partial and shifting similitude and dissimilitude."[78] It follows that broadcasting's powerful imaginative, expressive, and aesthetic potentials, its capacity to engage the emotions, and its mediation of other expressive cultural forms have both cultural and political value. These modes of experience can be a focal means of staging dialogical engagements between diverse groups; as such, they are central to the way that the media can generate empathy, recognition, and toleration in their audiences.[79]

Implicit and explicit in these writings is a realization of culture's central place in contemporary politics. But the converse must also be taken into account, and is surprisingly absent in the philosophical register of these debates: that is, the critical role that culture, and specifically broadcasting and new media, can play as arenas for staging just those dialogues and reciprocities that are fundamental to sustaining pluralist democracies. Such reasoning has led some to argue that cultural citizenship is the principal form for the exercise of citizenship in conditions of pluralism.[80] If we take seriously the role of media cultures in influencing audience tastes and conditioning the wider public culture, then, by analogy with the concern in democratic theory with the formation of an educated and informed citizenry, we might add a commitment to the formation of a culturally mature and aware and culturally pluralistic citizenry.[81] In this sense media organizations—both in their social makeup and in their output— can be understood as the primary "theaters" for contemporary pluralism. It follows that it should be a core function of public service communication to provide such diversity of cultural experience. As Stuart Hall has put it: "The quality of life for black or ethnic minorities depends on the *whole society* knowing more about the 'black experience.'"[82] In the present era, public service communication therefore has a vital role to play in fostering the processes of social and cultural development that underlie the general condition of citizenship.

If the principles of dialogue and self-representation mentioned earlier may seem to imply as their goal the resolution of differences and achievement of consensus, some writers demur from any such assumption. Chantal Mouffe conceives democratic politics as an unending process, arguing that it necessarily entails an agonistic pluralism that "implies the permanence of conflict and antagonism." The illusion that a final resolution of conflict is possible, she warns, puts democracy at risk because it carries "the desire for a reconciled society where pluralism would have been superseded."[83] Suggesting that antagonism is ontologically constitutive of human societies and of the political,[84] Mouffe contends that "to negate the ineradicable character of antagonism and aim at a universal rational consensus—this is the real threat to democracy."[85] Rather, the task of democracy is to "transform antagonism into agonism" via legitimate channels for passionate political engagement.[86] In a similar vein, Iris Marion Young advocates a communicative democracy based on understanding without identification, an irreducible plurality, emphasizing the way that a variety of language practices can be utilized to maintain that plurality.[87] In this light, broadcasting offers intriguing capacities, since the collagelike, parallel streaming, and temporally endless nature of multichannel programming engenders a multiplicity of discursive flows that—even if consensus is enacted within particular programs—together form a "super flow" without any overarching hierarchy of truth, that is, without any necessary commensurability or consensual closure.[88] Thus, if not directly airing constitutive antagonisms, the broadcast super flow has the potential to offer a semblance of the experience of what Bonnie Honig calls "dilemmas—situations in which two values, obligations, or commitments conflict" and that signal "the ineliminability of conflict and difference from the human condition."[89]

Broadcasting's importance in this context is not only its unequalled reach as a space for exhibiting and experiencing difference and diversity. It is also its inherent power, by virtue of the constant juxtaposition of genres and perspectives on mass channels, to relativize different kinds of knowledge and expression, sensitizing its audiences and augmenting their capacity for comparison and critical reflection.[90] In this way, broadcasting potentially compounds or "doubles" a property of cultural diversity itself, as identified by Parekh: "No culture embodies all that is valuable in human life and develops the full range of human possibilities. Different cultures thus … complement each other, [and] expand each other's horizon of thought." By giving access to other cultures, cultural diversity can enable people to "step out of their culture," to "see [its] contingency . . . and relate to it freely rather than as a fate … Since [it] fosters such vital preconditions of human freedom as self-knowledge [and] self-criticism, it is an objective good."[91] Moreover, the expanded universe of media attendant on digitization compounds the capacities I have attributed here to multichannel broadcasting. Where broadcast media tend merely to exhibit cultural diversity without eliciting response, digital media—with their interactive and participatory powers—have the potential to proffer something akin to the agonistic and open, expressive dialogism advocated by Mouffe, Young, and Honig.

What do these principles and observations contribute in terms of redefining public service broadcasting in the contemporary context? Most of the writers mentioned hold fastidiously to the "realms of ideal theory" and abjure any "institutional design."[92] However, Nancy Fraser, in an astute critical commentary on Habermasian universalism, provides some useful pointers. She offers, between the lines, a kind of normative architecture for public service communication in an age of diversity. It takes the form of a topological discussion of the optimum forms that could be taken and functions that could be fulfilled by democratic deliberation in multicultural and stratified societies. Strikingly, her technique is to shift productively between registers—between normative questions, on the one hand, and history and sociology, on the other. A first step is to argue that any formal ideal that a unitary public sphere could be fully inclusive is a fiction: "Declaring a deliberative arena to be a space where extant status distinctions are bracketed and neutralised is not sufficient to make it so."[93] Drawing on the evidence of historians, she notes that "[c]ontemporaneous with the bourgeois public sphere there arose a host of competing counter-publics" peopled by subordinate social groups (peasants, the working class, and elite women). Fraser then counters the view that a single, comprehensive public sphere is preferable to a nexus of multiple public spheres. Rather, "[i]n stratified societies, arrangements that accommodate contestation among a plurality of competing publics better promote the ideal of participatory parity than does a single, overarching public … Subordinate social groups … have repeatedly found it advantageous to constitute alternative publics [as] arenas for deliberation among themselves about their needs, objectives and strategies." She calls such arenas of deliberation "subaltern counter-publics," and she contends that "[i]n general, the proliferation of subaltern counter-publics means a widening of discursive contestation, and that is a good thing in stratified societies."[94] Moreover, only the existence of multiple public spheres allows marginal and subordinate groups to speak in their own voice and engage in their preferred expressive idioms. Multicultural societies, according to

Fraser, must allow for a plurality of public arenas in which groups with diverse values and rhetorics participate on their own terms. But—and here is the crux of her normative design—this "need not preclude the possibility of an additional, more comprehensive arena in which members of different ... publics talk across lines of cultural diversity," a public in which "participants can deliberate ... across lines of difference about policy that concerns them all."[95]

In this last assertion Fraser finds an echo in Hall's work when, discussing the imperative of pluralizing citizenship in contemporary Britain, he argues that a truly public culture requires that minoritarian cultural practices be brought together and made available for the majority.[96] The goal must be, therefore, to ensure the existence of channels for counter-public to speak to counter-public, and for their integration into an (always imperfect) unitary public culture. The alternative is the extreme segmentation characteristic of commercial media in the United States, where "the logic of segmentation emphasizes the value of difference over the value of commonality."[97] Hall's point is that contemporary media politics cannot only be about a proliferation of micropublics, but should be about achieving a unifying space in which are displayed and in which mutual encounters take place between expressions of the diverse and apparently incommensurable component cultures of the nation.

A Normative Architecture for
Pluralist Public Service Communication

How, then, can public service broadcasting be reinvented in digital conditions so as to provide channels for "mutual cultural recognition"? How can we flesh out the "politics of complex cultural dialogue" in relation to the future of public service communication? I want finally to sketch a normative typology of the several forms that such a pluralist communicative democracy might take in relation to both digital and "old" media; I thereby engage in some speculative, if rudimentary, "institutional design." My case is that different media—broadcast, niche and narrowcast, networked, point-to-point—have the potential to fulfill different normative purposes; that, as I stated at the outset, something of an elective affinity can be drawn between digital media and the politics of difference; but, emphatically, that the exploitation of digital media for pluralist ends must be supplemented and balanced by a continuation of mass or "universal" channels. In developing this typology, as well as utilizing Fraser's architecture and the principles discussed, I extrapolate conceptually from the inventive variety of the BBC's digital strategies. This is not to suggest that the BBC is alone in developing such initiatives, nor that it is a paragon, nor that it has covered all bases; simply that in their scope, they are suggestive of the normative functions of dialogical flows between sociocultural majority and minorities, or dominant and subordinate groups. There are five such forms; each is critically important for an extended communicative pluralism. The first three amount to structural variations on the mediated encounter between majority and minorities; they represent three basic vectors of dialogue or agonism.

The first is the established form in which the majority hosts divergent and contesting minority perspectives. It is well suited to broadcast networks and comes close to the long-standing liberal orthodoxy in which "diverse opinions" are presented for debate on current affairs, politics, or talk shows—an orthodoxy that, as Hall, Philip Schlesinger, and others have shown, was built on now unacceptable political and cultural exclusions.[98] This form can be revivified, after Mouffe and Young, in terms of the staging of more open-ended dialogues, and by stressing the necessity of hosting agonistic encounters between conflicting worldviews. For it is only in such a "universal" media space that the constitutive antagonisms of cosmopolitan societies can confront one another and be worked through, albeit without closure.[99]

A second form is when minority speaks both to the majority and to other minorities: *inter*cultural communication. It is well served by both broadcasting and the Internet. This is the core function of cultural-diversity-in-unity, of a plural public broadcast culture. As Hall puts it, seen in these terms broadcasting can become "the open space, the 'theatre,' in which [Britain's] cultural diversity is produced, displayed and represented, and the 'forum' in which the terms of its associative life together are negotiated."[100] Here, universal channels become the means of exposure to and connection with others' imaginative and expressive worlds, via the self-representation and self-expression of diverse groups in their own "voice." It encompasses minority programming on mass channels, such as black and Asian sitcoms, drama, or current affairs; access programming, like the BBC's video diary format on television or the Internet; and cross-platform events engaging the experiences of minorities, such as the BBC's Asylum Day.

A third form is when minority speaks to minority (or to itself): *intra*cultural communication. This equates with Fraser's alternative or counterpublic spheres, channels that act primarily as arenas for deliberation on the part of minorities about their own needs and strategies, and that can foster and augment self-expression and self-understanding. Such channels are often also accessible to others, who can thereby gain understanding of minority cultures as well as pleasure from these encounters. Media well suited to the purpose are radio, video, cable and satellite television, DTV, and the Internet. Examples are the many diasporic networks and ethnic minority niche media that foster intracultural self-reflection, association, and solidarity. The BBC's Asian and black music radio stations approximate these functions. But another powerful model is the innovative Australian network SBS, which offers a continuous series of niche broadcasts produced by and serving minority communities.[101]

The last two forms in my structural typology are of a different but complementary order and embody variants of mediated community. The fourth comprises territorially based local and regional community networks; they can be served by all media and by cross-media activities, as exemplified by the BBC's Hull Interactive project or, less elaborately, by experiments in online local democracy. A fifth form is when issue-based politics or associations become the basis for mediated point-to-point networks, a development particularly associated with the Internet. Here, nonterritorial thematic communities of interest are constituted by online networks, a potential facilitated by the BBC's iCan website, and exemplified by the countless self-generated, decentered online politicized scenes and activist networks.[102]

Conclusions

Together, these five forms have the potential to populate a new normatively grounded conception of public service communication. In light of them, a first concluding remark in relation to academic perspectives is the need to transcend the sterile assumptions of the "either-or" polarity: either universal *or* multiple public spheres; either the old, unreconstructed PSB—charged, depending on the orientation of the critique, with being irredeemably elitist, paternalistic, or hegemonic—*or* its inevitable demise. To concretize the arguments given by theorists of democratic pluralism, and to rejuvenate our collective technological imagination about what digital can bring to public service communication, I have proposed that we attend to the BBC's suggestive strategies, which transcend these polarities, rendering them redundant.

I have argued also that public service broadcasters have an overriding duty to respond to the redrawing of the social and constitutional contours of the nation-state, and to developments in the world, and to allow them to inform and enrich their cultural, political, and moral stance.[103] A Britain and a Europe "cosmopolitanized from within" demand of PSB that it should find a new engagement with its publics, one that meets head-on the formidable challenges of a progressive pluralism. Such a claim does not amount to a call for an unthinking multiculturalism, nor for the fixing or exacerbation of ethnic and cultural differences. It entails two complementary assertions: that mutual cultural recognition and the expansion of cultural referents, as opposed to assimilation, are dynamics essential to the well-being of pluralist societies;[104] but that this does not obviate the need also for integration—for the provision of common information and experience and the fostering of common identities, just as it does not gainsay the inevitable syncretisms and hybridities that will occur across cultural, ethnic, and religious boundaries.

For Britain, a message of this analysis is that the BBC's capacity in pluralist conditions to reinvent its remit, its institutional shape, and the configuration and substance of its platforms, services, and content is in good health. At present, the achievement of public media policy in the UK is highly dependent on the BBC's initiatives, an assessment that is multiplied when the success and significance of Freeview as a free-to-air DTV platform is taken into account.[105] Only the BBC can be expected to monitor the excesses of commercial and transnational media and on that basis intervene creatively, reorienting the market under no other imperative than the public interest, orchestrating a benign media ecology in order to secure democracy's expanded well-being. In turn, the BBC must expect to engage in self-reforms that respond to the changing social and cultural contours of contemporary Britain.[106]

For however constructive the BBC's current activities, they do not exhaust the possibilities. With much enhanced digital capacity, the corporation should develop its role as the hub of Britain's public culture writ large through "public-public partnerships." More can be done on two fronts in particular, directions in which the BBC has been surprisingly reticent. First, it should build facilitative connections with other cultural organizations, both national and local; for example, at the national level with bodies like the UK Film Council and the Arts Councils, and at the local level with galleries, museums, and universities. Such links would offer means to explore fertile interfaces between new media and the "old" arts and culture, and to further develop some of the products and creative talent nurtured by those organizations. In parallel, the corporation should take on the responsibility of animating and offering services to local and community media, aiding the creation of a plural public media space much wider than the BBC, so enabling Britons to benefit from the extraordinary potential offered by the expanding media ecology.[107] As an advocate puts it, such a space must be both local and universal, "individuated and collective ... inclusive, participative and connective."[108] With digital media, as the BBC's early steps imply, there are vast and complex possibilities to be imagined for the future, some of them unprecedented in the history of the BBC. Above all, the opportunities proffered by a new configuration of mass and niche networks fuelled by social and cultural pluralism can enable the BBC to support more spaces for originality, experimentation, and risk, provisions that are central to its remit but that throughout its existence—not least in the past decade—have been undersupplied. Of course, these suggestions, while based on observations about the BBC and the UK, are not limited in their relevance to the UK.

Finally, a general argument underlying this essay is the need to break down the boundaries between normative theories and the design of democratic institutions, including media systems suited to democratic pluralism. From a policy perspective, we need to take political philosophies seriously—to realize that they offer tangible bases on which to construct institutional arrangements; but also to acknowledge that our existing institutions embody political philosophies, which themselves deserve scrutiny and updating. More specifically, Fraser's commentary on Habermas points to the importance of orchestrating a differentiated, multitiered public service media system, one that is designed in answer to real sociological complexities and that can be enhanced by digitization. With reference to political theory I have argued that the challenge for public service communication in an age of diversity is to develop both instantiations of Hall's "theater" of the associative life of the nation, as in the universal orientation and ethical address of mass channels and "impartial" news functions, and to offer a rich array of communicative channels for the self-representation, participation, and expressive narrativization of minority and marginalized groups, addressed both to and among those groups and to the majority. In this way the architecture of public service communication will encompass both the politics of presence and an agonistic pluralism, and will contribute to the formation of a more adequate communicative democracy than we have yet seen.

Notes

1. See Jürgen Habermas, *The Structural Transformation of the Public Sphere* (Cambridge, 1992).
2. Jürgen Habermas, "Three Normative Models of Democracy," in *Democracy and Difference: Contesting the Boundaries of the Political*, ed. Seyla Benhabib (Princeton, NJ, 1996), pp. 21–30.
3. Paddy Scannell, "Public Service Broadcasting and Modern Public Life," *Media, Culture and Society* 11, no. 2 (1989): 135–66, and Nicholas Garnham, "The Media and the Public Sphere," in Calhoun, *Habermas and the Public Sphere*, pp. 359–76.
4. Scannell, "Public Service Broadcasting and Modern Public Life."

5. Britain's advertising-funded public service broadcasters are ITV, Channel Four, and *five*. Their status is presently in question as the British media regulator, Ofcom, considers whether their public service obligations are too onerous to allow them to flourish as businesses.

6. This, with reference to the BBC, is the theme of Born, *Uncertain Vision*.

7. See, for example, Marc Raboy and David Taras, "The Trial by Fire of the Canadian Broadcasting Corporation: Lessons for Public Broadcasting," and Robert Picard, "Audience Relations in the Changing Culture of Media Use: Why Should I Pay the Licence Fee?" both in *Cultural Dilemmas in Public Service Broadcasting*, ed. Gregory Ferrell Lowe and Per Jauert (Goteborg, 2005), pp. 251–76 and 277–92, respectively.

8. Philip Dodd and Wilf Stevenson, "Creative Industries and 'Joined-up' Culture," in *Culture and Communication: Perspectives on Broadcasting and the Information Society*, ed. Stuart Higdon (London, 2001), p. 130.

9. Ulrich Beck and Elisabeth Beck-Gernsheim, *Individualization: Institutionalized Individualism and Its Social and Political Consequences* (London, 2001).

10. Bhikhu Parekh, ed., *The Parekh Report: The Future of Multi-Ethnic Britain* (London, 2000), p. xiii.

11. Ulrich Beck, "Cosmopolitan Europe," lecture delivered to the London School of Economics (January 2003).

12. Philip Schlesinger, *Media, State and Nation: Political Violence and Collective Identities* (London, 1991), p. 173.

13. Ibid.

14. Daya Kishan Thussu, "Introduction," in *Media On The Move: Global Flow and Contra-Flow*, ed. Daya Kishan Thussu (London, 2007), pp. 1–8.

15. Myriad Georgiou and Roger Silverstone, "Diasporas and Contra-flows beyond Nation-centrism," in Thussu, *Media On The Move*, pp. 33–48.

16. Nabila Saddiq, "Young British Muslims and the Media" (MPhil dissertation, University of Cambridge, 2004). On Turkish diasporic and national media in Germany, see Kira Kosnick, *Migrant Media: Turkish Broadcasting and Multicultural Politics in Berlin* (Bloomington, IN, 2007).

17. Department of Culture, Media and Sport (DCMS), *The Communications Act*, London, 2003, para. 264(6)(b) and 264(6)(i). Available at http://www.opsi.gov.uk/acts/acts2003/20030021.htm.

18. DCMS, *A Public Service for All: The BBC in the Digital Age* (The White Paper), London, 2006, 3.5.1, p. 18. Available at http://www.bbccharterreview.org.uk/have_your_say/white_paper/bbc_whitepaper_march06.pdf.

19. See, for example, David Goodhart, "Discomfort of Strangers," *Prospect*, February 2004.

20. *A Public Service for All: The BBC in the Digital Age*, 2006, 3.5.1, p. 18.

21. Samir Shah, "Democracy, Diversity and Television News," in Higdon, *Culture and Communication*, p. 136.

22. Parekh, *The Parekh Report*, chap. 12. Similar findings are given in Andrea Millwood Hargrave, ed., *Multicultural Broadcasting: Concept and Reality* (London, 2002). For 2006 industry research on continuing discrimination in employment, see Creative Skillset, "Census 2006 Shows Changes in TV and Interactive Media Sectors," available at http://www.skillset.org/skillset/diversity/article_3777_1.asp. On institutional racism in the BBC, see Born, *Uncertain Vision*, chap. 5.

23. Seyla Benhabib, "Introduction: The Democratic Moment and the Problem of Difference," in Benhabib, *Democracy and Difference*, p. 5.

24. Her Majesty's Stationery Office (HMSO), *Report of the Committee on the Financing of the BBC* (The Peacock Report), London, Cmnd. 9824, 1986; and for an update

and discussion of this position, Alan Peacock, *Public Service Broadcasting Without the BBC?* (London, 2004).

25. Patrick Barwise, "What Are the Real Threats to Public Service Broadcasting?" and Steven Barnett, "Which End of the Telescope? From Market Failure to Cultural Value," both in *From Public Service Broadcasting to Public Service Communications*, ed. Damien Tambini and Jamie Cowling (London, 2004), pp. 16–33 and 34–45, respectively. See also Gavyn Davies and Andrew Graham, *Broadcasting, Society and Policy in the Multimedia Age* (Luton, 1997).

26. Cabinet Office Strategy Unit, *Connecting the UK: The Digital Strategy*, London, March 2005, p. 1. Available at http://www.strategy.gov.uk/downloads/work_areas/digital_strategy/report/index.htm.

27. See, for example, Jamie Cowling and Damien Tambini, eds., *Public Service Broadcasting to Public Service Communications: Choice, Competition and Public Interest on the Internet*—Seminar Summary (London, 2003), but also the tenor of the recent reviews commissioned by government of the BBC's digital television and radio services.

28. See, for example, Mark Armstrong, "Public Service Broadcasting in the Digital Age" (May 2005) and Martin Cave, "Review of the BBC's Royal Charter: Some Comments on the DCMS Green Paper" (May 2005), both of them written submissions to the House of Lords Select Committee on the BBC Charter Review.

29. Ed Richards, *Ofcom Annual Lecture: Trends in Television, Radio and Telecoms*, London, Westminster Media Forum, July 2005, p. 10. Available at http://www.ofcom.org.uk/media/speeches/2005/07/nr_20050720.

30. Ibid., p. 11.

31. DCMS, *Review of the BBC's Royal Charter: A Strong BBC, Independent of Government* (The Green Paper), London, 2005, quotes from p. 49, para. 2.5 and 2.6. Available at http://www.bbccharterreview.org.uk/publications/cr_pubs/pub_bbcgreenpaper.html.

32. Cabinet Office Strategy Unit, *Connecting the UK*, para. 2.9.

33. Cabinet Office, Office of the E-Envoy, *Digital Television: A Policy Framework for Accessing E-Government Services*, London, December 2003, p. 17. Available at http://www.govtalk.gov.uk/policydocs/policydocs_document.asp?docnum=833.

34. Cabinet Office Strategy Unit, *Connecting the UK*, p. 47 and p. 50.

35. Georgina Born, evidence to the House of Lords Select Committee, *Review of the BBC's Charter—A Strong BBC, Independent of Government* (London, 2005), vol. 2, pp. 279–84.

36. Mike Bracken, "Seeing the Little Picture: Public Service Interactivity, Investment and a Demand-based Re-ordering of Public Service Values," in Cowling and Tambini, *Public Service Broadcasting to Public Service Communications*, p. 24.

37. Cowling and Tambini, *Public Service Broadcasting to Public Service Communications*, but see below on Stephen Coleman's exceptional contribution to this seminar.

38. William Davies, *Modernising with Purpose: A Manifesto for Digital Britain* (London, 2005), p. 66.

39. Ibid., p. 68.

40. Ibid., pp. 70–71.

41. Cabinet Office Strategy Unit, *Connecting the UK*, para. 28.

42. The commentaries are numerous: see the summary in John B. Thompson, *The Media and Modernity* (Cambridge, 1995), and the contributions in Calhoun, *Habermas and the Public Sphere*.

43. Nancy Fraser, "Rethinking the Public Sphere: A Contribution to the Critique of Actually Existing Democracy," in Calhoun, *Habermas and the Public Sphere*, pp. 109–42. See also the arguments concerning critical and oppositional public spheres in Oscar

Negt and Alexander Kluge, *Public Sphere and Experience: Toward an Analysis of the Bourgeois and Proletarian Public Sphere* (Minneapolis, 1993).

44. Pippa Norris, *Digital Divide* (New York, 2001), p. 210.

45. Peter Dahlgren, "The Public Sphere and the Net: Structure, Space and Communication," in *Mediated Politics: Communication in the Future of Democracy*, ed. W. Lance Bennett and Robert M. Entman (Cambridge, 2001), pp. 33–55, and Noortje Marres, "No Issue, No Public: Democratic Deficits after the Displacement of Politics" (PhD dissertation, University of Amsterdam, June 2005).

46. Stephen Coleman, "From Service to Commons: Re-inventing a Space for Public Communication," in Tambini and Cowling, *From Public Service Broadcasting to Public Service Communications*, pp. 88–98.

47. Stephen Coleman, "New Mediation and Direct Representation: Reconceptualizing Representation in the Digital Age," *New Media and Society* 7, no. 2 (2005), 177–98.

48. Coleman, "From Service to Commons," p. 96. See also Coleman's contribution to Cowling and Tambini, *Public Service Broadcasting to Public Service Communications*.

49. John Keane, "Structural Transformations of the Public Sphere," *The Communication Review* 1 (1995): 4.

50. Ibid., p. 8.

51. Ibid., p. 15.

52. Ibid., p. 18.

53. Ibid., p. 5.

54. Damien Tambini, "New Media and Democracy: The Civic Networking Movement," *New Media and Society* 1, no. 3 (1999): 325. See also Mark Poster, "Cyberdemocracy: The Internet and the Public Sphere," 1998 (available at http://www.hnet.uci.edu/mposter/writings/democ.html) as well as Marres, *No Issue, No Public*, for additional perspectives on this issue.

55. Paddy Scannell, "The Meaning of *Broadcasting* in the Digital Era," in *Cultural Dilemmas in Public Service Broadcasting*, ed. Gregory Ferrell Lowe and Per Jauert (Goteburg, 2005), p. 7.

56. Ibid., p. 8.

57. John Hartley, "Television, Nation, and Indigenous Media," *Television and New Media* 5, no. 1 (2004): 7–25.

58. See also Graeme Turner, "Introduction: Global Television," *Television and New Media* 5, no. 1 (2004): 3–5.

59. James G. Webster, "Beneath the Veneer of Fragmentation: Television Audience Polarization in a Multichannel World," *Journal of Communication* 55 (2005): 366 and 378.

60. *Communications Market Report 2007* (London, 2007), pp. 161–67.

61. Mark Oliver, "The UK's Public Service Broadcasting Ecology," in *Can the Market Deliver? Funding Public Service Television in the Digital Age* (London, 2005), pp. 39 and 46.

62. For analysis of these processes, see Georgina Born, "Strategy, Positioning and Projection in Digital Television: Channel Four and the Commercialisation of Public Service Broadcasting in the UK," *Media, Culture and Society* 25 (2003): 773–99, and *Uncertain Futures: Public Service Television and the Transition to Digital—A Comparative Analysis of the Digital Television Strategies of the BBC and Channel Four*, Media@LSE Working Paper 3, London, LSE, 2003 (available at http://www.lse.ac.uk/collections/media@lse/mediaWorkingPapers/ewpNumber3.htm).

63. Stephen Coleman and H. Marsh, *From Public Service Broadcasting to Knowledge-sharing Commons: An Evaluation of the First Year of the iCan Project* (Oxford, 2004). The website was relaunched under a new name, Action Network, in July 2005.

64. See the Creative Archive homepage at www.bbc.co.uk/creativearchive.
65. Lawrence Lessig, *The Future of Ideas: The Fate of the Commons in a Connected World* (Harmondsworth, 2002).
66. Richard Paterson, "Creativity, Intellectual Property Rights and the Pragmatics of the Public Sphere in UK Television" (paper, Society for Cinema and Media Studies conference, Chicago, IL, March 2007).
67. For a sustained and insightful discussion of normative arguments in favor of cultural diversity as a social condition per se, see Bhikhu Parekh, *Rethinking Multiculturalism: Cultural Diversity and Political Theory* (London, 2000), chap. 5, esp. pp. 165–78.
68. A path-breaking example of this approach is Gerd Baumann, *Contesting Culture: Discourses of Identity in Multiethnic London* (Cambridge, 1996).
69. Anne Phillips, "Dealing with Difference: A Politics of Ideas, or a Politics of Presence?" in Benhabib, *Democracy and Difference*, p. 141.
70. Tully, *Strange Multiplicity*.
71. Onora O'Neill, "Practices of Toleration," in *Democracy and the Mass Media*, ed. Judith Lichtenberg (Cambridge, 1990), pp. 173 and 167.
72. Seyla Benhabib, *The Claims of Culture: Equality and Diversity in the Global Era* (Princeton, NJ, 2002), pp. 75, 79, and 115.
73. Tully, *Strange Multiplicity*, pp. 5, 10, and 205.
74. Parekh, *Rethinking Multiculturalism*, p. 312 and p. 223.
75. Fraser, "Rethinking the Public Sphere," p. 119.
76. Ibid., p. 126.
77. Martha Nussbaum, *Upheavals of Thought: The Intelligence of Emotions* (Cambridge, 2001).
78. Moira Gatens and Genevieve Lloyd, *Collective Imaginings: Spinoza, Past and Present* (London, 1999), pp. 78–79, 128, 125, and 149.
79. Born, *Uncertain Vision*, chap. 9.
80. Engin Isin and Patricia Wood, *Citizenship and Identity* (London, 1999), and Nick Stevenson, ed., *Culture and Citizenship* (London, 2001). See also the discussion in Georgina Born and Tony Prosser, "Culture and Consumerism: Citizenship, Public Service Broadcasting and the BBC's Fair Trading Obligations," *Modern Law Review* 64 (2001): 670–75.
81. Born and Prosser, "Culture and Consumerism," and Parekh, *Rethinking Multiculturalism*.
82. Stuart Hall, "Which Public, Whose Service?" in *All Our Futures: The Changing Role and Purpose of the BBC*, ed. Wilf Stevenson (London, 1993), p. 36.
83. Chantal Mouffe, "Democracy, Power and the 'Political,'" in Benhabib, *Democracy and Difference*, p. 254.
84. Chantal Mouffe, *On the Political* (London, 2005), pp. 8–34.
85. Mouffe, "Democracy, Power and the 'Political,'" p. 248.
86. Mouffe, *On the Political*, p. 20.
87. Iris Marion Young, "Communication and the Other: Beyond Deliberative Democracy," in Benhabib, *Democracy and Difference*, pp. 120–35.
88. On super flow see Klaus Bruhn Jensen et al., "Super Flow, Channel Flow and Audience Flows," *Nordic Review of Research on Media and Communication* 2 (1994): 1–13. Raymond Williams coined the term "flow" to characterize television as a medium; see his *Television: Technology and Cultural Form* (New York, 1975), chap. 4. On the hierarchization of discourses and its truth effects, see McCabe, "Realism and the Cinema," pp. 216–35.
89. Bonnie Honig, "Difference, Dilemmas, and the Politics of Home," in Benhabib, *Democracy and Difference*, pp. 258 and 273.

90. See an analogous argument for the "epistemic benefits of [mediated] diversity" in serving democratic practice, and specifically of heterogeneous deliberation and distributed and interactive collective cognition, in James Bohman, "Political Communication and the Epistemic Value of Diversity: Deliberation and Legitimation in Media Societies," *Communication Theory* 17 (2007): 348–55.

91. Parekh, *Rethinking Multiculturalism*, p. 167.

92. Judith Squires, "Culture, Equality and Diversity," in *Multiculturalism Reconsidered*, ed. Paul Kelly (Cambridge, 2002), p. 129. Squires criticizes the lack of any "detailed, practical account of the institutional arrangements required" (p. 130) by deliberative models of democracy in much of the philosophical literature.

93. Fraser, "Rethinking the Public Sphere," p. 115.

94. Ibid., pp. 122–23 and 124.

95. Ibid., pp. 126 and 127.

96. Hall, "Which Public, Whose Service?"

97. Oscar Gandy, "Dividing Practices: Segmentation and Targeting in the Emerging Public Sphere," in *Mediated Politics: Communication in the Future of Democracy*, ed. W. Lance Bennett and Robert M. Entman (Cambridge, 2001), p. 157. On the segmentation of new media audiences in the United States, see also Joseph Turow, *Breaking Up America: Advertisers and the New Media World* (Chicago, 1997).

98. Stuart Hall et al., "The 'Unity' of Current Affairs Television," in *Popular Television and Film*, ed. T. Bennett, S. Boyd-Bowman, C. Mercer, and J. Woolacott, pp. 215–37, and Philip Schlesinger, *Putting Reality Together* (London, 1987).

99. Mouffe, "Democracy, Power and the 'Political,'" and Young, "Communication and the Other." See my analysis of halting cultural changes in BBC News, which includes an account of such a confrontation: an edition of the flagship analysis program, *Newsnight*, focused on representatives of conflicting currents within British Islam, and on their televised encounter with Samuel Huntington (Born, *Uncertain Vision*, pp. 414–30, esp. 428–30).

100. Hall, "Which Public, Whose Service?" pp. 36–37.

101. Gay Hawkins, "SBS: Minority Television," *Culture and Policy* 7 (1996): 45–63.

102. For insights into new modes of political activism, see Marres, *No Issue, No Public*.

103. For a full discussion of this point, see Born, *Uncertain Vision*, "Epilogue."

104. Tully, *Strange Multiplicity*, and Parekh, *Rethinking Multiculturalism*.

105. On the development of Freeview, see Born, *Uncertain Futures*, and *Uncertain Vision*, chap. 10, esp. pp. 482–91.

106. Born, *Uncertain Vision*, chap. 10 and "Epilogue."

107. See also Davies, *Modernising with Purpose*, pp. 70–71.

108. Don Redding, "A Vision of a BBC that Serves Citizens to 2016," in *The Future of the BBC* (London, 2004), speaking on behalf of the NGOs 3WE and Public Voice.

Chapter 8

CRITIQUE OF PUBLIC REASON
Normativity, Legitimation, and Meaning in the Public Sphere

Steven G. Crowell

In his classic account, Jürgen Habermas describes the "structural trans-formation" of what he calls the "public sphere": in the eighteenth cen-tury, bourgeois literary and discursive practices gave rise to a new political constellation in which the public use of reason served to hold state poli-cies up for critical scrutiny. By the twentieth century, however, the public sphere had fundamentally altered. Succumbing to direct intervention by state and economic forces, the "principle of publicity"—Kant's expression for the politically normative commitment to public reasoning—was dis-placed by a "publicity machine" aimed at manipulating "public opinion" and transforming political actors into consumers.[1] Habermas constructed this narrative of structural transformation in part to answer Hannah Ar-endt's claim that in modernity the social had come to displace the po-litical altogether. On a purely descriptive level, however, his story did nothing to challenge that claim. While Habermas continued to maintain that the idea of the public sphere as a site of legitimating practices was *normatively* "indispensable" for democratic theory, in the late 1960s one might have been forgiven for thinking that the *actual* public sphere had been replaced by what Guy Debord called the "society of the spectacle."[2]

The emergence of the spectacular as a category of social analysis did not, however, mean the resurrection of the public sphere as Arendt had described it, namely, as a "common space of appearance" in which the real is "what appears" and politics involves exemplary self-showing through word and deed. Appealing implicitly to norms of authenticity and integrity, Arendt's notion of self-showing is eviscerated under conditions of "spectacular" social organization, in which identities are fungible products of identification with institutionally manipulated economic, religious, or social representations. As Debord put it, "[t]he spectacle is not a collection of images; rather, it is a social relationship between people that is mediated by images"[3]—hence mediated neither by Arendtian "action" nor by Habermasian "discourses."

Under such conditions, can the concept of the public sphere have any role in our thinking about politics? Is Arendt's conception merely nostalgic, as Dana Villa suggests —the basis for a "politics of mourning" and remembrance of the *res publica?*[4] Can we embrace Habermas's version of it as a counterfactual ideal whose normative force derives not from social reality but from communicative practices that are "distorted"—but contingently so—under contemporary conditions? I will argue that neither conception of the public sphere is plausible on its own, but that taken together they provide a useful window on the question of political legitimation. I will first contrast these conceptions under the headings of a "politics of meaning," governed by the norm of authenticity (Arendt), and a "politics of law," governed by the norm of autonomy (Habermas). I will then examine the sublimated remainder of Habermas's sociohistorical concept of the public sphere, namely, his account of the discursive legitimation of norms through argument. Identifying certain rationalistic assumptions in Habermas's approach, I will suggest a less rationalistic version of his legitimation strategy—one that links argumentation to processes of meaning constitution—and will illustrate it by examining the juridification of human rights. Here legitimation retains an element of the *performative* and shows why the politics of law cannot be divorced from the politics of meaning.

Hannah Arendt and the Politics of Meaning

In Arendt's account, the public sphere as *res publica* is a condition for the possibility of action; and because action is what defines us as human beings, the existence or nonexistence of a *res publica* determines whether a truly human life is possible. Action—a matter of both word and deed—is distinguished from work by its nonutilitarian character: whereas the entire purpose of work rests in fabricating a lasting product, action is not only goal oriented but is also carried out for its own sake. Thus, while work produces goods, action allows *meaning* to show forth.[5] Work fails if its end is not attained; "meaning, on the contrary, must be permanent and lose nothing of its character, whether it is achieved or, rather, found by man or fails man and is missed by him."[6] This permanence of meaning shares in the performative nature of selfhood: self-identity is neither a given nor a goal to be attained once and for all, but something permanently *at stake*. Since the meaning at stake in a life does not depend on whether one's goals are fulfilled, the possibility of a "failure" of meaning implies a norm—authenticity—that is not utilitarian in character, one that pertains to *how* life is lived rather than *what* life is lived.

For Arendt, the question of meaning is a political question. To ask who one is to not to ask what one's qualities, gifts, talents, and shortcomings are but to seek a "character" behind all such things. The "disclosure" of such character "can almost never be achieved as a wilful purpose," since typically "the 'who,' which appears so clearly and unmistakably to others, remains hidden from the person himself." It is in the *political* context of "acting and speaking" that "men show who they are, reveal actively their unique personal identities and thus make their appearance in the human world."[7] Acting and speaking take place in a "web of human relationships" that, through them, is constituted as a "public," a space in which identity shows itself, and is recognized, through contest (*agon*). This—the human "world" in the strict sense—"does not always exist."[8] States, laws, and institutions are the fabricated basis for such a world, but the world itself, the "common space of appearance," exists only in being cared for, only where "natality"—action's capacity for inaugurating the new—and the "boundlessness" or unpredictability accompanying it, are embraced as "fate."[9] The "frailty" of the world, of the *res publica*, lies in its being nowhere but in the "appearing to all."[10] Thus, when modernity began to think of action in terms of the "uncertainty" of its outcome, rather than the "frailty" of the world it both presupposes and constitutes, the political was lost and life became, in the strictest sense, "meaningless."[11]

Arendt's conception of the public sphere as a common space of appearance, and the corresponding vision of a politics of meaning, might recall certain positions sketched out by theorists of "spectacular" social reality. As Dana Villa remarked, "Arendt's theory reveals a narrative structure that hooks up, in unexpected ways, with the concerns of postmodern and poststructuralist critics."[12] Her thesis of the displacement of the political by the social, for instance, invokes the "normalizing" power of the social: "[t]he last stage of the laboring society, the society of jobholders, demands of its members a sheer automatic functioning"; the common space of appearance collapses when subjects do not act but "acquiesce in a dazed, 'tranquillized' functional type of behavior."[13] This recalls Michel Foucault's idea of a public sphere subjected to "power that substitutes an institutionally dispersed and normalizing regime of panoptic visibility for a centralized space in which action is seen and heard by all."[14] What "appears" in such a space is not a unique individual who constitutes meaning through self-disclosing action, but a "subject" who has turned social surveillance mechanisms on herself (become a spectacle for herself) in order *not* to stand out. The notion of exemplarity, which underwrote Arendt's original conception of the political, now belongs to the realm of fantasy, as Debord suggests, in the form of the "star system." The star is the "mere" appearance, or simulacrum, of exemplarity and individuality: "In entering the spectacle as a model to be identified with, he renounces all autonomy in order himself to identify with the general law of obedience to the course of things."[15] The exemplarity upon which meaning depends is deflated into the banal equality of all possible lifestyles of the rich and famous.

The point of identifying convergences between Arendtian and postmodern diagnoses of the fate of the public sphere is not to suggest that "spectacular logic" is the best way to understand social and political conditions. Rather, the kinship between Arendt's public spectacles and those of postmodernity reinforces the thought that a *global* politics of meaning is preposterous, indeed terrifying. Because a "universal" public sphere or world in Arendt's sense cannot be envisioned otherwise than as its simulacrum, the spectacle, Habermas's attempt to reconceive the political under conditions of modernity is salutary. For him, the birth of liberalism in the religious struggles of the seventeenth century signals the demise of a "thick" connection between politics and meaning: the former becomes the search for ways to live among strangers who want to remain strangers, while the latter, as identity formation and "pursuit of happiness," belongs within a space ideally free from the encroachment of politics.

For Habermas, then, no less than for Debord, Jean-François Lyotard, or Jean Baudrillard, "authenticity" has no political role. Indeed, Habermas's position is perhaps even further from a politics of meaning than theirs, since the postmodernists invoke notions like "resistance" and *"detournement"* that trade on the connection that once obtained between action and meaning. Such notions revive something of Arendt's positive conception of the public sphere, but when they are seen as alternatives to liberal politics they fail to do justice to the real basis of her pessimism. It is here that Habermas's conception of the public sphere as a site of *legitimation* proves indispensable.

Habermas and the Politics of Law

In contrast to Arendt's conception of the public sphere, which turns on authenticity as a norm of self-disclosure, Habermas's conception of the public sphere derives normative force from the idea of *autonomy*. While agreeing with Arendt that modernity is characterized by the emergence of "the social," Habermas finds in civil society a political potential that Arendt did not. He does so by shifting from a conception of politics that emphasizes narrative identity formation and agonistic meaning constitution to one that emphasizes rational will formation and the discursive legitimation of law.[16] In *The Structural Transformation of the Public Sphere* (1962), Habermas argued that the bourgeois public sphere introduced a new principle—the "principle of publicity"—into political life. By means of literature, broadside, and coffeehouse debates, the bourgeoisie became a new "functional element in the political realm," an instrument of post-conventional legitimation: "The 'domination' of the public, according to its own idea, was an order in which domination itself was dissolved." That is, "public debate was supposed to transform *voluntas* into a *ratio* that in the public competition of private arguments came into being as the consensus about what was practically necessary in the interest of all." The public use of reason produced a "consciousness of this, if you will, formless humanity" as the ultimate instance of legitimation.[17] Politics became a matter of submitting "arcane" state authority to the principle of publicity, thereby replacing it with the transparent authority of law legitimated through the force of the better argument.

Habermas did, of course, recognize the ideological character of this notion of "humanity"—its exclusions and its tendency to confuse class interests with "rational" principles—as it first emerged in the historical public sphere. And he also described how, in the subsequent structural transformation, the principle of publicity was translated into a media-dominated "public opinion," democratic participation was debased into ratification of prepackaged candidates, and political decisions were increasingly ceded to "experts" removed from supervision by rationally debating bodies.[18] Yet he continued to hold that the original legitimizing and steering functions of public reason had a role to play in the "democratization" of state and economy. No longer a matter of an "intact public of private people dealing with each other individually," the public sphere would be "replaced by a public of organized private people"—that is, by interest groups (social movements, unions)—that could "participate effectively in a process of public communication ... on the basis of an affirmation of publicity as regards the negotiations of organizations with the state and with one another."[19]

With the collapse of the labor movement, and with the increasing autonomization of state and economic "systems," Habermas turned away from the idea of direct intervention. However, he found a way to preserve the political potential of the principle of publicity by reconceiving public reason as a "democratic bulwark" against the "colonization" of the lifeworld by the system imperatives of state bureaucracy and market economy. Abandoning the last vestiges of the idea of revolutionary action—or political "steering"—Habermas now identified politics primarily with processes of legitimation. This required him to rethink the source of the normative force of the public sphere. No longer tied to the practices of a historical public nor to specific political institutions, that source was now found to lie in the rational potential contained in everyday communicative action. Language may be used merely rhetorically or placed in the service of manipulation of public opinion, but it also makes possible "discourses"—communicative action oriented toward mutual understanding (*Verständigung*)—that by their very nature, according to Habermas, commit all participants to certain normative constraints. Habermas's project of analyzing discourses to reveal these universal normative commitments—his proposal for an "ethics of discourse"—thus represents a philosophical sublimation of hopes previously placed in the public sphere, hopes for cognitive adjudication of normative claims through the public use of reason.

To what extent does this philosophical sublimation of the public sphere achieve its purpose? Arendt's conception of the public sphere as a site of authentic self-disclosure lost much of its normative force when the politics of meaning collapsed into a kind of simulacrum of itself, but the goal of autonomous will formation through rational argumentation can also seem parochial. Foucault, for instance, insists that conceiving politics as normatively beholden to an ethics of argumentation inevitably fails to acknowledge the reality of power.[20] And Lyotard maintains that consensual legitimation fails to recognize the *differend* between the cognitive and the normative in political discourse.[21] Finally, hermeneutic theorists suggest that autonomous will formation is itself a Western cultural ideal that may have no normative standing in other cultural contexts.

While these challenges to Habermas's conception of political legitimation raise many issues, the most pressing one, given an interest in the concept of the public sphere, concerns Habermas's radical distinction between the constitution of meaning and the process of legitimation. Whatever problems there may be with Arendt's conception of the public sphere, it acknowledges a phenomenon—identity formation—that motivates postmodern and hermeneutic objections to Habermas's political theory, and it suggests the presence of something like a *differend*: a dispute that cannot be resolved without doing an injustice to one or another of the disputants because their claims belong to normatively incommensurable language games. In what follows I will argue that a politically useful conception of the public sphere must accommodate this *differend* by recognizing the limits of argumentation in the legitimation process itself. Such a "critique" of public reason shows that we must deny the autonomy of law in order to make room for the claims of meaning.

Discourse Ethics: A Dialogical Approach to Legitimation

The aim of an ethics of discourse is to defend a form of moral cognitivism by identifying pragmatically necessary normative presuppositions in those forms of communicative action in which individuals with differing interests and values come together to decide what ought to be done. Moral cognitivism is the view that normative statements make cognitively redeemable claims to validity and are not reducible to expressions of individual or cultural preference. On what basis are such validity claims redeemable? Intuitionism treats normative statements as truth-functional in just the way statements of fact are, but Habermas rejects intuitionism. While claims to truth and to normative rightness can both be redeemed by adducing reasons, the reasons given in support of normative rightness are not moral facts. The statement "one ought not to discriminate against people on the basis of race" might reflect a fact about a particular society's normative commitments, but Habermas notes that "while there is an unequivocal relation between existing states of affairs and true propositions about them, the 'existence' or social currency of norms says nothing about whether the norms are valid."[22] Normative claims are only *"analogous to truth claims."*[23] The source of their validity, in Habermas's view, lies not in matters of moral fact but in the practice of giving and asking for reasons itself. It is the pragmatic context, where claims are advanced and reasons adduced, that underwrites moral cognitivism.

In treating argumentation as a form of communicative *action*, Habermas advances a conception of reason that breaks with the traditional "philosophy of consciousness" in two important ways. First, it links legitimation of normative claims to "a 'real' process of argumentation in which the individuals concerned co-operate." Because disputes over norms arise when a prior consensus has been disrupted, "the problems to be resolved in moral argumentation cannot be handled monologically."[24] A *plurality* of subjects must engage in argument to reach a new consensus. And second, because legitimation is intersubjective, the criterion that distinguishes a rational agreement from one that rests on coercion must involve something like the principle of publicity. These two points together yield a dialogical version of Kant's categorical imperative.

Because de facto agreement is not enough to establish normative validity, moral cognitivism requires—in analogy to the principle of induction, which authorizes one to move from a set of observations to a universal law—a "bridging principle" that allows one to anticipate the universal validity of a norm on the basis of a limited consensus. Habermas derives such a principle from the nature of public reasoning: a norm is valid if "*all* affected can accept the consequences and side-effects its *general* observance can be anticipated to have for the satisfaction of *everyone's* interests."[25] Where Kant's categorical imperative established "what each can will without contradiction to be a universal law," Habermas's principle picks out "what all can will in agreement to be a universal norm."[26] A norm is valid if it satisfies this dialogical "principle U," and such validity is *cognitively* grounded if U itself can be rationally legitimated.

Habermas begins his defense of U by acknowledging the pluralism of subjective interests characteristic of the prescientific cultural-historical lifeworld. These interests are asserted in a social context of asymmetrical power relations, and where conflict arises language use will reflect these asymmetries. One may have recourse to strategic or rhetorical speech acts, oriented exclusively toward making one's own view prevail. But other speech acts—discourses—aim at mutual understanding (or agreement; *Verständigung*) and involve a commitment to achieving decisions based solely on "the force of the better argument." In the "rules" of this practice Habermas purports to identify a set of ethical norms that *any* participant in argumentation must presuppose as valid, thereby establishing a "quasi-transcendental" check on normative pluralism. Such ethical rules are not logically entailed by the propositional content of what the various parties assert; nor are they semantic rules belonging to the truth-functional structure of argument. Rather, they are *pragmatically* implied in the argumentative speech act itself. Two questions thus present themselves: how are such normative commitments to be identified? And how can it be shown that they are binding on all participants in argumentation? The answer to both questions is found in Habermas's idea of a "performative contradiction." A performative contradiction is a contradiction between what one *does* by engaging in argument and the assertion, in that argument, of a statement that denies some norm governing argumentative practice. By "demonstrating the existence of performative contradictions," Habermas claims, we can "identify the rules necessary for any argumentation game to work."[27]

How, then, can performative contradictions be demonstrated? If they could be established by appeal to the propositional content of normative claims, Habermas's account would be uncontroversial. But the *pragmatic* rules of argumentation do not initially take the form of propositions that could directly come into contradiction with something asserted in the argument.

To demonstrate a performative contradiction one must instead "appeal to the *intuitive preunderstanding* that every subject competent in speech and action brings to a process of argumentation."[28] For instance, participants in discourses are said to be pragmatically committed to the rule that "everyone is allowed to question any assertion whatever," and that "every subject with the competence to speak and act is allowed to take part in a discourse."[29] These phrases supposedly express the intuitive preunderstanding of what he or she is up to possessed by anyone competent in argumentation. Thus, if a participant in argumentation claims to possess a revealed truth that others must simply accept, that claim exempts itself from the pragmatic rules contained in our intuitive preunderstanding of what we are doing when we argue. This means that making such a claim performatively contradicts the participant's commitment to the rule that "everyone is allowed to question any assertion whatsoever." Phrases expressing such rules would then be normatively binding on any participant in dialogue. No reason can be given for denying their validity, since the act of giving reasons is already committed to that very validity. On this basis principle U, which ties validity to unrestricted participation and to the consensus of all affected, can be legitimated. For, according to Habermas, the rules inherent in our intuitive preunderstanding are such that "everyone who seriously tries to *discursively* redeem normative claims to validity intuitively acknowledges procedural conditions that amount to implicitly acknowledging U."[30]

The appeal to intuitive preunderstanding is thus essential to the project, but it is also its most controversial feature. For, as Habermas acknowledges, "the description we employ to pass from knowing how to knowing that is a hypothetical reconstruction that can provide only a more or less correct rendering of intuitions." Thus, our certainty of what we are up to when, as competent speakers, we engage in argumentation does not transfer to "*our reconstruction* of this pretheoretical knowledge and the claim to universality we connect with it." Discourse ethics thus "takes its place among the reconstructive sciences concerned with the *rational bases* of knowing, speaking, and acting."[31] As rational reconstructions, however, the so-called "rules" of discourse—and so also the concept of a performative contradiction—remain "debatable," and critics of Habermas who favor a more hermeneutic approach to dialogue have joined that debate.

Denying that any sharp distinction between strategic and argumentative discourses can be drawn, these critics hold that by conceiving the pragmatics of dialogue through the prism of logical universality, Habermas rationalistically distorts the concrete discursive situation and obscures the peculiar *reasonableness* that belongs to real dialogue. Hermeneutic critics deny that pragmatic preunderstandings are like semantic or truth-functional rules of logic: they cannot be reconstructed as rules at all without distorting their character. And because, as even Habermas admits, they are not *constitutive* rules,[32] what discourse ethics reconstructs are merely *ideal* symmetry conditions descriptive of "a speech situation immune to repression and inequality." It then imputes to participants in argumentation commitment to the "rule" that *real* speech situations must be assumed to adequately approximate these ideal conditions.[33] For hermeneutic theorists, however, as we shall see in the next section, such "reconstructions" are nothing but rationalistic assumptions, and the "rule" they establish is demonstrably not part of actual discourses.

Hermeneutic Critique of Habermas's Rationalistic Assumptions

Habermas maintains that reconstruction of our intuitive preunderstanding reveals *universally* valid norms. For instance, the practice of giving and asking for reasons is said to entail that a norm or action is legitimate only if its justifying reasons could be objects of agreement among all actual and potential participants, no matter what their local situation might be. Reconstructive reflection thus suspends the hermeneutic circle to identify principles that break through every local solidarity, transcend in principle every limited interpretive context, and underwrite claims to "universal" or unconditional normative and cognitive validity.[34] Hans-Georg Gadamer and other hermeneutic theorists, however, deny that reasons can be fully context transcendent, cleanly separated from the interpretations in which they are embedded. For them, Habermas's reconstructions are idealizations that ignore the way reflection depends on the play of meanings that sustain the practice of argumentation, the "tradition" or background—historically particular, never fully transparent—that gives questions of normative validity their specific sense. The idea that reflection can break free of its contingent meaning-context would be self-contradictory, a rationalistic distortion that takes reasoning to be more autonomous than it could ever be.[35] The idea of universal agreement is actually an *irrational* idealization because, as David Hoy notes, "it would be irrational for one to aim at an ideal if one knew that in principle it could never be attained."[36] An account of the public use of reason must therefore focus on the *real*—local, tradition-bound—situation of dialogue, eschewing "reconstructions" that attribute to participants in such dialogues a commitment to an unreasonable ideal of universal validity.

The critical theorist's response—that this equates validity with a de facto agreement, which can come about in nonrational ways—is not to the point, for hermeneutic theorists do not deny that validity claims should be legitimated through reasoning. They deny only that a valid outcome of such reasoning demands the kind of universality characteristic of the rules of logic. In making it the *telos* of all communicative practices, Hoy writes, "Habermas is overextending the formal or logical notion of validity," imposing on discourses a "critical monism" which holds that reasonable dialogue is possible only if there is one right interpretation with which everyone could in principle be brought to agree.[37] On the contrary, a plurality of acceptable ("valid") interpretations, equally well supported by reasons, is possible. As Hoy puts it, "an interpreter can offer an interpretation to others and expect them to find it reasonable and insightful without also expecting them to drop their differing interpretations."[38] Reasoning belongs *within* the agonistic space of meaning, not at a remove from it.

The critical theorist responds that, politically, such pluralism leaves us with no principled way to resist a relapse from argument into violence. Merely local solidarities cannot insure mutual understanding, and if universal consensus is impossible in principle, then conflicts of interpretation cannot finally be rationally adjudicated. Thus, Thomas McCarthy argues that local differences can be transcended on the basis of our "background of common humanity," which provides concrete support for "the boundless claims of reason" and for a politics of rational adjudication through argument. For the hermeneutic theorist, however, this background of common humanity—which has no culturally specific content and so no meaning in the political sense—is a rationalistic assumption, too thin to establish any a priori limit on interpretive tolerance.[39] In the course of real dialogues, limits to tolerance make themselves felt, and the fact that all our reason giving takes place in a finite situation, where only local agreements can be expected, is no reason to dismiss the reasonableness of conclusions reached in this way. Indeed, it is only possible to distinguish between reasonable and unreasonable interpretations *within* such a situation. The idea that practical reason is oriented toward universal consensus merely reflects the rationalization and functionalization of the lifeworld.[40]

This argument finds an echo in the phenomenological critique of the role Habermas assigns to the lifeworld. According to Bernhard Waldenfels, Habermas begins by identifying the lifeworld as the *background* to

all reasoning practices (thus agreeing with hermeneutic and phenomenological theories), but in the end it becomes a mere "vestibule" (*Vorhof*)
of reason, such that reason stands *opposed* to its own background.[41] This
is because Habermas construes reason in a narrow, uniform way. Specifically, reason—*logos*, the order of things—is reduced to "rationality" as
it finds itself "pressed through the narrow filter of human opinions, actions, and assertions." Thus, the different sorts of validity claims associated with three types of discourse—cognitive truth, moral rightness, and
subjective truthfulness or authenticity—become identified with substantive ontological "regions" that rationalistically replace the imbricated
texture of the actual lifeworld:[42] "Under the directive of differentiation
and formalization of validity claims, traditional forms of life appear as
undifferentiated *mixture*, and under the simultaneous directive of univer-
salization they are turned into *mere tradition and convention* that does not
rise above particularistic validity."[43] In imagining that one should pass,
via argument, from the "vestibule" to what is supposed to be a genuinely
"rational" order of things, Habermas's theory conceals the reasonableness
that already belongs to the lifeworld's own play of meanings.

Habermas counters with the claim that such rationalization is not ne-
gotiable in "post-conventional" cultures, where one can "no longer appeal
to the naive validity of the context of the lifeworld."[44] For the phenom-
enologist, however, this only appears necessary because Habermas identifies reason with argument, thereby overlooking the reasonableness that
characterizes "naïve" lifeworld practices. The prediscursive lifeworld is
already a *form* of reason, "the material rationality of an order of things."[45]
Whereas Habermas marginalizes as nonrational everything that cannot
come to word, hermeneutics and phenomenology hold that discursive
reasoning is nourished upon bodily habitualities, skillful comportments,
perceptual formations, and other such "merely subjective" phenomena.
The "naïve" distinctions drawn within particular cultural lifeworlds—between us and them, nature and culture, persons and things—are not mere
confusions awaiting rationalistic adjudication but the very way that the
"symbiosis" between reason and *meaning* takes place.[46]

Public Reason Without Rationalism

Waldenfels's argument returns us to the contrast between a politics of
law and a politics of meaning, for it highlights the main problem with
Habermas's discourse ethics: it has no place for the "subjectivity" through
which the practice of giving and asking for reasons gains its ethicopo-
litical *meaning*. Habermas draws the principles of discourse ethics from

the pragmatics of argumentation, but he understands "pragmatics" in a narrow linguistic sense, thus occluding the *full* pragmatic situation that informs our intuitive preunderstanding of what we are doing when we engage in argumentation. Hermeneutic and phenomenological critics are right to identify a rationalistic distortion here, one that ignores the way reason giving is bound up with other linguistic strategies, nondiscursive practices, and pre-predicative experiences. Reason giving always draws upon a "hermeneutic surplus" of meaning. Thus, while argumentative legitimation of normative validity claims may be politically indispensable, any reconstruction of the accompanying intuitive preunderstanding must be able to *integrate* meaning and validity, on pain of becoming an irrelevant idealization. Can discourse ethics survive without its rationalistic assumptions?

To begin with, the main claim of discourse ethics—that someone engaged in the practice of argumentation implicitly acknowledges that a normative claim is valid only if it could be the object of a universal consensus—is defensible apart from any such assumptions. Habermas's response to the hermeneutic argument that validity always concerns a local "fusion of horizons" is persuasive. He grants that argumentative discourses are never pure, and that actual agreement will always be achieved through the context-bound faculty of *phronesis*. Thus, "as long as problems of application are viewed from a *third person perspective*," orientation toward a universal consensus will appear unnecessary. However, "no participant in argumentation can escape this claim [to universality] as long as he takes a *performative attitude*," the first-person perspective of one engaged in the practice.[47] Hermeneutics adopts the third-person stance to argue that the performative attitude is mistaken, but this only shifts the question to the "meta" level where the validity of hermeneutic theory itself is argumentatively debated. At this level, hermeneutics argues—in the performative attitude and so with its ineluctable claim to universal validity—for a metatheory that claims there can be no universally valid interpretations. Because the hermeneutic account involves a performative contradiction, its idea of limited agreement does not do justice to the performative *meaning* of argumentation. In the performative attitude any such limit will be experienced as a prejudice in the negative sense: an arbitrary exclusion of potential discourse partners. Thus, Habermas is right to hold that the practice of argumentation involves commitment to the idea of a universal consensus.

However, the second presupposition Habermas attributes to participants in public reasoning—the claim that "there are general symmetry conditions that every competent speaker who believes he is engaging in argumentation must presuppose as *adequately fulfilled*"[48]—cannot be justified by an appeal to the performative attitude. Participants in real dialogue are fully aware of social and political asymmetries, and for this reason they draw linguistically upon the various "rhetorical" elements that distinguish informal argumentation from formal deductions. Nor can a "counterfactual" presupposition of symmetry be likened to the principle of charity, which concerns the propositional content of what is said. For without the principle of charity I could not even understand the other as speaking a language at all, whereas the practice of argumentation is perfectly intelligible even in the face of plainly acknowledged asymmetries. To see the *practice* as a meaningful one, in other words, it is not necessary that the participant's intuitive preunderstanding in the performative attitude include any *counterfactual* presuppositions. Habermas's second presupposition, then, is a rationalistic distortion of the performative meaning of argumentation. Why does he insist on it? A clue is found in his description of it as a "presupposition about relations of *mutual recognition*."[49] For without this assumption it might seem that one could arbitrarily exclude discourse partners with whom one disagreed simply by denying that they were engaging in argumentation at all, i.e., by claiming that they were acting under "motives other than the co-operative search for truth."[50] The presupposition that ideal symmetry conditions are adequately fulfilled thus reflects the fact that argument rests upon relations of mutual recognition.

But the failure of performative contradiction arguments to establish this presupposition does not mean that mutual recognition is *not* a condition of argumentative practice. It only means that insight into the relation between recognition and argumentation must be sought elsewhere, defended otherwise than through appeal to our intuitive preunderstanding. And in fact its defense belongs to the "philosophical anthropology" (theory of meaning) that discourse ethics (as a theory of validity) tries to avoid. Only by tracing the practice of giving and asking for reasons back to its "ontological" ground does the nature of the mutual recognition that belongs to the practice of argumentation become clear.

An example of this is Frederick Olafson's recent use of Heideggerian ontology to define an ethically relevant notion of mutual recognition. Martin Heidegger's thesis that human beings "disclose" a "world"—that is, constitute a space of meaning through their practices—provides the key. For Heidegger, as for Ludwig Wittgenstein, there can be no meaning (because no norms or rules) without a social context. World disclosure is always a codisclosure with others.[51] Olafson shows how such codisclosure entails a form of mutual recognition that serves as the "foundation for morality."[52]

Prior to any particular project—including that of argumentation—I have always already acknowledged the other as one *with* whom I must coconstitute a meaningful world. This ontological recognition does not entail a set of moral rules, but it does entail that I have a particular sort of *responsibility* to the other when I deliberate: "My being responsible means that my choice must be such that it can be presented as being at least compatible with some wider form of life in which there is a place for others that is arguably consistent with their interests."[53] If, as we argued, the ideal of universal consensus belongs to the performative attitude of discourses, it would not be hard to expand this notion of responsibility into Habermas's principle U.[54] Along with such responsibility comes a *trust* that others place in me; "[t]he fundamental relation of one human being to another is one in which trust is paired with responsibility," and this grounds the normative force of ethics: "The authority of the ethical limits within which we live is owed to the fact that a failure to respect them would be a violation of the trust placed in us by the people to whom we are responsible."[55] If that is so, it should be possible to trace both the practice of giving and asking for reasons and any ethical commitments it entails—for instance, its normative universalism—to the disclosive or meaning-constituting aspect of our being.

From the ontological point of view, defending the validity of one's claims by giving reasons is one of many meaning-constituting practices. Still, it is not a *contingent* practice, but one embedded in the social relation that constitutes human beings as responsible. As Olafson notes, "a responsible person must offer some reason to himself and to ... others for the priority that has been assigned to his own interests over theirs."[56] Because I do not constitute the meaningful world by myself, it is not possible to dismiss the question of how I can *legitimate* the assertion of my own interests. To recognize the other as codisclosive just *is* to treat my own inclinations as potential *reasons* that I can offer to the other as justifying my acting in one way rather than another.[57] Constituting meaning brings with it an obligation to enter into the practice of giving and asking for reasons, and because the others with whom I codisclose the world are not restricted to any particular community, that practice involves an ethical commitment to universal participation and consensus.

Reconceiving public reason ontologically also addresses Waldenfels's objection that in Habermas reason is too narrowly tied to linguistic practices. Codisclosure does entail an obligation to be ready to state one's reasons, but these assertions must draw on something that already belongs to an "order of things," a *logos*. For instance, if I am able to offer my inclination (or some traditional usage) as a reason for what I do, it must already have a protorational form. Its "reasonableness" is not first constituted by my asserting it *as* a reason. The pre-predicative level of prototypical perception, sedimented meanings, and traditional taxonomies is not a terrain devoid of reason but the very sort of thing that can take the *form* of a justifying reason. The significance of argumentation does not lie in its being the exclusive locus of rationality, but in the fact that through it the reasonableness of lifeworld meanings becomes a public theme. Because the processes of meaning constitution and legitimation thus complement each other, there is no need to pass from the lifeworld "vestibule" of nonrationality to some rationalized world constructed in argument. Interestingly, Habermas himself offers an example of a legitimation procedure that illustrates just this complementarity between the politics of law and the politics of meaning.

Between Meaning and Validity: The Unprincipled Normativity of Rights

Habermas's hermeneutic critics argue that the individualism and secularism embedded in an autonomous argumentative legitimation process embody Western cultural ideals that lack normative force outside that context. For Habermas, however, "the decisive alternatives lie not at the cultural but at the socioeconomic level."[58] Global modernization is the basic fact, and no society can "participate in capitalistic modernization without taking advantage of the achievements of an individualistic legal order," since modernization requires modes of social integration and regulation for which law supplies the necessary condition: "Complex societies, whether Asian or European, seem to have no functional equivalent for the integrative achievements of law," an "artificially created norm, at once compulsory and freedom-guaranteeing" that "has also proven its worth for producing an abstract form of civic solidarity among strangers who want to remain strangers."[59] Societies *must* engage in legitimation through public reason because their own economic modernization requires it.

From this perspective, the idea of the public sphere no longer involves *any* cultural particulars but is functionalized into two institutions that sustain the process of legitimation itself: popular sovereignty and human rights. The idea of popular sovereignty "lays down a procedure that, because of its democratic features, justifies the presumption of legitimate outcomes," while the idea of human rights supplies the normative force for these procedural guarantees by delineating the concept of a "legal person." Habermas recognizes the tension between these two notions: fear of the "tyranny of the majority" leads one to assert one's basic, democracy-trumping, human rights; but this assertion can only be legitimated through a democratic process of argumentation. Habermas tries to resolve this tension with "the idea of a constitution-making practice."[60]

Habermas argues that such a practice, through which "an inherently legitimate rule of law itself" arises, entails certain human rights. The legal order produced by a constitution-making practice can be legitimate only if "all those possibly affected could consent to it after participating in rational discourses." If this is so, then "popular sovereignty"—that is, "the forms of communication [and participation] necessary for a reasonable will-formation of the political lawgiver"—must *itself* be legally instituted, and this is just to establish human rights: "[h]uman rights institutionalize the communicative conditions for a reasonable political will-formation"; they are conditions "which make the exercise of popular sovereignty possible."[61]

This result is important, but it is also extremely limited. Habermas himself notes that the set of rights that can be legitimated by appeal to the idea of a constitution-making practice contains *only* the "political" rights of "communication and participation." The wider set of human rights—which "guarantee everyone a comprehensive legal protection and an equal opportunity to pursue her life plans"—cannot be justified in this way. But then, how is political theory to conceive the legitimation of this broader set of rights? Habermas notes that they "clearly have an intrinsic value" and that they are "not reducible to their instrumental value for democratic will-formation," but this just points to the problem: the existence of a kind of "intrinsic value," or *meaning*, that lies beyond the politics of law and is not open to discursive legitimation.[62] With this, Arendt's notion of the public sphere achieves new relevance.

The key point is that "human rights are not pregiven moral truths to be discovered but rather are *constructions*."[63] Whatever their "intrinsic" value, such rights must be legislated if they are to be politically binding, and in this they are indistinguishable from positive laws. Thus human rights, too, are subject to the demand for discursive legitimation. But because such rights are supposed to serve as a *check* on what can be legislated through discursive legitimation procedures, their normative validity cannot be established *through* such procedures. Where rights are already embodied explicitly in a legal order, one can appeal to them as a check on argumentative outcomes. But when such rights are not in place—that is, when some legislation is contested in the name of a right that has not yet been institutionally codified—the discourse that contests such legislation will be, in a certain sense, *unprincipled*. One cannot assume, even ideally, that the legitimate outcome will be the one that emerges from the force of the better argument alone, since to determine which argument is "better" one must appeal to something that cannot be argumentatively justified, namely, the putative right that one argumentative outcome would transgress. The assertion of rights thus belongs to agonistic *meaning-constituting* practices, as individuals and groups who constitute *themselves* in terms of the supposed right contest with others who do not recognize such a right.

Habermas acknowledges that rights emerge from practices. The human rights of communication and participation emerge from the practice of rational argumentation, but other rights will emerge from other practices. For instance, changes in the way many people in the United States lived their lives, together with the emergence of social movements, such as the women's movement, that made those changes politically urgent, led to the legal construction of a right to privacy not explicitly asserted in the US constitution. The right to privacy became law not because it had stronger arguments on its side but because practices entailing such a right, carried out by actors in the public sphere, came to appear "exemplary." The Supreme Court might well have decided differently in *Roe v. Wade*, but since their decision *constituted* the right to privacy as law that decision could not, strictly speaking, be seen as *legitimated* by the existence of such a right. What legitimated it, if anything did, were the practices in which it was implicated and the identity-asserting political action that made that dimension of those practices salient.

This point is illustrated by one recent attempt to construe the process of "juridification" or "institutionalization of new rights" entirely within a Habermasian framework.[64] Jean Cohen and Andrew Arato take their point of departure from Habermas's conclusion, in *The Structural Transformation of the Public Sphere*, that the functions of the public sphere are increasingly carried out not by individuals but by groups: "democratic publics *within* the firm or state," such as "social movements, associations, and publics" concerned with "new identities, new norms, and new solidarities."[65] Cohen and Arato conceive legitimation of the norms governing such movements in classically Habermasian terms: social integration is "communicative coordination" whose "relationship to norms" is "open to discursive testing," and such a communicatively organized civil society can "be stabilized, in institutional terms, only as a framework of fundamental rights."[66] What, then, is the relation between the norms—"open to discursive testing"—that constitute these different groups and the rights that provide the institutional framework for such testing? Can these rights be postconventionally legitimated?

Cohen and Arato apparently believe so, for they argue that "the structure of a given catalogue of fundamental rights allows one to distinguish empirically *and normatively* among different types of modern civil society"—something possible only if rights are capable of postconventional legitimation.[67] But they also argue that rights "can be guaranteed by positive law but are not equivalent to law or derivable from it."[68] What, then, is the normative status of a right prior to its constitution as law? If only very few rights—the purely "political" ones entailed by the practice of argumentative legitimation itself—can be justified by performative contradiction arguments, how can Cohen and Arato cognitively assert the normative superiority of one "catalogue" of rights over another? For instance, on what basis can they hold that "a new centrality of rights guaranteeing intimacy and personal autonomy" *ought* to replace "the current primacy and model character of property rights"?[69] Why isn't this normative judgment merely an expression of the norms of their own political culture, as postmodern and hermeneutic theorists claim?

Cohen and Arato identify the central point: "[r]ights begin as *claims asserted* by groups and individuals in the public sphere of an emerging civil society,"[70] but we must take this thought one step further. Although rights may subsequently come to be inscribed in law, they never lose their ontological character as *claims* that are integral to specific practices. They are normative only for the identities that are constituted when individuals and groups *engage* in such practices, and their validity can therefore never be established through argument alone.[71] As long as practices involve incommensurable moments of meaning or identity constitution, rights remain *inherently contestable*, a contest decided—if it is decided at all, and does not remain a more or less ongoing bone of contention in society—by what ultimately comes to be seen as "exemplary." Their legitimation is a matter, finally, of how we choose to *live*.

If this is correct, the struggle of individuals and groups for rights is something like a remnant, within the modern public sphere, of the ancient *res publica* as a space of self-disclosure in which meaning is constituted. According to Arendt, the question of "who one is" can be answered only in the "common space of appearance" where I reveal what I am committed to. The example of rights shows that this space—where the substantive commitments or "identities" that lie beyond the reach of procedural legitimation are at stake—belongs to modern politics as well. Despite the universalistic rhetoric that it borrows from the idea of legitimation through argumentation, the modern discourse of rights belongs to the politics of meaning. This suggests that any politically relevant concept of the public sphere must draw on a less linear history of the concept and a more nuanced understanding of the legacy of modernity.

Notes

1. Jürgen Habermas, *The Structural Transformation of the Public Sphere*, trans. Thomas Burger and Frederick Lawrence (Cambridge, MA, 1989).
2. Guy Debord, *The Society of the Spectacle*, trans. Donald Nicholson-Smith (New York, 1995).
3. Ibid., p. 12.
4. Dana Villa, "Postmodernism and the Public Sphere," *The American Political Science Review* 86, no. 3 (September 1992): 719.
5. Hannah Arendt, *The Human Condition*, 2nd edn., intro. Margaret Conovan (Chicago, 1998), p. 154.
6. Ibid., p. 155.
7. Ibid., p. 179.
8. Ibid., p. 199.
9. Ibid., p. 190.
10. Ibid., p. 199.
11. Ibid., pp. 232 and 300.
12. Villa, "Postmodernism and the Public Sphere," 717.
13. Arendt, *The Human Condition*, p. 322.
14. Villa, "Postmodernism and the Public Sphere," 718.
15. Debord, *Society of the Spectacle*, p. 39.
16. Habermas, *The Structural Transformation of the Public Sphere*, p. 52.
17. Ibid., pp. 82–85.
18. Ibid., p. 233.
19. Ibid., p. 232.
20. Michel Foucault, "What Is Enlightenment?" in *The Foucault Reader*, ed. Paul Rabinow (New York, 1984), pp. 32–50.
21. Jean-François Lyotard, *The Differend: Phrases in Dispute*, trans. Georges van den Abbeele (Minneapolis, 1989), and Jean-François Lyotard and Jean-Loup Thébaud, *Just Gaming*, trans. Wlad Godzich (Minneapolis, 1985). See also Steven Crowell, "Who Is the Political Actor? An Existential-Phenomenological Approach," in *The Phenomenology of the Political*, ed. Kevin Thompson and Lester Embree (Dordrecht, 2000), pp. 11–28.
22. Jürgen Habermas, "Discourse Ethics: Notes on a Program of Philosophical Justification," in *Moral Consciousness and Communicative Action*, trans. Christian Lenhardt and Shierry Weber Nicholsen (Cambridge, MA, 1990), pp. 43–115: 61.
23. Ibid., p. 56.
24. Ibid., p. 67.
25. Ibid., p. 65.
26. Ibid., p. 67.
27. Ibid., p. 95.
28. Ibid., p. 89 (my emphasis).
29. Ibid.
30. Ibid., pp. 92–93.
31. Ibid., pp. 97–98.
32. Ibid., p. 91. Such rules "are not *constitutive* of discourses in the sense in which chess rules are constitutive of real chess games. Whereas chess rules *determine* the playing of actual chess games"—that is, you are not playing chess if you are not following the rules—"discourse rules are merely the *form* in which we present the implic-

itly adopted and intuitively known pragmatic presuppositions of a special type of speech."

33. Ibid., p. 88.
34. David Couzens Hoy and Thomas McCarthy, *Critical Theory* (Cambridge, MA, 1994), p. 254.
35. David Hoy, *The Critical Circle* (Berkeley, CA, 1982), pp. 118 and 126.
36. Hoy and McCarthy, *Critical Theory*, p. 255.
37. Ibid., p. 184.
38. Ibid., p. 264.
39. Ibid.
40. Ibid., pp. 270–71.
41. Bernhard Waldenfels, "Rationalisierung der Lebenswelt—Ein Projekt: Kritische Überlegungen zu Habermas' Theorie des kommunikativen Handelns," in *In den Netzen der Lebenswelt* (Frankfurt am Main, 1985), p. 107. Translations are mine.
42. Ibid., pp. 95 and 102.
43. Ibid., p. 107.
44. Habermas, "Discourse Ethics," p. 109.
45. Waldenfels, "Rationalisierung der Lebenswelt," p. 116.
46. Ibid., pp. 113–14.
47. Habermas, "Discourse Ethics," pp. 104–5.
48. Ibid., p. 88.
49. Ibid.
50. Ibid., p. 89.
51. For an early discussion of the connection between Wittgenstein and Heidegger that similarly seeks something like a pragmatic "anthropological" approach to transcendental questions, see Karl-Otto Apel, *Transformation der Philosophie, I: Sprachanalytik, Semiotik, Hermeneutik* (Frankfurt am Main, 1976), especially the essays in Section II, "Hermeneutik und Sinnkritik." A more recent treatment of Heidegger's analysis of meaning and normativity along Wittgensteinian lines can be found in Hubert Dreyfus, *Being-in-the-World: A Commentary on Heidegger's "Being and Time," Division I* (Cambridge, MA, 1991).
52. Frederick Olafson, *Heidegger and the Ground of Ethics* (Cambridge, 1998), pp. 51 and 58.
53. Ibid., pp. 51–53.
54. Olafson does not himself go so far, but he does speak of the "convergence" between "the conclusions [Habermas] draws" and "those reached here"—that is, in his own ontological account (*Heidegger and the Ground of Ethics*, p. 63).
55. Ibid., p. 61.
56. Ibid., p. 53.
57. Steven Crowell, "Conscience and Reason: Heidegger and the Grounds of Intentionality," in *Transcendental Heidegger*, ed. Steven Crowell and Jeff Malpas (Stanford, CA, 2007), pp. 43–62.
58. Jürgen Habermas, "Remarks on Legitimation Through Human Rights," in *The Postnational Constellation*, trans. Max Pensky (Cambridge, MA, 2001), p. 124.
59. Ibid., pp. 124 and 122.
60. Ibid., pp. 115–16.
61. Ibid., pp. 116–17.
62. Ibid., p. 117.
63. Ibid., p. 122.

64. Jean Cohen and Andrew Arato, "Politics and the Reconstruction of the Concept of Civil Society," in *Cultural-Political Interventions in the Unfinished Project of Enlightenment*, ed. Axel Honneth, Thomas McCarthy, Claus Offe, and Albrecht Wellmer (Cambridge, MA, 1992), p. 135.
65. Ibid., p. 137.
66. Ibid., pp. 132–33.
67. Ibid., p. 133 (my emphasis).
68. Ibid., p. 138. They further recognize that the state is "neither the source nor the basis of their validity."
69. Ibid.
70. Ibid. (my emphasis).
71. This extends a point about "practical identities" made by Christine Korsgaard in *The Sources of Normativity* (Cambridge, 1996). A practical identity is "a description under which you value yourself"; more particularly, it is like a role—student, lover, friend, test pilot, feminist—and such "identities give rise to reasons and obligations" because "normativity is built right into the role" (p. 101). However, "such identities are contingent," and "you may stop caring whether you live up to [their] demands" (p. 120). This means that these demands have no more normative force for one who no longer cares. Only an act of commitment to them—an act of will or choice—can make them normative, i.e., can make them have validity for *you*. It follows that there can be no *sufficient* reason for adopting one identity or another, and so the validity of their norms (and the "rights" that derive from such practices) cannot be legitimated through the "force of the better argument" alone.

Chapter 9

ON THE GLOBAL MULTIPLICITY OF PUBLIC SPHERES
The Democratic Transformation of the Public Sphere?

James Tully

All concepts in which an entire process is semiotically concentrated elude definition: only that which has no history
is definable.
                    —Nietzsche, *On the Genealogy of Morals*

The Practical and Semantic Field of a Global Multiplicity of Public Spheres

One of the most spectacular *events* of our time is the emergence and proliferation of a multiplicity of public spheres and the correlative multiple
uses or senses of the vocabulary of public spheres around the world.[1] This
dawning global plenitude of public spheres composes an immensely complex practical and semantic field of public activities. When public activists and researchers comment on this multiplicity they usually mention
four observable features of the field.[2]

The practical and semantic field does not only comprise many examples of one kind of public sphere and one corresponding conceptualization
of the public sphere. It is composed of a large *variety* of kinds of public
spheres and senses of the public sphere terminology employed in them.[3]

For example, public spheres are local, regional, national, transnational, global, and glocal,[4] official and unofficial, publics and counter-publics, and Western and non-Western. They can be institutional, networked and ad-hoc, face-to-face and mediated, secular, religious, and mixed; and relatively powerful and powerless. Some are limited to opinion formation and communication by prespecified procedures; yet others involve negotiation with the powers that be, and some include the exercise of public powers themselves. Some are separate while others overlap locally and globally, and often new public spheres spring up within existing ones, questioning and publicizing their exclusions, either transforming them from within or branching off in new directions. The public sphere, in its most familiar sense, is a composite public sphere of the historical conglomeration of this ever-changing kaleidoscope of diverse public spheres.

Second, the particular instances of different varieties of public spheres are not stable institutions or structures operating in accord with fixed sets of rules and roles. Their practical and semantic features—such as institutionalization, rules, activities, internal and external relationships, and public scripts—*vary* as they develop. For example, the hypothesis of the stages of historical development of public spheres toward an ideal form in Europe and the spread of this module to the less-developed world by means of the promotion of Western economic, democratic, and public sphere globalization is now widely seen as only one among many ways of classifying the temporal variability of public spheres.

Third, while the number, types, and electronically mediated reach of local/global public spheres in the *present* may well be unprecedented, the field of overlapping varieties and variability of multiple publics and public spheres has a much longer history. The editors of the *Oxford English Dictionary* remind their readers that the semantic field of publics and public spheres has always been various and variable in the English-speaking world (and, by extension, in all language communities of the world):

> The varieties of sense [of public] are numerous and pass into each other by many intermediate shades of meaning. The exact shade often depends upon the substantive qualified, and in some expressions more than one sense is vaguely present; in others the usage is traditional, and it is difficult to determine in what sense precisely the thing in question was originally called "public."[5]

The editors are saying that there is neither an observable set of essential features present in every instance of a public and public sphere nor a single prototype from which the diverse instances appear to be derived. Rather, there is only a network of overlapping intermediate shades or similarities of meaning among the various uses that enable us to see the various resemblances among the instances to which the terms are applied.

Therefore, all the editors can do is to list various senses of the terms, the contexts in which they are used, and the similarities that justify the application of the terms in particular cases. Any instances of publics and public spheres always share at least some similarities or criteria with others, but no one set of criteria is shared by all. In a word, public, public sphere, and cognate terms are what we now call *family resemblance* concepts.[6]

Fourth, public spheres and their vocabulary are various and variable *because* they are *negotiated practices*. Citizens do not engage in public spheres only to form public opinions, take up public problems, address public audiences, and care for public goods. In participating in these standard public sphere activities, they also engage in the critical and reflective activity of calling into question, testing the adequacy, negotiating and modifying the given rules, scripts, roles, and relationships of the public spheres in which they act. As a consequence they also vary the public sphere vocabulary so it can be predicated on the new arrangements.

This critical public freedom of turning, calling into question, testing, negotiating, and modifying the *given* features of a public sphere en passant is perhaps the most commonplace of all four features of public spheres.[7] Moreover, it is itself the activity of creating a new public sphere within the existing one—a new public sphere that often outlasts its immediate task and takes on a life of its own. For this activity is just the application of the classic democratic public sphere activity of citizens assembling together in a forum and having a say over the rules to which they are subject (thereby rendering their government "democratic") to the rules of an existing public sphere. The variety and variability features can thus be explained, at least in part, by the global manifestation of this uniquely creative and democratic public freedom of both engagement *in* and engagement *with* public spheres. It might be called the democratic transformation of the public sphere.

According to both Nietzsche and Hannah Arendt, this ongoing free activity of institutional and conceptual negotiation explains both why and how an association such as a public sphere does not appear to have a fixed definition or trajectory but, rather, the complex, unpredictable, and miraculous phenomenon called human history.[8] That is, the public sphere is an essentially contested concept and practice.[9] Yet, as we will now see, this too is a contested claim.

Two Approaches to the Multiplicity of Public Spheres

Given the four empirical features of the field of public spheres introduced above, the question is how such a field should be approached to understand and study it comparatively and critically. I want to explore the field through two general approaches that have grown up with the field of public spheres and are interwoven into its history. Both approaches accept the multiplicity I have outlined but each responds to it in a different way. One seeks to reconstruct theoretically the essential features of the public sphere that are discoverable in an unfinished form within the observable multiplicity, whereas the other sees the multiplicity as irreducible. Both claim to be critical, yet in different senses of this semiotically concentrated term. One aims to develop a *universal* critical *theory* of the field of public spheres from a theoretical and reconstructive perspective, based on the Western experience of public spheres, whereas the other aims to foster a critical and comparative *relationship* between academic research and citizens in the plurality of public spheres, based on global public sphere pluralism, and from perspectives within the field. While their analyses of public spheres overlap, the former tends to take a broadly liberal orientation to the field, whereas the latter takes a broadly democratic orientation, and the terms "liberal" and "democratic" are used, respectively, to name the two approaches.

These two approaches have long and intertwined histories in the West and non-West. However, they took their present formation in response to the postwar proliferation of multiple public spheres and along with Jürgen Habermas's influential study of what he saw at the time as the rise and decline of the official public sphere in western Europe, which he called the bourgeois public sphere.[10] One of the most constructive criticisms of his study of the official bourgeois public sphere is that it did not take into account the "multiplicity" of nonofficial public spheres that other researchers were beginning to notice.[11] The criticism is not that he either denied or overlooked the plenitude of public spheres in Europe. Habermas acknowledged the existence of other types of modern public spheres, such as "plebeian" (working class, anarchist, radical democratic) and "plebiscitary" (popular), and he discussed other senses of "public sphere" in European languages (German, French, and English).[12] Rather, he chose not to study them, but to concentrate almost exclusively on the history, normative reconstruction, and emancipatory potential of the official bourgeois public sphere. In conjunction with other important factors, the "multiplicity criticism," as I will call it, has proven to be immensely constructive in stimulating the study of public spheres under both approaches.

On one hand, it has helped to spur legal, political, and postcolonial theorists, sociologists, political scientists, historians, feminists, anthropologists, cultural and media scholars, critical race theorists, critical digital public sphere scholars, and public sphere activists to study the multiplicity of public spheres in Europe and other Western societies, in non-Western societies, among indigenous peoples, in the international and global realms, at the World Social Forum, in immigrant and refugee communities, and so on. From the perspectives of other public spheres, as Craig Calhoun initially summarized in 1992, these more pluralistic studies expose the exclusions and restrictions of the official public sphere and its private/public distinction in the past and present, as well as the mechanisms of inclusion and assimilation into bourgeois, male, and Eurocentric norms of subjectivity and public reasoning built into the official public sphere. They thus question its emancipatory potential and suggest that emancipatory steps often come from outside the official public sphere or from contesting its allegedly universal norms of recognition from within. In addition, they bring to light the variegated lived experiences of concrete democratic cooperation, solidarity, and contestation in public spheres that is missing from the predominantly procedural and abstract reconstruction of the bourgeois public sphere.[13] These studies also present different interpretations of the official public spheres than the one Habermas originally advanced, suggesting that they form a plurality of types with a diversity of internal features and external relationships to alternative public spheres, not one single type.[14] Finally, these studies tend to emphasize the irreducible variety and variability of public spheres historically and in the present, and hence the correlative inability to construct a comprehensive theory of the field of public spheres.[15] These multidisciplinary studies in global public sphere pluralism are the avant-garde of the critical democratic and pluralist approach.[16]

On the other hand, the multiplicity criticism and the studies that followed have been important factors in Habermas's more recent reconstruction and elaboration of his theory of the official public sphere, which he now calls the "liberal" public sphere.[17] While his particular project is not endorsed by all critical liberals, it is nevertheless the single most influential and comprehensive example of a universal critical liberal theory of the field of public spheres. As such, it has played a formative role in developing the postwar critical liberal approach, within which variations on its central theses are discussed and debated by a wide range of scholars from different disciplines who share its general orientation.[18] Accordingly, I will employ it to explicate the central features of the approach.[19]

The Critical Liberal and Universal Approach to the Multiplicity of Public Spheres

Between Facticity and Normativity

The critical liberal approach discloses the field of the public sphere as an integral part of the broader field of the historical development and differentiation of the institutions and spheres (or subsystems) of the modern Western constitutional nation-state and the world system of similar constitutional orders under international law. These institutions and spheres include the private and public spheres, capitalist economy, representative government, the institutions of public government and administration, the military sphere, the general liberal public sphere of the multiplicity of public spheres throughout civil society, the specific liberal public sphere at the center, and the official channels of communication among them.[20] These separate and functionally differentiated spheres of modern constitutional states are formally constituted by the underlying legal system that guarantees the modern "system of rights": the individual rights of private autonomy (negative liberty and market freedoms) and public autonomy (public participation) that regulate participation in the private and public spheres, respectively, and that are extended from the core experience within European states and their colonies to public spheres within supranational constitutional organizations, with the European Union as a prototype, and transnational public spheres relative to global publics and the legal institutions of international law and global governance.[21]

This terrain of the public sphere is approached critically under two aspects: facticity and normativity. The task is to "reconstruct the normative ideal that is already present to some extent in the social facticity of 'existing reason' already incorporated in political processes, however distorted these may be."[22] In this approach, there is not an "*opposition* between the ideal and real," for the ideal is the abstraction and idealization of features already present in the basic institutions, processes, and procedures of the real, not yet fully realized.[23] The normative ideal is used as a critical standard to delineate, judge, and reform the distortions of the real relative to their immanent potential. It is a reformist approach in contrast to those who *oppose* their critical ideal to the real and aim to transform structural features of it. The relationship between the real and the critical ideal is, in Habermas's succinct phrase, one of an "unfinished project."[24]

While this type of critical approach does not "need a philosophy of history to support it,"[25] it is usually underpinned by a progressive liberal philosophy of history that portrays Europeans and their European legal, economic, and political institutions as if they are moving forward in time through (uneven) stages and processes of historical and cognitive development toward their ideal form. These universal processes and institutions—referred to as civilization, modernization, globalization, and democratization—are simultaneously portrayed as spreading out to the less-developed non-European world by means of European overseas expansion over the last half millennium and continuing by the promotion of market freedoms, representative democratization, and civil society building in the postcolonial world today. Situated within this broader world-historical narrative the unfinished project of the liberal public sphere can be seen as the continuation of the Enlightenment project set out by Immanuel Kant in his "Idea for a Universal History with a Cosmopolitan Purpose" (1784) and *Perpetual Peace: A Philosophical Sketch* (1795).[26]

Discourse Ethics and Opinion Formation in the Liberal Public Sphere

The general liberal public sphere is a large constitutionally ordered network of nodes (specific public spheres) "for communicating information and points of view (i.e., opinions expressing affirmative or negative attitudes); the streams of communication are, in the process, filtered and synthesized in such a way that they coalesce into bundles of topically specified *public* opinions." It is a "communication structure." The general public sphere emerges out of a basic form of everyday communication, namely, local dialogues in which humans exchange opinions and bystanders are free to join in. Such intersubjective dialogues bring into being a linguistically constituted "public space." Episodic public spaces are then "abstracted" from both the local place in which they occur and the locally accepted norms of validation, extended and rendered more permanent, and structured into "assemblies" of various kinds that are called "public spheres." Yet even these remain attached to the physical presence of audiences and local modes of argumentation. These specific public spheres become more general by further argumentation and the use of extensive public media to link the "virtual presence of scattered readers, listeners or viewers" into the abstract and general liberal public sphere.[27]

By starting in this way, Habermas is able to acknowledge and recognize within the general public sphere the multiplicity of alternative, unofficial, professional, and specific public spheres that emerge out of the everyday exchange of views in public spaces.[28] Yet, at the same time, he is able to argue that there is an ideal form of the public sphere immanent in yet distorted forms in the factual multiplicity. Between the publication of *The Structural Transformation of the Public Sphere* (1962) and the reconstruction of the liberal public sphere in *Between Facts and Norms* (1992), Habermas developed a theory (discourse ethics) of this ideal. He argued in *The Theory of Communicative Action* (1981) and *Moral Consciousness and Communicative Action* (1983) that there is an ideal set of procedures, implicit in any and every communicative exchange of opinions that ought to govern the open exchange of public reasons pro and contra among free and equal participants oriented toward reaching agreement by the force of the better argument. The theory of discourse ethics sets out a universal set of procedures that govern participation in an idealized public sphere: the conditions for entrance into the public sphere, how participants should relate to one another in the exchange of reasons over a proposition (proposed public opinion), the canonical forms of argumentation they should employ, and the type of agreement they should aim to reach. These rules constitute the essence of an ideal specific liberal public sphere that underlies the empirical multiplicity.[29]

Since all public spheres grow out of this basic form of dialogue, it follows that this set of procedures is the norm by which to construct the official liberal public sphere at the center of the network of multiple public spheres and relative to which all other public spheres in civil society can be judged and arranged.

The Functions of the Central or Specific Liberal Public Sphere

The liberal public sphere at the center of the network, which embodies the ideal procedures to the highest degree, performs three main strategic functions within the modern constitutional system of private and public spheres. It alerts the political system to public problems that need to be addressed by it "because they cannot be solved elsewhere." It brings these problems from alternative public spheres at the periphery of civil society to the center, identifies, dramatizes, and directs them to the official agency that is suited to deal with them. This is its "signal function." By means of its procedures of public opinion formation, it translates and transforms the often radical problems from the periphery into an official form of problem (a well-formulated public opinion) that the official audience (fellow citizens and potential voters) and government agencies can handle. This is its "problematizing" function. It also "oversees" how the government deals with the problem.[30]

In signaling, problematizing, and overseeing, the official liberal public sphere exercises a type of power called "influence." Publics do not make decisions or exercise public powers other than communicative capacities. Rather, they seek to employ communicatively generated public opinions through "institutionalised procedures" to influence "the beliefs and decisions of authorized members of the political system" and to determine "the behavior of voters, legislators, officials and so forth." This "public audience" of "spectators" is a constitutive feature of any public sphere. In the final analysis, the influence of the public sphere rests on gaining the approval and conviction of the lay public, and so influencing their voting behavior. Hence, public audiences, not the small deliberating publics, "possess final authority."[31]

The Role of the Variety of Public Spheres within the General Liberal Public Sphere

The varieties of unofficial public spheres on the "periphery" of civil society are also a constitutive feature of the general liberal public sphere. These multiple specialized public spheres are characterized by legally guaranteed rights of participation on the one hand and the actual ongoing practices of publics generating public opinions on the other.[32] They range from world-disclosing religious, artistic, and cultural public spheres of the broad "literary public sphere" to specialized public spheres of scientific experts, health care workers, environmentalists, feminists, and so on.[33] The quality of the bundles of public opinion they generate can be ranked relative to their closeness to the liberal procedural ideal. The liberal public sphere is designed to channel and reformulate this strange multiplicity of citizen-generated public opinions through the legally prescribed channels and procedures of communicative power so they are not excluded or disregarded, but, rather, are included and have the opportunity to influence voters and governments. As Habermas explains:

> I develop a sociological model that focuses on the empirical weight of the constitutionally prescribed, hence official, circulation of power. This weight depends primarily on whether civil society, through resonant and autonomous public spheres, develops impulses with enough vitality to bring conflicts from the periphery into the center of the political system.[34]

Many public problems that modern representative governments and their bureaucracies deal with are formulated by officeholders and political leaders within the political system and do not pass through the public sphere. Other problems are initiated from the inside, and then the public sphere is mobilized to deliberate, legitimate, and oversee solutions often already decided upon.[35] These can be perfectly legitimate functions, and not the manufacturing of public consent, as long as the public sphere procedures retain their structural autonomy.[36] Yet other problems are orchestrated by powerful media, money, and administrative interests that manipulate public opinion for their own strategic purposes.[37] Last but not least, an important class of problems is initiated by the alternative public spheres on the outskirts of civil society. These problems are often formulated in a radical way that conflicts with and opposes both the factual status quo and its liberal normative framework. The strategic role of such alternative and activist public spheres is to ferret out these new problems and direct them through sluicelike legal channels into the official liberal public sphere for translation and procedural processing into a language of manageable public problems and reforms for voters and officials to consider.[38]

According to Habermas, many of "the great issues of the last decades" were initiated on the periphery in this manner. Once they were directed into the channels of official communicative power, they influenced the "entire system's mode of problem solving." The problems of the arms race, genetic engineering, ecological threats, Third World poverty, feminism, and immigration were initiated by intellectuals, concerned citizens, radical professionals, and advocates at the margins. Just like suffragettes in relation to the bourgeois public sphere, they dramatized these problems in various public ways and forced them onto the "public agenda," where they then received "formal consideration."[39] These events on the periphery succeed by evoking a kind of "crisis consciousness" that enables the new problems to break through the closed circuit of the other two types of problem initiation above and so to influence "institutionalised opinion- and will-formation" in the central liberal public sphere and official institutions of representative government.[40] Citizens tolerate and learn from the multiplicity of religious statements in the general public sphere, yet they too have to be translated into the liberal public language before they can be processed.[41] In sending their issues into the official channels, these resonant alternative public spheres enable the liberal public sphere to hold out against manipulation and subordination by mass media and administrative power.[42]

Essential Limits and Institutional Bases of the General Public Sphere

There are several constitutionally prescribed limitations to participation in the liberal public sphere. First, the condition of stepping out of the private sphere and into alternative or official public spheres is the acceptance of the shared "liberal political culture and the corresponding patterns of socialization." These liberal socialization patterns include the acceptance of a separate "integral private sphere," the "already rationalized lifeworld" and "capitalist modernization."[43] They also require that the specific "public texts" employed in any public sphere must be open to the application of the universal text—the procedures of argumentation of the liberal public sphere—by other citizens.[44]

Second, the communicatively unstructured opinions of alternative public spheres, as we have seen, have no legitimate public influence (public communicative power) whatsoever on their own. They acquire public influence only when they are fed into and filtered through the procedures of the liberal public sphere and on to voters and governments through the legally prescribed channels: "Not influence per se, but influence transformed into communicative power legitimates political decisions."[45]

Third, publics must abjure the democratic premise of popular sovereignty that the people have the public capacity to assemble together as publics, as "we the people," and exercise public powers themselves if they judge that their representatives fail to exercise these powers for the public good as they are entrusted to do. Citizens must accept the differentiation of modern capitalist societies into the various subsystems and spheres as they are set out in the liberal theory of law and representative democracy and limit their public participation to the functional public spheres assigned to it.

> Democratic movements emerging from civil society must give up holistic aspirations to a self-organizing society, aspirations that also undergirded Marxist ideas of social revolution. Civil society can directly transform only itself, and it can have at most an indirect effect on the self-transformation of the political system; generally, it has an influence only on the personnel and programming of this system.[46]

It is not only Marxists that are excluded. Any liberal, democratic, socialist, feminist, or anarchist movement of a people as a whole or as various organizations of publics that aspire to act democratically in *any* way different from those prescribed in this critical liberal reconstruction are excluded from the public sphere.

Fourth, the sole exception is a nonviolent act of civil disobedience. However, civil disobedience is severely limited. It is not part of the public sphere but of civil society. And, it is permissible only if performed to extend the unfinished project of realizing the liberal constitutional "system of [private and public] rights" to those who have been excluded or discriminated against:

> [T]he justification of civil disobedience relies on a dynamic understanding of the constitution as an unfinished project. From this long-term perspective, the constitutional state does not represent a finished structure but a delicate and sensitive—above all fallible and revisable—enterprise, whose purpose is to realize the system of rights anew in changing circumstance, that is, to interpret the system of rights better, to institutionalize it more appropriately, and to draw out its contents more radically.[47]

In addition to these four limitations on public sphere conduct, there are constitutionally protected institutions and subsystems that constitute the necessary *preconditions* of the liberal public sphere. These must be accepted by all participants in public affairs. First, politics and the public sphere take place within and on the basis of the background constitutional structure. Politics is always "constituted in a legal form" that specifies its functions and that is not open to question in the political arenas. "This is because the conditions that make the production of legitimate law possible are ultimately not at the disposition of politics." The constitutional order is the "enabling condition" of politics.[48] Second, the constitution legally orders the other functional subsystems of modern constitutional states, of which the liberal public sphere is only one. These other private and public spheres and institutions of the modern capitalist state have their own logics of organization and development and publics are barred from "direct political interventions" in them.[49] Third, the democratic legitimacy of this constitutional system of subsystems comes from representative government and circulation of communicative influence through the liberal public sphere. The "constitutionally regulated circulation of power is nullified if the administrative system becomes independent of communicatively generated power" of the public sphere, or if large private organizations overwhelm public communication, and the system suffers a democratic deficit.[50]

Fourth and finally, citizens must both think and act within all these discursive and institutional limits and not think of alternatives, at all times but especially in times of crises. The constitutionally regulated "structures of functionally differentiated societies" constitute the form of "self-empowerment undertaken by a society of free and equal subjects who bind themselves by law."[51] The reason why all public actors must accept these institutional limits and the critical liberal normative reconstruction of their essential and not yet fully realized features as their own "participant perspective" is that they constitute the universal constitutional form of self-determination. The critical liberal theoretical reconstruction is "the paradigmatic *understanding* of law and democracy that guides citizens whenever they form an idea of the structural constraints on the self-organization of the legal community in their society."[52] Although it may appear in changing social circumstances that, especially in moments of legitimation or steering crises, there is "a spectrum of legal paradigms," these alternatives are actually various interpretations of the ideal system of rights.[53] And this is true of legal pluralism more generally. Historical constitutions can be seen as so many ways of construing one and "the *same* practice—the practice of self-determination on the part of free and equal citizens."[54] Hence, the discourse theory of law and democracy makes explicit the ideal constitutional form in which the practice of self-determination must take place and which is already present in a permanent yet unfinished form in the Western constitutional state:

> From a reconstructive standpoint, we have seen that constitutional rights and principles merely explicate the performative character of the self-constitution of a society of free and equal citizens. The organizational forms of the constitutional state make this practice permanent.[55]

Hence, while the liberal public sphere is universal in the sense of being open to all individuals in principle, and opened historically in practice by public actors extending the system of rights to excluded groups,[56] they are allowed to enter only if they become liberal capitalist subjects in their public thought and action. These limits and institutional preconditions constitute the essential features of the general liberal public sphere.

The Unfinished Project of Globalizing the Liberal Public Sphere

The promotion of this universal model of the liberal public sphere in the liberal constitutional state is only one part of the larger unfinished global project. The constitutional structure and the functional roles of the liberal public sphere within it (of socializing citizens and legitimating public decisions) can be detached from states and applied to transnational constitutional orders, such as the European Union.[57] The EU in turn can function as a model for supranational constitutions and public spheres in "Asia, Latin America, Africa, and the Arab World."[58] It can also function as a prototype for the constitutionalization of existing international law and the Charter of the United Nations.[59] Political decisions within these constitutional orders do not have anywhere near the same degree of public sphere legitimacy as decisions within constitutional states, because their transnational and global public spheres and circuits of communicative power are not well developed. Yet these emerging constitutional structures can be said to gain democratic legitimacy as "the channels of democratic legitimation are progressively extended 'upwards' from the level of existing liberal nation-states to the level of continental regimes," again with the European Union as the possible prototype.[60] The spread and institutionalization of these new constitutional orders and their weak liberal public spheres around the world should be seen as a further stage in the realization of the unfinished project initiated by Kant of bringing global constitutional facticity in line with Western constitutionalism as the normative ideal.[61] Europe has a "second chance" to promote this global project in a different way than in its imperial past.[62]

The Intermediate Step to the Critical Democratic Approach

In response to democratic critics of this new theory of the liberal public sphere, Habermas claims that the limits he lays down do not constitute the "incapacitation" of citizens.[63] In Kantian terms, these limits do not disable citizens from exercising their public capacities as mature and autonomous agents and treat them as dependent and immature, because they are self-limiting: the intrinsic conditions of the exercise of public capacities of self-determination by free and equal citizens under the rule of law. In one sense this is correct. The liberal public sphere constrains and enables public actors to develop and exercise the public communicative capacities of liberal citizens and to develop the corresponding liberal form of subjectivity and self-consciousness. It integrates and assimilates them into the constitutional order through their free public use of communicative reason and, simultaneously, it channels their public opinions into influences on political decisions. And, in so doing, it reproduces the basic constitutional structure of a liberal capitalist society and reforms it toward its immanent ideal. In this sense, it enables citizens to exercise a set of capacities of self-determination within a legal form.

Notwithstanding its merits, from the perspective of critical democratic pluralists the liberal public sphere nevertheless incapacitates democratic citizens and researchers. To begin, it confines the repertoire of public capacities of self-determination that citizens can exercise to a narrow skill set of communicative capacities within the uncontestable limits and institutional preconditions of one particular historical example of a public sphere, namely, the general liberal public sphere interpretation of the official public sphere of Western constitutional states and its global projection. The only change possible is reform within the bounds of the liberal capitalist state and world order by influencing its officials, on the presumption that public problems cannot be "solved elsewhere." The general liberal public sphere is presented as universal, yet this claim is based on the self-referential first step that the ideal features of all public spheres can be discovered by reflection on the features that are present in an unfinished form in a particular example. This sort of universalizing from one or two senses of "public sphere" is precisely the approach that the editors of the OED encourage their readers to deuniversalize (or "provincialize") and see beyond its horizons to the wider field by giving other undeniable examples of public spheres that share some features but not others.[64]

Imagine that democratic citizens in a liberal public sphere or a democratic people in a global liberal public sphere raise a tentative question about the validity of any of the limits and institutional preconditions placed upon the exercise of their public capacities for addressing a public problem. For example, is the limit really necessary and enabling or is it a cause of the public problem they are trying to address and an obstacle to its solution?[65] To raise this kind of question is, as Rainer Forst points out, to do no more than invoke the democratic right to ask for a justification of the rules that govern their conduct in this system of government (the liberal public sphere), as in any other.[66] It also can be seen as a public responsibility from the democratic perspective.[67] Reciprocally, those who are responsible for imposing and enforcing the limit (the government) have a democratic duty to respond: to enter into a dialogue over the validity of the limit in question. This question-and-answer dialogue between governors and governed renders their form of government "democratic" in the classic sense: those subject to the rules have an effective say over them. This democratic test of the validity is the enactment of the democratic public freedom of bringing a given rule into the space of public questions and submitting it to public scrutiny, rather than unquestionably submitting to it.

The initiation of this kind of question brings a *democratic* public sphere into being, in this case around the public discussion of a limit of the liberal public sphere. That is, it treats the critical liberal as a fellow citizen and his or her claim of a limit as one (liberal) proposal to be examined in the broader democratic public sphere, along with conservative, socialist, anarchist, ecologist, feminist, religious, nonviolent, and other proposals, not as a legislative imperative imposed from outside the public sphere that must be obeyed without question. The critical liberal forecloses this reflexive democratic question by claiming that the limits of the liberal public sphere are the background enabling conditions of questioning within the public sphere. However, in raising this kind of question a citizen simply invokes a basic criterion of legitimacy that critical liberals—and Habermas in particular—share with the critical democrat. The principle is the equiprimordiality of the rule of law (constitutionalism) and democracy (or popular sovereignty).[68] That is, the elaboration of constitutionally prescribed limits to the exercise of democratic capacities of self-determination of free and equal citizens and peoples should be coarticulated in relationships in which those who are subject to them can have a democratic say over them. This coarticulation norm combines the rule of law and the consent of the governed. Yet, the critical liberal claims that a complex constitutional framework, a system of underlying institutions, and a discursive script in which to think about them are all exempt from the coarticulation requirement. The citizens who raise the question are simply asking that this justification be presented and discussed in the public sphere.

The justification of the exemption of all these limits from the democratic test is that they could be proved to be, from the theoretical perspective, outside the public sphere, the universal and obligatory *form* of the exercise of the democratic capacities of free and equal citizens for self-determination always and everywhere. They are "self-limiting": constitutive rules of the public sphere, not a regulative rule that could be discussed within it. Yet, the constitutive *status* of the limits of the public sphere is *presupposed* in the first step of the critical liberal approach, in *taking* the normatively reconstructed implicit limits of the particular given or factual liberal public sphere as the universal background conditions of participation in any public sphere. And this presupposition runs throughout the argument, insulating the limits from democratic testing as they are explicated. The democratic question opens this closed circle by bringing the limit and the presupposition that serves to justify its exception into the space of questions and submits it to the test of public reason. In so doing the questioner does no more than hold the critical liberal to his or her own criterion of legitimacy in the very institution that is designed for this purpose, the public sphere.

The critical liberal who disallows the question in the public sphere places a whole framework of the constitutional rule of law and the underlying institutions it orders *prior to and insulated from* the practice of democratic examination and thereby violates the equiprimordiality criterion. This view of the relation between constitutionalism and democracy is correctly called the *juridical containment* premise. The constitution contains democratic activity to reform within the boundaries of the constitutionally protected system of spheres and institutions, which are off-limits.[69] This is a classic "liberal" approach, rather than the "liberal-democratic" approach of combining the rule of law and democracy equally. Critical democratic citizens and free peoples who insist on their democratic right to question what is given to them as universal, necessary, or obligatory limits to democracy, and critical liberal democrats who think twice and accept the invitation to join in the public discussions, are the upholders of the equiprimordiality criterion.[70]

Critical democrats are not only saying that a presumptive limit of the liberal public sphere and the corresponding vocabulary *could* be questioned, negotiated, and gone beyond by some step. Such free citizens and free peoples actually *take* the intermediate step and go beyond a limit by asking the question and invoking the shared equiprimordiality criterion to justify it. This practice of public questioning *is* the exercise of a democratic public capacity that is supposed to be off limits. In bringing a limit into the space of public questions, it is transformed from its status as an untouchable structure of domination beyond the reach of the liberal public sphere into its status as a regulative relationship of power open to testing, negotiation, and modification within the democratic public sphere.[71]

The Critical Democratic and Pluralist Approach

Bringing a Public Sphere Into Being Here and Now

Like the liberal, the democrat begins from the everyday Socratic scene of a couple of people and bystanders raising questions about the way they are governed. From the democratic perspective of citizens, a public sphere is brought into being when some of those who are subject to a system of government turn around and call some *aspect* of it into the space of public questions.[72] In engaging in this *practice* they transform themselves from subjects of a form of government to *active agents*—or "citizens" in the classic or "active" sense—*in and of* the form of government.[73] In entering into dialogue relationships with each other, in taking up and discussing the public question (or questions), they form a "public" in one of the many senses of this term. Their form of cooperative public questioning is a "sphere" in at least three senses: (1) it "takes place" here and now in this particular questionable relationship of this government, this locale, and this ecosystem; (2) their association is a definite sphere or form of public activity; and (3) they extend and hyperextend by various means a "sphere of influence" to immediate bystanders and audiences near and far. In Hannah Arendt's famous formulation, they bring a "public world" into being.[74]

Unlike the liberal approach, this concrete public space does not need to be "abstracted" from its local context, and the particular question of injustice does not to be "generalized" into an abstract problem from the vernacular languages in which it is articulated for it to become a public sphere. As journalists, novelists, historians, anthropologists, and public philosophers have known for centuries, sufficient criteria of publicness are already present at hand for this situation to be an effective public sphere.[75]

When subjects engage in the difficult yet commonplace practice of turning and reflecting on an aspect of the relationships of power, knowledge, and subjectification that govern their conduct, they bring that aspect into the immediate public sphere they create. They take the questionable relationship out of the "private" realm of its place in the routine and taken-for-granted background of everyday life and submit it to the light of public scrutiny. They publicize it. When women turn and call into question a patriarchal relationship in the household, children demand a voice in family relations, workers bring forth an arbitrary condition in the workplace, civil servants go public with a document, students demand a say in the educational system, soldiers seek to democratize the military, consumers refuse to buy sweatshop products, or a colonized people turn and challenge an imperial relationship of subordination, they bring to public awareness in a public sphere what lies in the unquestioned background sphere of the given system of norms of recognition and action coordination, where the governing relationship "goes without saying." These are the democratic senses of the "private" (goes without saying) and "public" (having a say) spheres.

The democratic senses of private and public differ from the liberal senses; yet both derive from the Greek practice of calling the household private and the political realm public. Early modern state builders and the liberal tradition interpreted this as a reference to two separate institutionalized spheres or subsystems and continued to use the terms in this way, constructing a system of private and public rights around them that shielded autocratic relationships in the family and private corporations from change. The democratic tradition interpreted this as a reference to two different kinds of *relationships* and continued to use the terms in this sense, regardless of their institutional location. A private relationship is one of command and obedience (monological), whereas a public relationship is open to the free speech and negotiation of the partners.[76] Over the last two hundred years, feminists, advocates of the rights of the child, workers demanding a say in the workplace, abolitionists, anti-imperialists, and so on have employed this sense to make *public* and *democratize* relationships within the liberal institutional private sphere, often without any official right to do so and at great cost to themselves.[77] Democratic governments and courts have occasionally responded to these struggles by granting subjects in the so-called liberal private sphere public rights of consultation and negotiation over the governance relationships they bear, thereby helping to transform the liberal private sphere beyond recognition.

Public Spheres and Forms of Government

The Arendtian moment of the irruption of a democratic public sphere can occur in any system of governance in which we find ourselves, across the institutionalized liberal public and private spheres. This is difficult to see due to the peculiar development of public spheres in the West. On the one hand, in the early modern period "government" was used in a broad sense to refer to any practice of some people governing the conduct of others, from households, schools, churches, guilds, poorhouses, and local parishes to navies, city-states, emerging centralized states, leagues, and empires. According to Michel Foucault, the critical democratic tradition in the West emerged in innumerable acts of insubordination and counterconduct in these diverse forms of government, often successfully transforming them from unilateral master-servant relationships to forms of government in which the subordinate partner had an effective say to the principal about the character of their relationship in tailor-made public spheres.[78]

On the other hand, as modern states gradually claimed to centralize all power relationships under their juridical auspices, the term "government" tended to be restricted to the central representative government and "public participation" to engagement in the corresponding official or bourgeois public sphere at the national level, as both Habermas and Foucault show. The multiplicity of local forms of government and their correlative public spheres were subordinated to central authority, not without continual resistance to this usurpation of local authority. Modern political theory went along with this trend. It took the centralized institutions of representative government and the official public sphere as its central and virtually exclusive focus and downplayed and denigrated the local. The everyday public world of diverse forms of governments and public spheres was concealed by the widely held fiction that individuals or peoples moved from a state of nature directly to members of centralized nation-states with rights of participation in the national or federal public sphere. Moreover, as Hobbes recommended, the central state claimed to establish the public sphere and its rules of participation, and thus to be the necessary precondition of its existence. Thus, the juridical containment premise appeared to be accurate.

Notwithstanding this centralist revolution, the crazy quilt of practices of government and companion public spheres not only continued but expanded exponentially, as the historians of the multiplicity of the public sphere have pointed out. As Foucault puts the general point, the "forms and the specific situations of the government of some by others in a given society are *multiple:* they are superimposed, they cross over, limit and in some cases annul, in others reinforce, one another." And, in any form of government, from a master-servant relationship to an empire-colony relationship, there is always an internally related or co-original public sphere game created by the agonism between governors and governed: the limited yet ongoing freedom of negotiation of the relationship between them.[79] From the perspective of the democratic and popular sovereignty traditions, this multiplicity of public spheres is seen as the sovereign people exercising their constituent powers as publics in practices of government. Yet, as we have seen, even today the multiplicity of other types of public spheres continue to be seen as peripheral or "subaltern counter-publics" relative to the hegemony of the official central public sphere in practice and theory.[80]

The Global Pluralism of Public Spheres and Forms of Government

These local public spheres might be called "specific" or "customized" public spheres because they involve a specific number of people and are centered around a specific public good of their specific form and situation of government. Yet, the local public goods that they discuss are generalizable around the world: fair wage, pay equity, environmentally friendly work conditions and products, fair trade between North and South and, of course, the guarantee of the freedom to enter into these kinds of public spheres around issues of common concern with the relevant powers that be. A customized (and often customary) public sphere in one place speaks to the similarly situated public audiences all along global networks of production, consumption, and volunteer activities, and their voices are amplified by electronic networks of e-mail, YouTube, Facebook, and so on. Public audiences learn from the shared experiences and create their own public spheres with the ways and means appropriate to their niche. Perhaps, as Raj Patel argues, one of the most spectacular examples is the rapid rise of a glocal network of public spheres throughout the global chain of food production, consumption, disposal, and reuse around caring for the public good of food sovereignty.[81] Of course, the networking of public spheres began well before what Manuel Castells calls the "network revolution" of the late twentieth century.[82] The most successful example is the "international" public spheres of the nineteenth and twentieth centuries that brought together citizens from the imperial and colonial worlds to discuss the abolition of imperialism and liberation.[83] However, the creation of the World Wide Web has increased glocal public sphere networking astronomically, again in tandem with networked forms of global governance. In turn, these digitized public spheres have given rise to a whole new academic field of research, critical digital studies.[84]

The *variety or plurality* of public spheres follows from the features enumerated so far. Public spheres are not exclusive to a particular kind of government, such as Western constitutional representative government and its underlying institutions. Public spheres develop in interaction with the specific forms and situations of government that publics submit to the test of public reasons in various ways. Their development, internal organization, types and degrees of institutionalization, networkization, and rationalization, and relationships to other public spheres, audiences, and governments are accordingly various, variable, and open-ended. Moreover, there is not only a pluralism of public spheres within and across Western-style constitutional associations, both national and transnational, but also a pluralism of non-Western public spheres in critical relationships with their corresponding forms of government. These persist in damaged forms after centuries of colonial imposition of Western institutions and public spheres.[85] In each particular case, the public sphere "democratizes" the form of government by bringing it under the public discussion of those subject to it. This is the grassroots sense of "democratization" of the democratic approach. This kind of democratization is as various and pluralistic as the forms of government it is tailored to democratize. In contrast, the critical liberal sense of "democratization" is the global projection of one modular form of government (representative government), public sphere (the general liberal public sphere), institutional preconditions, and constitutional container.

From the critical democratic perspective, therefore, we can distinguish four historically interrelated kinds of global pluralism: legal, governmental, democratic, and public sphere pluralisms. This is not only a conceptual conclusion, but the conclusion of multidisciplinary empirical research on democratization since decolonization.[86] Moreover, this research also shows that since the Cold War, the "low intensity democracy" of the liberal public sphere and its multilayered legal regimes and economic institutions have been relentlessly promoted by the powerful agents of neoliberal globalization in tension with the pluralism of "alternative democracies" from below.[87] The most dangerous aspect of this globalizing project from the democratic perspective is the argument that it can be imposed throughout the former colonial world without the agreement of the governed because it simply establishes the legal and institutional preconditions of democratic participation, of giving public agreement. The right of the self-determination of peoples was specifically designed during the decolonization period to check this imperial justification. But, as we have seen, the critical liberal tradition has absorbed this challenge in the postcolonial period by counterarguing that the liberal module of the system of rights of representative democracy and market freedoms is the universally legitimate form of self-determination, thereby legitimating its implantation and delegitimating resistance to it.[88]

Nothing illustrates the interrelated pluralism of the field of public spheres better than the public life and influence of Mahatma Gandhi. From the publication of *Hind Swaraj* (Home Self-Government) in 1909 to his death, Gandhi brought to the attention of the world the non-violent and self-governing public spheres in and among Indian villages and adapted them to contest imperialism, economic exploitation, gender inequality, religious intolerance, and environmental degradation.[89] His followers, from Ernst Friedrich Schumacher to the Chipko and living democracy movements today, have continued to revive and extend concentric circles of these homespun village public spheres and general public goods.[90] These alternative democracies and public spheres have been studied and voluntarily adapted in Africa, Latin America, North America, and Europe.[91]

Popular Sovereignty, Public Spheres, and Public Goods

The classical way to formulate any public question in a public sphere about its corresponding form of government and for a public audience is in terms of "public goods." In other words: "Is this aspect of the way we are governed that we are bringing to the attention of the public actually serving public goods or is it harming them in some way?" This is, as John Locke restated at the beginning of the modern period, the general description under which citizens have a right and duty to appraise and judge their governors in any form of government and to overthrow them if they violate the public good and fail to amend their ways. The premise that underlies this form of argument is that the citizens, the people, have the public capacities to govern themselves in accordance with the public good if they so wish, in the form of direct democracy. The people are sovereign. In forms of government where the governed and governors are different people, the citizens delegate and entrust some of their public capacities to exercise powers of self-government to their governors on the condition that they exercise these delegated powers in accord with the public good or goods. Citizens retain a range of capacities that they exercise directly in their various activities (e.g., in the private sphere in the liberal sense), regulated by the government. The range of delegated capacities differs in different forms of government (e.g., socialist, capitalist, or cooperative economic organization) and with different political parties within one form of government, yet the people always retain the public capacities to appraise and judge the performance of their governors in serving the public as they entrust them to do so, and to remove and replace them if they fail. They are thus never "incapacitated" (treated as subjects rather than active citizens) because, ultimately, they determine which public capacities they exercise themselves and which they delegate to governors, and they literally govern the way their governors exercise these powers (by judging their performance and calling them to account if necessary). This is the popular sovereignty representation of public capacities and the powers of government.[92]

In this democratic representation of the exercise of public capacities, the public sphere plays an *indispensable* role. It is the place where citizens exercise their public capacities to judge and hold to account their governors in accord with the public good. Governors cannot govern in accord with the public good unless they are guided to do so by the public discussion of their governance by the governed and by the threat of removal if they fail to learn from the public dialogue. If the governed fail to engage in the public sphere and turn to private affairs (that is, do not raise any public question about the form of government), then the unrestrained (or "ungoverned") governors are unable to exercise public capacities in accord with the public good on their own, and they exercise them in accord with their private good. The governors become corrupt. Conversely, if the governed fail to enter into the public sphere, speak truth to power, and engage in the public dialogue with their governors, they fail to develop their public democratic capacities as citizens to speak frankly and act in accord with the public good. They turn to their private affairs or they treat their governors as unrestrained masters and toady up to them, rather than developing the public courage to speak truthfully to the powerful. They become servile rather than mature public actors. The relationship of self-interested masters and servile servants permeates the relationships of governance in all areas of society, from childrearing and early education to higher education, gender relations, the work place, the church, and the military, as Mary Wollstonecraft famously argued.[93] Hence, the public sphere is a sphere of mutual subjectivization, where the continuous *dialogue* between the governed and their entrusted governors over the delegation of capacities of self-government and the public good in public spheres creates good citizens and good governors.[94] In other words, the popular sovereignty understanding of public spheres is the discursive feature that enables subjects to take the very first step of bringing into being a democratic question, a democratic public, and a democratic public sphere.

Public Reasoning in Conditions of Plurality

At the center of the liberal public sphere is a particular form of the exchange of public reasons. It consists of arguing pro and contra propositions in ascending steps of abstraction and generalization in accordance with a set of universal rules and with the aim of reaching agreement on a generalizable public opinion. In contrast, if the free exchange of public reasons is approached from the democratic perspective, this deliberative model is seen as one limited mode of public reasoning, as Iris Marion Young shows in her path-breaking studies of contemporary public spheres. It is appropriate for a small number of well-focused public propositions for which a pro and contra form of reasoning is appropriate. Most public issues are much more multiplex than this. Rather, she goes on to suggest, a more appropriate and disclosive critical hypothesis of the field as a whole is the one initially advanced by Hannah Arendt: of an irreducible *plurality* of genres of public reasoning and intersecting public judgments by differentially situated citizens over the contested public goods of their shared public world. The underlying idea is that the public sphere should always open to the public freedom of the plurality of voices that it excludes or misrecognizes to challenge the prevailing rules of recognition and participation.[95]

The reason for the plurality is that public judgments are evaluative descriptions of public problems concerning the exercise of delegated powers of government from the contextual perspectives of citizens. They bring to public light problematic *aspects* of their shared world from their different locales (places) and identities (cultural, religious, etc.) and they formulate them in the vernacular public language or languages. This is the very condition of having one's own public voice, as David Owen argues.[96] It solicits other participants to learn to listen and attend to the specific aspects of the situation that matter for each speaker and constitute the reason for exercising the civic courage to speak publicly, as well as attend to and demand a fair hearing for those who are legally excluded from a public sphere but are massively affected by the political decisions that the privileged participants are discussing.

Presenting and listening to plural public judgments over public problems and public goods requires the linguistic skills of using and understanding the complex semantic range of shades of meaning of the shared public languages that the editors of the OED, Wittgenstein, and ordinary language philosophers of reason and rhetoric have investigated over the last century. These difficult intersubjective public skills of learning one's way around in this irreducible plurality of public judgments of fellow citizens and all affected noncitizens, of making critical and comparative judgments relative to variously interpreted public goods, and of extending the uses of public terms in new ways are not something to be transcended. They are the only means to democratic public education and enlightenment about the multifaceted public problems of the common world that diverse citizens share with each other in the global webs of relationships they inhabit. Rather than homogenizing the plurality of public judgments that survive critical comparative reasoning, they respect the irreducible diversity of views and begin the difficult task of negotiating a provisional agreement that incorporates aspects of each, yet which is always open to question, revision, and renegotiation as they move forward.[97]

If, conversely, they are constrained to shed their differences and deliberate toward agreement on a general public opinion, public reasoning and judgments can become detached from and cover over the specific injustices from which they arise and to which they are supposed to respond. Less adversarial modes of public engagement can be relegated to the periphery. Public deliberation tends toward the amateur or professional disengaged manipulation of general principles and opinions divorced from and irrelevant to practice.[98] The turn to modes of critical, contextual, and engaged public reasoning in conditions of plurality by democratic publics and critical democratic researchers in our time is a response to the deficiencies of the abstract model of public reasoning of the liberal public sphere and the corresponding detachment of critical theory from practice.[99] Like critical liberals, critical democrats are concerned with the manipulation of the public sphere and the manufacturing of public opinion by powerful actors, such as media, corporations, co-opted civil society organizations, security agencies, propaganda ministries, and terrorist organizations. They also support legislative remedies. However, with their stubbornly realistic orientation, critical democratic publics and researchers do not imagine ideal public spheres free of power and ideal legislation. Instead, they act with respect to these forms of distorting power in the public sphere as they do with respect to any other relationship of power that governs their conduct.

Citizens bring a public sphere into being and reason critically and plurally together about the public good of some aspect of the way they are governed in their various activities. As we saw earlier, this exercise of their public capacities of judging their government has to reach out and establish a dialogue with their governors. This is unlike the liberal public sphere, whose primary audience is the electorate. Such a dialogue is the only way that citizens can effectively oversee the way their governors exercise the powers of self-government that the people entrusted to them to be employed in accord with the public good. Governors in any form of governance have yet other perspectives on public problems, and these need to be part of public discussions to gain fuller and more enlightened views of what the public good requires. They become good governors and good citizens only by being mutual subjects of these reciprocally enlightening relationships of democratic interdependency and mutual aid. Otherwise, they tend to pursue their private interests and public goods are not upheld.

The Ethical Basis of the Democratic Public Sphere

The last and most important feature of a public sphere is its ethical basis. According to the critical liberal approach, a person steps out of the private sphere and directly into the public sphere, acts in accord with the liberal public culture, and is socially integrated into it. From the democratic perspective this overlooks the intermediate step into the *ethical* public sphere between the private and (liberal or democratic) public sphere. This is the public sphere of citizens' daily lives in relationships with others and the environment where they can care for the same public goods that they argue for in the democratic public sphere. For example, in their everyday public activities environmentalists take care of the environment, peace and nonviolent public actors act peacefully and nonviolently in their relationships, feminists enact nonpatriarchal relationships, localists act locally, anti-imperialists buy and sell in nonexploitive and democratic relationships between workers in the global North and South, and democrats treat their everyday relationships as partnerships open to negotiation among diverse partners. In engaging in these daily ethical practices of the self in relationships with others, they gradually *become* in their own lives the change they advocate and hope to bring about through participation in democratic public spheres. As a result, they bring into being another world, an ethical public world, that provides the practical basis of and motivation for going on and struggling for these public goods in the ways surveyed in the previous sections.

Public spheres are resonant and independent only if the publics who participate in them are grounded in the actual daily experience of ethical practices of caring for the public goods they wish to bring about in the democratic public spheres. They would not be able to problematize the dominant for and against discourses and present other possibilities unless they had alternative forms of living together to draw on. This internal relationship between ethical practices of caring for public goods and participation in public spheres has been one of the central teachings of the democratic tradition, from Socrates admonishing his fellow citizens to take care of their ethical being as a prelude to taking care of public goods in the *Apology*, to Mary Wollstonecraft on early education, Gandhi's ashrams, Martin Luther King Jr.'s practices of purification and self-discipline, and the later Michel Foucault's rediscovery of ethical practices of the care of the self in relationships with others.[100]

When citizens engage directly in practices of caring for public goods in their everyday activities they do so, as much as possible, in accord with these goods as they articulate them in democratic public spheres. These radical articulations of public goods are located, from the liberal perspective, on the periphery of the liberal public sphere. Because they usually problematize some limit of the liberal public sphere and its underlying institutions and suggest that it is part of the problem, rather than the enabling condition of addressing the problem squarely, these articulations have to be filtered and translated into the official public problem language of the liberal public sphere to have any legitimate influence whatsoever.

From the democratic perspective, this officially sanctioned influence is just the tip of the iceberg; just the tip of the *effectiveness* of the full, unofficial articulation of public goods and the underlying public world of alternative ethical practices on which they rest and gain their transgenerational endurance. The unofficial version and its underlying ethical practices remain as an irreducible standing critique of one or more limits of the liberal public sphere and its underlying institutions to deal with the public problems. For over a century, publics have raised these critical problematizations, enacted another world in ethical practices, and passed them on to the next generation. Many were raised initially in public spheres within imperial states and the colonized world, then in international public spheres, such as socialist internationals and liberal democratic peace and freedom leagues, and now in glocal public spheres vis-à-vis the institutions of global governance. The history of peace and anti-imperial publics and public problems illustrates how general critical problematizations, publics, and ethical public practices endure on the rim of official public spheres.[101]

From the democratic perspective, the critical public problems and their underlying ethical practices have their greatest influence and effectiveness outside the official channels of the liberal public sphere. The citizens engaged in them change the world directly by changing their life-styles and the relationships that govern their conduct in their everyday activities. These practices in the ethical public sphere then provide the resources for engagement in democratic public sphere communication and action. In engaging in ethical and democratic public spheres, citizens work in, on (by negotiation), and around the limits of the liberal public sphere in ways that the critical liberal approach overlooks, yet, taken all together, they may well make up the largest and most practically effective, yet unnamed, composite public sphere of ethical and democratic publics and public spheres in the world.[102]

The main critical liberal criterion for judging the knowledge produced in a public sphere is the procedures of public argument. Critical democrats agree that this is one standard. Yet, because they include a plurality of modes of public reasoning, this is a more complex judgment than it is for the critical liberals. However, they have another criterion that is at least as important. They judge the validity and truthfulness of what citizens say and do in the public sphere in relation to their ethical conduct in the ethical public sphere. To what extent do they embody in their ethical practices the principles and goods they claim to profess in the public sphere? This is the oldest democratic test in the Western world, coextensive with the birth of the public sphere. It is probably the most common test employed by public sphere participants and audiences throughout the world today—does this speaker walk the talk?

From a democratic perspective, the failure of the critical liberal approach to see the relationship between ethical practice and public speech and to judge public speakers relative to their own practice is part of the larger problem of the abstraction of public discussion from concrete practice in contemporary democracies. It leaves free-floating public speech in the public sphere open to manipulation and watering-down on one hand and unconnected to concrete struggles to make the world a better place on the other. The democratic approach of connecting together, as tightly as possible, ethical practices in ethical public spheres and democratic practices in democratic public spheres reunites the two complementary senses of democratic self-government that Gandhi called *swaraj*. The delegation of powers of self-government to representatives must always be linked reciprocally to individual ethical practices of self-government of citizens (and governors) in their daily relationships. The link between the two is the relationship of negotiation and mutual subjection manifested in the public sphere. As Gandhi noted:

> I have therefore endeavored to show in word and deed that political self-government—that is self-government for a large number of men and women—is no better than individual self-government, and therefore, it is to be attained by precisely the same means that are required for individual self-government.[103]

As a result, a democratic public sphere has a different relationship to public audiences than the liberal public sphere. The function of the liberal public sphere is to influence the voting behavior of the public audience. While influencing voting behavior is one aim of democratic public spheres, it is not the primary aim. The primary objective is to bring members of the public audience to consider changing their ethical lives by changing their daily habits with respect to the public goods at issue, thereby directly participating in changing the world from the ground up. Publics in public spheres engage in this relationship not only by presenting good public reasons for all to see and hear, but also by bringing their own daily ethical public sphere practices in conformity with what they say in the democratic public sphere. They act as exemplary role models to public audiences by walking their talk. Public audiences judge them accordingly and are moved, not only by the better argument to change their opinion, but also by the better *ethos* to change themselves.

This revolutionary understanding of public spheres as democratic practices of citizens and governors discussing, negotiating, and transforming the relationships of governance between them freely, openly, and peacefully, and the reciprocal relationship of these to practices of the self in ethical public spheres, only came to widespread public consciousness in the mid-twentieth century. The first step was the realization that the recourse to violence to resolve disputes is the antonym of a public sphere (as darkness is to light). It terminates the nonviolent public sphere relationship of discussion and negotiation and the background threat or possibility of recourse to violence to resolve the dispute erodes and subverts the trust relationship between partners that is a condition of a public sphere. This was not a new discovery, but the horrors of a century of global wars brought into being the biggest peace movement in history with this insight as its challenging public problem.[104]

The second step follows from the first as its antidote. The only way citizens can bring an end to war is to organize, discuss, and negotiate *non-violently* in public spheres with armed governments (and other organizations based on the use of violence). Publics have to embody in all their democratic and ethical public sphere activities the nonviolent way of life they promote publicly if they are to convert governments to disarmament and nonviolence on the one hand and gain the respect and support of the global public audience on the other, and thereby to build a nonviolent world from the ground up. Peace has to be the way as well as the end. Nonviolence is not one public good among many, but the public good that makes possible the multiplicity of practices of discussing and negotiating our differences that we call public spheres. This is the truth that Gandhi in the colonial world, Martin Luther King Jr. in North America, and Petra Kelly in Europe proposed in the public sphere and manifested in their public ethical lives.[105]

Conclusion

We have seen that the present general crisis of global governance does not only refer to the healthy discontent of citizens with the undemocratic character of the institutions of global governance and the foreign policies of the great powers. It also refers to a general discontent with many forms and situations of governments around the world. Finally, it refers to a parallel discontent with the official public spheres in which citizens can express their discontents and do something about them. I have attempted to show that the liberal and democratic public spheres and their two critical approaches are responses to this general crisis. How they will fare in the twenty-first century does not seem to be a project whose defining features we already know, but the unpredictable phenomenon Nietzsche and Hannah Arendt call history.

Notes

1. By public sphere vocabulary I mean "public sphere," "publics," "public reason," "public audiences," "public capacities," "publicness," "public goods," and the like, as well as their contrastive vocabularies of private, nonpublic, and so on. I also include in "public speech activities" all forms of public expression, such as acting, mime, film, witnessing, listening, signing, electronic media, and so on.
2. The term "multiplicity" was originally introduced by Nancy Fraser and Craig Calhoun to refer to these features.

3. For recent introductions to the global field, see Daniel Drache with Marc D. Froese, *Defiant Publics: The Unprecedented Reach of the Global Citizen* (Cambridge, 2008) and Michael A. Peters, Alan Britton, and Harry Blee, eds., *Global Citizenship Education: Philosophy, Theory and Pedagogy* (Rotterdam, 2008).

4. "Glocal" publics are grounded in a local public sphere yet hyperextend their public activities and spheres globally through networking and other means.

5. "Public," in *The Oxford English Dictionary*.

6. The use of the term "family resemblance" to describe nonessential concepts was famously introduced by Wittgenstein in a section of the *Philosophical Investigations* that almost reads like a gloss on the above quotation from the OED. See Ludwig Wittgenstein, *Philosophical Investigations*, ed. and trans. G. E. M. Anscombe (Oxford, 2002), §§ 65–67 and 75. The discovery of nonessential concepts and the kind of reasoning and understanding that is appropriate to them is much older. It is the core teaching of the classical humanist tradition from Aristotle to the early seventeenth century, under the concept of *paradiastole*. See Quentin Skinner, *Reason and Rhetoric in the Philosophy of Hobbes* (Cambridge, 1996), pp. 138–80. This is the general form of public reasoning characteristic of the democratic approach to public spheres.

7. For a path-breaking global survey that focuses on this feature, see Volker Heins, *Nongovernmental Organizations in International Society: Struggles Over Recognition* (New York, 2008).

8. Hannah Arendt, "What Is Freedom?" in *Between Past and Future: Eight Exercises in Political Thought* (New York, 1968), pp. 170–71. For Nietzsche, see the epigraph: Friedrich Nietzsche, *On the Genealogy of Morals*, ed. Keith Ansell-Pearson, trans. Carol Diethe (Cambridge, 1996), p. 57.

9. The idea of an essentially contested concept was first introduced by Bryce Gallie, in reference to the concept of democracy. See Walter B. Gallie, "Essentially Contested Concepts," *Proceedings of the Aristotelian Society* 56 (1956): 167–98, and developed by William Connolly, *The Terms of Political Discourse* (Lexington, MA, 1974).

10. See Jürgen Habermas, *The Structural Transformation of the Public Sphere: An Inquiry into a Category of Bourgeois Society*, trans. Thomas Burger with Frederick Lawrence (Cambridge, MA, 1992).

11. The multiplicity criticism was summarized and presented to Habermas in 1992 by Craig Calhoun in his "Introduction: Habermas and the Public Sphere," in Calhoun, *Habermas and the Public Sphere*, pp. 37–39. Calhoun also sketches out possible responses to the criticism, which are taken up by Habermas in his more recent work. Several authors in the volume raise the issue of multiplicity, but the single most influential chapter is that by Nancy Fraser, "Rethinking the Public Sphere: A Contribution to the Critique of Actual Existing Democracy," in Calhoun, *Habermas and the Public Sphere*, pp. 109–42. While Johanna Meehan, ed., *Feminists Read Habermas: Gendering the Subject of Discourse* (London, 1995), is primarily directed at "the principal blindspots of Habermas' theory with respect to gender"—as Nancy Fraser puts it in her contribution to Meehan's volume, "What's Critical about Critical Theory?" pp. 21–47—several authors also take up the multiplicity issue.

12. Habermas, *The Structural Transformation of the Public Sphere*, pp. 1–26. Habermas is sensitive to linguistic change throughout the work. Compare Calhoun, "Introduction," pp. 7–9.

13. Calhoun, "Introduction," pp. 33–39, and Fraser, "Rethinking the Public Sphere." Calhoun's summary is based on the early phase of this critical and alternative scholarship.

14. See Georgina Born's chapter in this volume for more recent work on this issue.
15. For a recent survey of this aspect of the global field, see Julia Paley, "Toward an Anthropology of Democracy," *Annual Review of Anthropology* 31 (2002): 469–96.
16. See, for example, Nick Crossley and John Michael Roberts (ed.), *After Habermas: New Perspectives on the Public Sphere* (Oxford, 2004).
17. See Jürgen Habermas, *Between Facts and Norms: Contributions to a Discourse Theory of Law and Democracy*, trans. William Rehg (Cambridge, MA, 1996), pp. 287–387.
18. For an excellent introduction to Habermas's theory of the liberal public sphere, see Pauline Johnson, *Habermas: Rescuing the Public Sphere* (London, 2006), and, more generally, Alan McKee, *The Public Sphere: An Introduction* (Cambridge, 2004).
19. I follow Habermas in calling it a theory of the "liberal" public sphere. He distinguishes his "discourse theory" of the liberal public sphere—and of democracy and law more generally—from a specific kind of "liberal" theory of the liberal public sphere. He argues that he gives more weight to citizen participation in deliberative public spheres than the liberal tradition, yet he gives a more limited and legally constituted role to participation than the "republican" tradition, thus creating a hybrid, discourse theory that combines the best features of both traditions. See Habermas, "Three Normative Models of Democracy" and "On the Internal Relation between the Rule of Law and Democracy," both in Habermas's *The Inclusion of the Other: Studies in Political Theory*, ed. Ciaran Cronin and Pablo De Greiff (Cambridge, MA, 1998), pp. 239–52 and 253–64, respectively.
20. I use the terms "general liberal public sphere" to refer to the sphere comprising the multiplicity of public spheres and "specific liberal public sphere" to refer to the deliberative public sphere at the center of the general public sphere, around which all other kinds of public sphere are arranged. They are sometimes called "two levels" of the public sphere, but this does not accord as well with the network of "communication sluices" from the general to the specific that Habermas employs.
21. The international projection of the liberal public sphere is taken up in Jürgen Habermas, *The Divided West*, ed. and trans. Ciaran Cronin (Cambridge, 2006).
22. Habermas, *Between Facts and Norms*, p. 287.
23. Ibid.
24. Ibid., p. 384.
25. Ibid., p. 387.
26. Habermas, "The Kantian Project and the Divided West," in *The Divided West*, pp. 113–93, and the contributions in James Bohman and Matthias Lutz-Bachman, eds., *Perpetual Peace: Essays on Kant's Cosmopolitan Ideal* (Cambridge, MA, 1997).
27. Habermas, *Between Facts and Norms*, pp. 359–61.
28. Ibid., p. 374. This is a direct response to this feature of the multiplicity criticism.
29. Jürgen Habermas, *The Theory of Communicative Action*, trans. Thomas McCarthy (Boston, 1984–87), and *Moral Consciousness and Communicative Action*, trans. Christian Lenhardt and Shierry Weber Nicholson (Cambridge, 1990). The theory is applied to the public sphere in *Between Facts and Norms*, pp. 287–328.
30. Habermas, *Between Facts and Norms*, p. 359.
31. Ibid., p. 363–64.
32. Ibid., pp. 368–69 and 364.
33. Ibid., pp. 374, 367, and 363.
34. Ibid., p. 330.
35. Ibid., pp. 379–80.
36. Ibid., p. 364.

37. Ibid. These powers led to the decline of the bourgeois public sphere. The "structure of communication" that he sets forth has the possibility of holding out against capture by powerful strategic actors (pp. 364 and 369).
38. Ibid., pp. 354–56.
39. Ibid., p. 381.
40. Ibid., pp. 382 and 355.
41. Jürgen Habermas, "Religious Toleration—The Pacemaker for Cultural Rights," in Cultural Politics in a Global Age: Uncertainty, Solidarity and Innovation, ed. David Held and Henrietta L. Moore with Kevin Young (Oxford, 2008), pp. 68–76.
42. Habermas, Between Facts and Norms, p. 179.
43. Ibid., p. 371.
44. Ibid., p. 369. All public spheres are thus "porous" to one another because, although they differ, they share universal background structures of argumentation.
45. Ibid., p. 371.
46. Ibid., p. 372.
47. Ibid., p. 384. That is, the protesters must be able to describe their reasons for disobedience in terms of a recognized constitutional principle.
48. Ibid., p. 385.
49. Ibid.
50. Ibid., pp. 385–86.
51. Ibid., p. 386.
52. Ibid., p. 384.
53. Ibid., p. 386.
54. Ibid., pp. 386–87. For a general discussion of Habermas on pluralism, see Michel Rosenfeld, "Habermas's Call for Cosmopolitan Constitutional Patriotism in an Age of Global Terror: A Pluralist Appraisal," Constellations 1 (2000): 159–81.
55. Habermas, Between Facts and Norms, p. 384. This is also Kant's view of how a citizen must stand to the constitutional order and to Kant's theoretical reconstruction of it.
56. Ibid., p. 300.
57. Habermas, The Divided West, pp. 139–43.
58. Ibid., pp. 177.
59. Ibid., pp. 115–93.
60. Ibid., p. 141.
61. Ibid., pp. 143–93.
62. Habermas, Between Facts and Norms, p. 512. This path is laid out in The Divided West, pp. 147–93. It consists in spreading the liberal public sphere and its underlying institutions multilaterally and by means of extending international law, following Kant and Woodrow Wilson, rather than the unilateral and often unlawful approach of the United States under the last two Bush administrations.
63. Habermas, Between Facts and Norms, p. 372. "Incapacitation" is the English translation of the German Entmündigung, which means to take someone's authority over him- or herself away. It is the opposite of Mündigkeit, "maturity," as Kant uses the term. I am grateful to Rainer Forst for clarification of this and other points.
64. For the term "provincialize" to describe the critical step of debunking various imperious Western claims to universality based on parochial examples, see Dipesh Chakrabarty, Provincializing Europe: Postcolonial Thought and Historical Difference (Princeton, NJ, 2000). Wittgenstein discusses this temptation to universalize one's local examples and how to overcome it. See Wittgenstein, Philosophical Investigations, § 3.
65. For example, these are the sorts of questions feminists raise to the limits, especially the private/public distinction that protects the differentiation of institutional spheres

underneath the liberal public sphere. See the contributions in Meehan, *Feminists Read Habermas*.

66. Rainer Forst, "Towards a Critical Theory of Transnational Justice," in *Global Justice*, ed. Thomas W. Pogge (Oxford, 2001), pp. 169–87.

67. Michel Foucault, "Confronting Governments: Human Rights," in Michel Foucault, *Power: Essential Works III*, ed. James D. Faubion (New York, 2000), pp. 474–75.

68. Habermas defends this principle in "On the Internal Relationship between the Rule of Law and Democracy," in *The Political*, ed. David Ingram (Oxford, 2002), pp. 160–67, and *Between Facts and Norms*, pp. 82–193.

69. For recent analyses of the juridical containment and the equiprimordiality theses, see the contributions in Martin Loughlin and Neil Walker, eds., *The Paradox of Constitutionalism: Constituent Power and Constitutional Form* (Oxford, 2008), especially that of Rainer Nickel, "Private and Public Autonomy Revisited: Habermas' Concept of Co-originality in Times of Globalization and the Militant Security State" (pp. 147–69).

70. Commentators have pointed out that the same issue of equiprimordiality arises in discourse ethics. The rules for the exchange of public reasons are claimed to be the universal enabling conditions of free and equal deliberation and therefore beyond question by the deliberators who are subject to them. Rainer Forst suggests that Habermas does allow for this kind of democratic testing of some of the limits of the liberal public sphere that I interpret as regulative limits in the section on essential limits and institutional bases above. Insofar as this is the case, the liberal public sphere is correspondingly closer to the democratic public sphere.

71. For a familiar formulation of this distinction between democratic and liberal forms of critique, see Michel Foucault, "So Is it Important to Think?" in Foucault, *Power*, pp. 456–57.

72. By "subject to" I mean both official members of the form of government and anyone subject to its affects (that is, all affected).

73. For a careful analysis of this transformative practice to which I am indebted, see Aletta Norval, *Aversive Democracy: Inheritance and Originality in the Democratic Tradition* (Cambridge, 2007).

74. Arendt, "What Is Freedom?" pp. 151–56.

75. When, for example, Halima Bashir wrote her terrifying memoir of rape and violence in Darfur, *Tears of the Desert* (2008), she realized that the personal stories of the female victims would create a much more effective global public sphere than the recounting of statistics and the abstract and arcane manipulation of universal principles of justice. Richard Rorty has probably done the most to advance this defence of concrete democratic public spheres and the corresponding criticism of the liberal public sphere as abstract and idle.

76. The classic interpretations in this democratic tradition are Hannah Arendt, *The Human Condition*, 2nd edn., ed. Margaret Canovan (Chicago, 1998); Moses I. Finley, *Democracy: Ancient and Modern* (London, 1973); and Benjamin Barber, *Strong Democracy: Participatory Politics for a New Age*, 2nd ed. (Berkeley, CA, 2003).

77. See the contributions in Calhoun, *Habermas and the Public Sphere*, and Meehan, *Feminists Read Habermas*.

78. Michel Foucault, "What Is Critique?" in Foucault, *The Politics of Truth*, ed. Sylvère Lotringer, intro. John Rajchman, trans. Lysa Hochrith and Catherine Porter (Los Angeles, 2007), pp. 41–82. This article is drawn from his Lectures at the Collège de France 1977–78. See also Michel Foucault, *Security, Territory, Population*, ed. Michel Senellart, trans. Graham Burchell (New York, 2007).

79. Foucault, "The Subject and Power," in Foucault, *Power*, p. 345.
80. Fraser, "Rethinking the Public Sphere."
81. Raj Patel, *Stuffed or Starved: The Hidden Battle for the World Food System* (New York, 2008).
82. Manuel Castells, *The Rise of Network Society* (Oxford, 1996).
83. Robert Young, *Postcolonialism: An Historical Introduction* (Oxford, 2001), pp. 113–58. These public spheres would be illegal according to the limits of the liberal public sphere.
84. For an introduction to the field of digitized public spheres see the contributions in Arthur Kroker and Marilouise Kroker, eds., *Critical Digital Studies: A Reader* (Toronto, 2008). See also Georgina Born's contribution in the present volume and Drache, *Defiant Publics*, pp. 89–114.
85. See, for example, Mahmood Mamdani, *Citizen and Subject: Contemporary Africa and the Legacy of Late Colonialism* (Princeton, NJ, 1996).
86. The best introduction to this global research is Paley, "Toward an Anthropology of Democracy," and Drache, *Defiant Publics*. For an introduction to legal and governmental pluralism, see Boaventura de Sousa Santos, *Toward a New Legal Common Sense: Law, Globalization and Emancipation*, 2nd ed. (London, 2002), and Boaventura de Sousa Santos and Cesar A. Rodriguez-Garavito, eds., *Law and Globalization from Below: Towards a Cosmopolitan Legality* (Cambridge, 2005). For specific studies of alternative democracies and public spheres in addition to references in the above works, see Janine Brodie, "Introduction: Globalization and Citizenship Beyond the Nation State," and Janet Conway, "Citizenship in Time of Empire: The World Social Forum as a New Public Space," both in *Citizenship Studies* 8 (2004): 323–32 and 367–81, respectively; Bridgett Williams-Searle and Harvey Amani Whitfield, "Introduction: Citizenship Struggles in North America and the Caribbean," *Citizenship Studies* 10 (2006): 1–4; Patricia K. Wood, "Aboriginal/Indigenous Citizenship: An Introduction," *Citizenship Studies* 7 (2003): 371–78; and Niger Dower, *An Introduction to Global Citizenship* (Edinburgh, 2003).
87. Alison J. Ayers, "Imperial Liberties: Democratization and Governance in the 'New' Imperial Order," *Political Studies* 57, no. 3 (2009): 1–27; Tony Evans and Alison J. Ayers, "In the Service of Power: The Global Political Economy of Citizenship and Human Rights," *Citizenship Studies* 10 (2006): 289–308; Paul Cammack, "U.N. Imperialism: Unleashing Entrepreneurship in the Developing World," in *The New Imperialists: Ideologies of Empire*, ed. Colin Moers (Oxford, 2006), pp. 229–60; Eric Hershberg, "Democracy Promotion in Latin America," *Democracy and Society* 4, no. 2 (2007): 3–5; and Tanya Basok and Suzan Ilcan, "In the Name of Human Rights: Global Organizations and Participating Citizens," *Citizenship Studies* 10 (2006): 309–27.
88. The subsumption of the right of self-determination into the constitutional container of liberal capitalism during decolonization is standardly attributed to Woodrow Wilson and the tradition of Wilsonian liberal imperialism. See Chalmers Johnson, *Sorrows of Empire: Militarism, Secrecy, and the End of the Republic* (New York, 2003). For an important response to the imperial uses of this argument from a leading critical liberal theorist, see Jean Cohen, "Rethinking Human Rights, Democracy and Sovereignty in an Age of Globalization," *Political Theory* 36 (2008): 578–606.
89. M. K. Gandhi, *Hind Swaraj and Other Writings*, ed. Anthony J. Parel (Cambridge, 1997).
90. For an introduction to these Gandhian movements and their public sphere activities and influences, see Young, *Postcolonialism*, pp. 93–121, and Thomas Weber, *Hugging the Trees: The Story of the Chipko Movement* (Harmondsworth, 1988).

91. For an introduction to the global influence of Gandhi's public sphere activities, see David Hardiman, *Gandhi in His Time and Ours: Resisting the Politics of Hate* (London, 2003), and Thomas Weber, *Gandhi as Disciple and Mentor* (Cambridge, 2004).

92. By far the most influential articulation of popular sovereignty and delegated government is John Locke, *Two Treatises of Government*, ed. Peter Laslett (Cambridge, 1994). For this interpretation of it, see James Tully, "An Introduction to Locke's Political Philosophy," in *An Approach to Political Philosophy: Locke in Contexts* (Cambridge, 1994), pp. 9–70. This doctrine is excluded from the liberal public sphere. It is the doctrine that brought liberalism to power in the democratic revolutions of the eighteenth and nineteenth centuries in Europe, North America, and Latin America. But once liberals gained power, and since Kant in theory, they outlawed the democratic theory and practice of popular sovereignty and subsumed popular sovereignty under liberal institutions and constitutions. See Immanuel Kant, "On the Proverb: That it may be True in Theory, But is of No Practical Use," in *Perpetual Peace and Other Essays on Politics, History, and Morals*, trans. and intro. Ted Humphrey (Indianapolis, IN, 1983), pp. 78–84.

93. Mary Wollstonecraft, *The Vindication of the Rights of Woman*, ed. Sylvana Tomaselli (Cambridge, 1995).

94. This modern Lockean account of the dynamics of popular sovereignty and democratic government in the public sphere has its roots in the Athenian practice of partners speaking freely and critically *(parrhesia)* in relationships of governance. This was called a *parrhesiastic* pact. The classic statement of it, on which I have drawn, is the dialogue between Jocasta and Polyneices in Euripides, *The Phoenician Women*, in *Orestes and Other Plays*, trans. Phillip Vellacott (Harmondsworth, 1983), lines 386–94. For a contextual survey of this complex practice in the classical period, see Michel Foucault, *Fearless Speech*, ed. Joseph Pearson (Los Angeles, 2001). For the development of free and critical speaking *(parrhesia)* in public spheres in early modern England, see David Colclough, *Freedom of Speech in Early Stuart England* (Cambridge, 2005).

95. Iris Marion Young, *Intersecting Voices: Dilemmas of Gender, Political Philosophy, and Policy* (Princeton, NJ, 1997). In this section I also draw on Norval, *Aversive Democracy*; Linda M. Zerilli, *Feminism and the Abyss of Freedom* (Chicago, 2008); and Rosemary Coombe, "Introduction: Identifying and Engendering the Forms of Emergent Civil Societies: New Directions in Political Anthropology," *Political and Legal Anthropology Review*, 20 (1997): 1–12. For a comparison of Arendt and Habermas on the public sphere, see Steven G. Crowell's chapter in the present volume.

96. See also David Owen, "The Expressive Agon: On Political Agency in a Constitutional Democratic Polity," in *Law and Agonistic Politics*, ed. Andrew Schaap (Aldershot, 2009), pp. 71–86.

97. See John Stuart Mill, *On Liberty*, ed. Edward Alexander (Toronto, 1999), pp. 90–121 for a strong endorsement of nonreductive public reasoning and the eclectic negotiating of differences over time from within the critical liberal tradition.

98. See Charles Spinosa, Fernando Flores, and Hubert L. Dreyfus, *Disclosing New Worlds: Entrepreneurship, Democratic Action, and the Cultivation of Solidarity* (Cambridge, MA, 1997), pp. 85–88, for a forceful presentation of these criticisms.

99. In many respects, this turn is a *return* to the more engaged and open-ended form of public reasoning typical of classical humanism from Aristotle to Montaigne. See Skinner, *Reason and Rhetoric in the Philosophy of Hobbes*, and Stephen Toulmin, *Return to Reason* (Cambridge, MA, 2001).

100. For the historical and philosophical argument that this internal relationship between ethical practices of the self and public practices of caring for public goods has been generally overlooked in the modern West, with a few notable exceptions, see Michel Foucault, *The Hermeneutics of the Subject: Lectures at the Collège de France, 1981–1982*, trans. Graham Burchell (New York, 2005), esp. pp. 251–52.
101. David Cortright, *Peace: A History of Movements and Ideas* (Cambridge, 2008).
102. Paul Hawken, *Blessed Unrest: How the Largest Movement in the World Came into Being, and Why No One Saw It Coming* (New York, 2007), for this opinion. It is shared by Drache, *Defiant Publics*.
103. M. K. Gandhi, *All Men are Brothers*, ed. Krishna Kripalani (New York, 1982), p. 134. In her study of contemporary India, Martha Nussbaum concludes that the decoupling of these two senses of self-government (ethical and democratic) is the fundamental problem today, not only in India but in other contemporary representative democracies. See Martha Nussbaum, *The Clash Within: Democracy, Religious Violence, and India's Future* (Cambridge, MA, 2007), and the review by Pankaj Mishra, "The Impasse in India," *New York Review of Books* 54, no. 11 (28 June 2007).
104. One of the public intellectuals who did the most to publicize the first step in the early twentieth-century literary public sphere was Leo Tolstoy, *The Kingdom of God Is Within You: Christianity not as a Mystic Religion but as a New Theory of Life*, trans. Constance Garnett (New York, 2005).
105. These two steps are drawn from Cortright's *Peace*, pp. 211–32. For Petra Kelly's relation to Gandhi and King, see Hardiman, *Gandhi in His Time and Ours*, pp. 238–93. All three were murdered.

BIBLIOGRAPHY

Abelson, Harold, and Gerald J. Sussman. *The Structure and Interpretation of Computer Programs*. Cambridge, MA, 1985.

Adams, John, and Katie Schmuecker, eds. *Devolution in Practice 2006*. London, 2005.

Adams, John, and Peter Robinson, eds. *Devolution in Practice: Public Policy Differences within the UK*. London, 2002.

Alderman, Ellen, and Caroline Kennedy. *The Right to Privacy*. New York, 1995.

Apel, Karl-Otto. *Transformation der Philosophie, I: Sprachanalytik, Semiotik, Hermeneutik*. Frankfurt am Main, 1976.

Arendt, Hannah. *Between Past and Future: Eight Exercises in Political Thought*. New York, 1968.

———. *The Human Condition*. 2nd ed. Edited by Margaret Canovan. Chicago, 1998.

Ayers, Alison J. "Imperial Liberties: Democratization and Governance in the 'New' Imperial Order." *Political Studies* 57, no. 3 (2009): 1–27.

Ayres, Jack, ed. *Paupers and Pig Killers: The Diary of William Holland, a Somerset Parson, 1799–1818*. Gloucester, 1984.

Bachelard, Gaston. *Le Rationalisme appliqué*. 3rd ed. Paris, 1998.

Baker, David, and David Seawright, eds. *Britain For and Against Europe: British Politics and the Question of European Integration*. Oxford, 1998.

Baldwin, Peter. *Contagion and the State in Europe 1830–1930*. Cambridge, 1999.

Barber, Benjamin. *Strong Democracy: Participatory Politics for a New Age*. 2nd ed. Berkeley, CA, 2003.

Basok, Tanya, and Suzan Ilcan. "In the Name of Human Rights: Global Organizations and Participating Citizens." *Citizenship Studies* 10 (2006): 309–27.

Baumann, Gerd. *Contesting Culture: Discourses of Identity in Multiethnic London*. Cambridge, 1996.

Bazerman, Charles. "Forums of Validation and Forms of Knowledge: The Magical Rhetoric of Otto von Guericke's Sulfur Globe." *Configurations* 1 (1993): 201–27.

Beaulieu, Anne. "Images Are Not the (Only) Truth: Brain Mapping, Visual Knowledge, and Iconoclasm." *Science, Technology, and Human Values* 27 (2002): 53–86.

Beck, Ann. "Issues in the Anti-vaccination Movement in England." *Medical History* 4 (1960): 310–21.

Beck, Ulrich, and Elisabeth Beck-Gernsheim. *Individualization: Institutionalized Individualism and Its Social and Political Consequences*. London, 2001.

Benhabib, Seyla. *The Claims of Culture: Equality and Diversity in the Global Era*. Princeton, NJ, 2002.

Benhabib, Seyla, ed. *Democracy and Difference: Contesting the Boundaries of the Political*. Princeton, NJ, 1996.

Bennett, W. Lance, and Robert M. Eltman, eds. *Mediated Politics: Communication in the Future of Democracy*. Cambridge, 2001.

Berlin, Isaiah. *Four Essays on Liberty*. New York, 1969.

Bogdanor, Vernon. *Devolution in the United Kingdom*. Oxford, 2001.

Bohman, James. "Political Communication and the Epistemic Value of Diversity: Deliberation and Legitimation in Media Societies." *Communication Theory* 17 (2007): 348–55.

Bohman, James, and Matthias Lutz-Bachman, eds. *Perpetual Peace: Essays on Kant's Cosmopolitan Ideal*. Cambridge, MA, 1997.

Born, Georgina. "Strategy, Positioning and Projection in Digital Television: Channel Four and the Commercialisation of Public Service Broadcasting in the UK." *Media, Culture and Society* 25 (2003): 773–99.

———. *Uncertain Vision: Birt, Dyke and the Reinvention of the BBC*. London, 2005.

Born, Georgina, and Tony Prosser. "Culture and Consumerism: Citizenship, Public Service Broadcasting and the BBC's Fair Trading Obligations." *Modern Law Review* 64 (2001): 670–75.

Boyle, James. "Mertonianism Unbound? Imagining Free, Decentralized Access to Most Cultural and Scientific Material." In *Understanding Knowledge as a Common: From Theory to Practice*, edited by Charlotte Hess and Elinor Ostrom, pp. 123–44. Cambridge, MA, 2006.

———. "The Second Enclosure Movement and the Construction of the Public Domain." *Law and Contemporary Problems* 66 (2003): 33–74.

Breidbach, Olaf. *Bilder des Wissens: Zur Kulturgeschichte der wissenschaftlichen Wahrnehmung*. Munich, 2005.

Broman, Thomas H. "The Habermasian Public Sphere and Eighteenth-Century Historiography: A New Look at 'Science in the Enlightenment.'" *History of Science* 36 (1998): 123–49.

Bromwich, David, and George Kateb, eds. *On Liberty*. New Haven, CT, 2003.

Brooke, John. "Reason and Passion in the Public Sphere: Habermas and the Cultural Historians." *Journal of Interdisciplinary History* 29 (1998–99): 43–67.

Buchstein, Hubertus. "Bytes that Bite: The Internet and Deliberative Democracy." *Constellations* 4 (1997): 248–63.

Cairncross, Alec. *The British Economy since 1945*. 2nd ed. Oxford, 1995.

Calhoun, Craig. "Civil Society and the Public Sphere." *Public Culture* 5 (1993): 267–80.

———, ed. *Habermas and the Public Sphere*. Cambridge, MA, 1992.

Cartwright, Lisa. *Screening the Body: Tracing Medicine's Visual Culture*. Minneapolis, 1995.

Castelao-Lawless, Teresa. "Phenomenotechnique in Historical Perspective: Its Origins and Implications for Philosophy of Science." *Philosophy of Science* 62 (1995): 44–59.

Castells, Manuel. *The Rise of Network Society*. Oxford, 1996.

Chakrabarty, Dipesh. *Provincializing Europe: Postcolonial Thought and Historical Difference*. Princeton, NJ, 2000.

Cohen, Jean, and Andrew Arato. "Politics and the Reconstruction of the Concept of Civil Society." In *Cultural-Political Interventions in the Unfinished Project of Enlightenment*, edited by Axel Honneth, Thomas McCarthy, Claus Offe, and Albrecht Wellmer, pp. 121–43. Cambridge, MA, 1992.

Colclough, David. *Freedom of Speech in Early Stuart England*. Cambridge, 2005.

Coleman, Stephen. "New Mediation and Direct Representation: Reconceptualizing Representation in the Digital Age." *New Media and Society* 7, no. 2 (2005): 177–98.

Coleman, Stephen, and H. Marsh. *From Public Service Broadcasting to Knowledge-sharing Commons: An Evaluation of the First Year of the iCan Project*. Oxford, 2004.

Connolly, William. *The Terms of Political Discourse*. Lexington, MA, 1974.

Conway, Janet. "Citizenship in Times of Empire: The World Social Forum as a New Public Space." *Citizenship Studies* 8 (2004): 367–81.

Coombe, Rosemary. "Introduction: Identifying and Engendering the Forms of Emergent Civil Societies: New Directions in Political Anthropology." *Political and Legal Anthropology Review* 20 (1997): 1–12.

Cooter, Roger, and Stephen Punfrey. "Separate Spheres and Public Spaces: Reflections on the History of Science Popularization and Science in Popular Culture." *History of Science* 32 (1994): 237–67.

Cortright, David. *Peace: A History of Movements and Ideas*. Cambridge, 2008.

Crary, Jonathan. *Techniques of the Observer: On Vision and Modernity in the Nineteenth Century*. Cambridge, MA, 1990.

Crossley, Nick, and John Michael Roberts, eds. *After Habermas: New Perspectives on the Public Sphere*. Oxford, 2004.

Crouch, Colin. *Post-Democracy*. Cambridge, 2004.

Crowell, Steven. "Conscience and Reason: Heidegger and the Grounds of Intentionality." In *Transcendental Heidegger*, edited by Steven Crowell and Jeff Malpas, pp. 43–62. Stanford, CA, 2007.

———. "Who Is the Political Actor? An Existential-Phenomenological Approach." In *The Phenomenology of the Political*, edited by Kevin Thompson and Lester Embree, pp. 11–28. Dordrecht, The Netherlands, 2000.

Dahlberg, Lincoln. "Cyberspace and the Public Sphere: Exploring the Democratic Potential of the Net." *Convergence* 4 (1998): 70–84.

Dahlgren, Peter. "The Public Sphere and the Net: Structure, Space and Communication." In *Mediated Politics: Communication in the Future of Democracy*, edited by W. Lance Bennett and Robert M. Entman, pp. 33–55. Cambridge, 2001.

Daston, Lorraine, and Peter Galison. *Objectivity*. New York, 2007.

Daum, Andreas W. *Wissenschaftspopularisierung im 19. Jahrhundert: Bürgerliche Kultur, naturwissenschaftliche Bildung und die deutsche Öffentlichkeit, 1848–1914*. Munich, 1998.

Davidson, Roger, and Lesley Hall, eds. *Sex, Sin and Suffering: Venereal Disease and European Society since 1870*. London, 2001.

Davies, Gavyn, and Andrew Graham, *Broadcasting, Society and Policy in the Multimedia Age*. Luton, 1997.

Davies, William. *Modernising with Purpose: A Manifesto for Digital Britain*. London, 2005.

Dean, Jodi. "Cybersalons and Civil Society: Rethinking the Public Sphere in Transnational Technoculture." *Public Culture* 13 (2001): 243–65.

———. "Why the Net is Not a Public Sphere." *Constellations* 10 (2003): 95–112.

Dear, Peter, ed. *The Literary Structure of Scientific Argument: Historical Studies*. Philadelphia, 1991.

Debord, Guy. *The Society of the Spectacle*. Translated by Donald Nicholson-Smith. New York, 1995.

Dörner, Andreas. *Politainment: Politik in der medialen Erlebnisgesellschaft*. Frankfurt am Main, 2001.

Dower, Nigel. *An Introduction to Global Citizenship*. Edinburgh, 2003.

Drache, Daniel, with Marc D. Froese. *Defiant Publics: The Unprecedented Reach of the Global Citizen*. Cambridge, 2008.

Dreyfus, Hubert. *Being-in-the-World: A Commentary on Heidegger's "Being and Time," Division I*. Cambridge, MA, 1991.

Dumit, Joseph. *Picturing Personhood: Brain Scans and Biomedical Identity*. Princeton, NJ, 2004.

Durbach, Nadja. *Bodily Matters: The Anti-vaccination Movement in England 1853–1907*. Durham, NC, 2005.

Dworkin, Ronald. *Life's Dominion: An Argument About Abortion, Euthanasia, and Individual Freedom*. New York, 1994.

———. "Unenumerated Rights: Whether and How *Roe* Should be Overruled." *University of Chicago Law Review* 59, no. 1 (Winter 1992): 381–432.

Ely, Geoff. "Politics, Culture, and the Public Sphere." *Positions* 10 (2002): 219–36.

Emden, Christian J. "Scanned Brains, Dyed Bacteria, and Magnified Flies: On Scientific Images and Things." In *ImageScapes: Studies in Intermediality*, edited by Christian J. Emden and Gabriele Rippl, pp. 148-52. Oxford, 2010.

———. "Epistemische Konstellationen, 1800–1900: Nerven, Telegrafen und die Netzwerke des Wissens." In *Netzwerke: Eine Kulturtechnik der Moderne*, edited by Jürgen Barkhoff, Hartmut Böhme, and Jeanne Riou, pp. 127–54. Cologne, 2004.

Emirbayer, Mustafa, and Jeff Goodwin. "Network Analysis, Culture, and the Problem of Agency." *American Journal of Sociology* 99 (1994): 1411–54.

Emirbayer, Mustafa, and Mimi Sheller. "Publics in History." *Theory and Society* 27 (1998): 727–79.

Erikson, Robert, and Kent Tedin. *American Public Opinion: Its Origins, Content, and Impact*. 7th ed. New York, 2006.

Evans, Tony, and Alison J. Ayers. "In the Service of Power: The Global Political Economy of Citizenship and Human Rights." *Citizenship Studies* 10 (2006): 289–308.

Findlen, Paula. "Masculine Prerogatives: Gender, Space, and Knowledge in the Early Modern Museum." In *The Architecture of Science*, edited by Peter Galison and Emily Thompson, pp. 29–57. Cambridge, MA, 1999.

Finer, Samuel E. *The Life and Times of Sir Edwin Chadwick*. London, 1952.

Finley, Moses I. *Democracy: Ancient and Modern*. London, 1973.

Fischer, Michael M. J. "Worlding Cyberspace." In *Critical Anthropology Now*, edited by George Marcus, pp. 245–304. Santa Fe, NM, 1999.

Fleck, Ludwik. *Genesis and Devlopment of a Scientific Fact*. Translated by Thaddeus J. Trenn and Robert K. Merton. Chicago, 1975.

Flinn, Michael W., ed. *Report on the Sanitary Condition of the Labouring Population of Great Britain by Edwin Chadwick*. Edinburgh, 1965.

Forman, Nigel. *Constitutional Change in the UK*. London, 2002.

Forst, Rainer. "Towards a Critical Theory of Transnational Justice." In *Global Justice*, edited by Thomas W. Pogge, pp. 169–87. Oxford, 2001.

Foucault, Michel. *Fearless Speech*. Edited by Joseph Pearson. Los Angeles, 2001.

———. *The Hermeneutics of the Subject: Lectures at the Collège de France, 1981–1982*. Translated by Graham Burchell. New York, 2005.

———. *The Politics of Truth*. Edited by Sylvère Lotringer. Translated by Lysa Hochrith and Catherine Porter. Introduction by John Rajchman. Los Angeles, 2007.

———. *Power: Essential Works III*. Edited by James D. Faubion. New York, 2000.

———. *Security, Territory, Population*. Edited by Michel Senellart. Translated by Graham Burchell. New York, 2007.

———. "What Is Enlightenment?" In *The Foucault Reader*, edited by Paul Rabinow, pp. 32–50. New York, 1984.

Frängsmyr, Tore, John L. Heilbron, and Robin E. Rider, eds. *The Quantifying Spirit in the Eighteenth Century*. Berkeley, CA, 1990.

Fraser, Derek. *Power and Authority in the Victorian City*. Oxford, 1979.

Friedman, Sharon M., Sharon Dunwoody, and Carol L. Rogers, eds. *Scientists and Journalits: Reporting Science as News*. New York, 1986.

Fry, Geoffrey K. "Whitehall in the 1950s and 1960s." *Public Policy and Administration* 13, no. 2 (1998): 2–25.

Galison, Peter. *Einstein's Clocks, Poincaré's Maps: Empires of Time*. New York, 2004.

———. *Image and Logic: A Material Culture of Microphysics*. Chicago, 1997.

———. "Removing Knowledge." *Critical Inquiry* 31 (2004): 229–43.

Gallie, Walter B. "Essentially Contested Concepts." *Proceedings of the Aristotelian Society* 56 (1956): 167–98.

Gandhi, Mohandas K. *All Men are Brothers*. Edited by Krishna Kripalani. New York, 1982.

———. *Hind Swaraj and Other Writings*. Edited by Anthony J. Parel. Cambridge, 1997.

Gatens, Moira, and Genevieve Lloyd. *Collective Imaginings: Spinoza, Past and Present*. London, 1999.

Gaukroger, Stephen W. "Bachelard and the Problem of Epistemological Analysis." *Studies in the History and Philosophy of Science* 7 (1976): 189–244.

Geertz, Clifford. *The Interpretation of Cultures*. New York, 1973.

George, Stephen, ed. *Britain and the European Community: The Politics of Semi-detachment*. Oxford, 1992.

Gestrich, Andreas. "The Public Sphere and the Habermas Debate." *German History* 24 (2006): 413–30.

Geuss, Raymond. *Philosophy and Real Politics*. Princeton, NJ, 2008.

———. *Public Goods, Private Goods*. Princeton, NJ, 2001.

Gieryn, Thomas F. "Boundaries of Science." In *Handbook of Science and Technology Studies*, edited by Sheila Jasanoff, Gerald E. Markle, James C. Peterson, and Trevor J. Pinch, pp. 393–443. Thousand Oaks, CA, 1994.

———. "Boundary-Work and the Demarcation of Science from Non-Science: Strains and Interests in Professional Ideologies of Scientists." *American Sociological Review* 48 (1983): 781–95.

———. *Cultural Boundaries of Science: Credibility on the Line*. Chicago, 1999.

Goldenbaum, Ursula, ed. *Appell an das Publikum: Die öffentliche Debatte in der deutschen Aufklärung, 1687-1796*. Berlin, 2004.

Golinski, Jan. *British Weather and the Climate of Enlightenment*. Chicago, 2007.

———. *Making Natural Knowledge: Constructivism and the History of Science*. Cambridge, 1998.

———. *Science as Public Culture: Chemistry and Enlightenment in Britain, 1760–1829*. Cambridge, 1992.

———. "The Theory of Practice and the Practice of Theory: Sociological Approaches in the History of Science." *Isis* 81 (1990): 492–505.

Green, Sarah, Penny Harvey, and Hannah Knox. "Scales of Place and Networks: An Ethnography of the Imperative to Connect through Information and Communication Technologies." *Current Anthropology* 46 (2005): 805–26.

Grell, Ole Peter, and Andrew Cunningham, eds. *Health Care and Poor Relief in 18th- and 19th-Century Northern Europe*. Aldershot, 2002.

Gronin, Sara Stidstone. "Imagining Inoculation: Smallpox, the Body and Social Relations of Healing in the Eighteenth Century." *Bulletin of the History of Medicine* 80 (2006): 247–68.

Gross, Alan G. *The Rhetoric of Science*. Cambridge, MA, 1990.

Großklaus, Götz. *Medien-Zeit, Medien-Raum: Zum Wandel der Wahrnehmung in der Moderne*. Frankfurt am Main, 1987.

Grundy, Isobel. *Lady Mary Wortley Montagu*. Oxford, 1999.

Habermas, Jürgen. *Between Facts and Norms: Contributions to a Discourse Theory of Law and Democracy*. Translated by William Rehg. Cambridge, MA, 1996.

———. *The Divided West*. Edited and translated by Ciaran Cronin. Cambridge, 2006.

———. *The Inclusion of the Other: Studies in Political Theory*. Edited by Ciaran Cronin and Pablo De Greiff. Cambridge, MA, 1998.

———. *Moral Consciousness and Communicative Action*. Translated by Christian Lenhardt and Shierry Weber Nicholsen. Cambridge, MA, 1990.

———. "On the Internal Relationship between the Rule of Law and Democracy." In *The Political*, edited by David Ingram, pp. 160–67. Oxford, 2002.

———. "The Public Sphere." In *Contemporary Political Philosophy: An Anthology*, edited by Robert E. Goodin and Philip Pettit, pp. 103–7. Oxford, 1997.

———. "Religious Toleration—The Pacemaker for Cultural Rights." In *Cultural Politics in a Global Age: Uncertainty, Solidarity and Innovation*, edited by David Held and Henrietta L. Moore with Kevin Young, pp. 68–76. Oxford, 2008.

———. "Remarks on Legitimation Through Human Rights." In *The Postnational Constellation*, translated by Max Pensky, pp. 113–29. Cambridge, MA, 2001.

———. *The Structural Transformation of the Public Sphere*. Translated by Thomas Burger and Frederick Lawrence. Cambridge, MA, 1989.

———. *The Theory of Communicative Action*. Translated by Thomas McCarthy. Boston, 1984–87.

Hacking, Ian. *Representing and Intervening*. Cambridge, 1983.

———. *The Social Construction of What?* Cambridge, MA, 1999.

Haedrick, Daniel R. *The Tentacles of Progress: Technology Transfer in the Age of Imperialism, 1850–1940*. Oxford, 1988.

Hamlin, Christopher. *Public Health and Social Justice in the Age of Chadwick*. Cambridge, 1998.

Hamlin, Christopher, and Sally Sheard. "Revolutions in Public Health: 1848, and 1998?" *British Medical Journal* 317 (1998): 592–96.

Hankins, Thomas L. *Science and the Enlightenment*. Cambridge, 1985.

Hanley, James G. "The Public's Reaction to Public Health: Petitions Submitted to Parliament, 1847–1848." *Social History of Medicine* 15 (2002): 393–411.

Hannaway, Owen. "Laboratory Design and the Aim of Science: Andreas Libavius versus Tycho Brahe." *Isis* 77 (1986): 585–610.

Hardiman, David. *Gandhi in His Time and Ours: Resisting the Politics of Hate*. London, 2003.

Hardy, Anne. *The Epidemic Streets: Infectious Disease and the Rise of Preventive Medicine*. Oxford, 1993.

———. "Pioneers in the Victorian Provinces: Veterinarians and Public Health and the Urban Animal Economy." *Urban History* 29 (2002): 372–87.

Hartley, John. "Television, Nation, and Indigenous Media." *Television and New Media* 5, no. 1 (2004): 7–25.

Hawken, Paul. *Blessed Unrest: How the Largest Movement in the World Came into Being, and Why No One Saw It Coming*. New York, 2007.

Hawkins, Gay. "SBS: Minority Television." *Culture and Policy* 7 (1996): 45–63.

Hegel, Georg Wilhelm Friedrich. *Elements of the Philosophy of Right*, edited by Allen W. Wood, translated by H. B. Nisbet. Cambridge, 1991.

Heins, Volker. *Nongovernmental Organizations in International Society: Struggles Over Recognition*. New York, 2008.

Hershberg, Eric. "Democracy Promotion in Latin America." *Democracy and Society* 4, no. 2 (2007): 3–5.

Higdon, Stuart, ed. *Culture and Communication: Perspectives on Broadcasting and the Information Society*. London, 2001.

Hohendahl, Peter Uwe. "Critical Theory, Public Sphere and Culture: Jürgen Habermas and His Critics." *New German Critique* 16 (1979): 89–118.

Holtzmann Kevles, Bettyann. *Naked to the Bone: Medical Imaging in the Twentieth Century*. New Brunswick, NJ, 1997.

Honderich, Ted. *Political Violence*. Ithaca, NY, 1976.

Hoy, David. *The Critical Circle*. Berkeley, CA, 1982.

Hoy, David Couzans, and Thomas McCarthy. *Critical Theory*. Cambridge, MA, 1994.

Isin, Engin, and Patricia Wood. *Citizenship and Identity*. London, 1999.

Jacob, Margaret C. "The Mental Landscape of the Public Sphere: A European Perspective." *Eighteenth-Century Studies* 28 (1994): 95–113.

Jardine, Lisa. *Ingenious Pursuits: Building the Scientific Revolution*. London, 1999.

Johnson, Chalmers. *Sorrows of Empire: Militarism, Secrecy, and the End of the Republic*. New York, 2003.

Johnson, Pauline. *Habermas: Rescuing the Public Sphere*. London, 2006.

Jordanova, Ludmilla. *Images of Gender in Science and Medicine between the Eighteenth and Twentieth Centuries*. New York, 1989.

Kant, Immanuel. *Political Writings*. 2nd ed. Edited by Hans Reiss, translated by H. B. Nisbet, 2nd ed. Cambridge, 1991.

———. *Perpetual Peace and Other Essays on Politics, History, and Morals*. Translated by and introduction by Ted Humphrey. Indianapolis, 1983.

Keane, John. "Structural Transformations of the Public Sphere." *The Communication Review* 1 (1995): 1–22.

Kellner, Douglas. "Globalization from Below? Toward a Radical Democratic Technopolitics." *Angelaki* 4 (1999): 101–13.

Kelty, Christopher. *Two Bits: The Cultural Significance of Free Software*. Durham, NC, 2008.

Kern, Stephen. *The Culture of Time and Space, 1880–1918*. 2nd ed. Cambridge, MA, 2003.

Knorr-Cetina, Karin. *Epistemic Cultures: How the Sciences Make Knowledge*. Cambridge, MA, 1999.

Korsgaard, Christine. *The Sources of Normativity*. Cambridge, 1996.

Kosnick, Kira. *Migrant Media: Turkish Broadcasting and Multicultural Politics in Berlin*. Bloomington, IN, 2007.

Kroker, Arthur, and Marilouise Kroker, eds. *Critical Digital Studies: A Reader*. Toronto, 2008.

Ku, Agnes S. "Boundary Politics in the Public Sphere: Openness, Secrecy, and Leak." *Sociological Theory* 16 (1998): 172–92.

Kuhn, Thomas S. *The Structure of Scientific Revolutions*. 3rd ed. Chicago, 1996.

La Berge, Ann F. "Debate as Scientific Practice in Nineteenth-Century France: The Controversy over the Microscope." *Perspectives on Science* 12 (2004): 424–53.

Lacy, Mark J., and Peter Wilkin, eds. *Global Publics in the Information Age*. Manchester, 2005.

Landes, David S. *Revolution in Time: Clocks and the Making of the Modern World*. Cambridge, MA, 1983.

Latour, Bruno. *Reassembling the Social: An Introduction to Actor-Network-Theory*. Oxford, 2005.

———. *Science in Action: How to Follow Scientists and Engineers through Society*. Cambridge, MA, 1987.

Latour, Bruno, and Peter Weibel, eds. *Iconoclash: Beyond the Image Wars in Science, Religion, and Art*. Cambridge, MA, 2002.

Latour, Bruno, and Steve Woolgar. *Laboratory Life: The Construction of Scientific Facts*. 2nd ed. Princeton, NJ, 1986.

LaVopa, Anthony. "Conceiving a Public: Ideas and Society in Eighteenth-Century Europe." *Journal of Modern History* 64 (1992): 79–116.

Lenoir, Timothy. "Models and Instruments in the Development of Electrophysiology, 1845–1912." *Historical Studies in the Physical and Biological Sciences* 17 (1986): 1–54.

———. *Politik im Tempel der Wissenschaft: Forschung und Machtausübung im deutschen Kaiserreich*. Translated by Horst Brühmann. Frankfurt am Main, 1992.

Lessig, Lawrence. *The Future of Ideas: The Fate of the Commons in a Connected World*. Harmondsworth, 2002.

Levy, Steven. *Hackers: Heroes of the Computer Revolution*. New York, 1984.

Lewis, Jane. *The Politics of Motherhood: Child and Maternal Welfare in England 1900–1939*. London, 1980.

Lewis, Richard A. *Edwin Chadwick and the Public Health Movement, 1832–48*. London, 1952.

Lippmann, Walter. *The Phantom Public*. New Brunswick, NJ, 1993.

Locke, John. *Two Treatises of Government*. Edited by Peter Laslett. Cambridge, 1994.

Loughlin, Martin, and Neil Walker, eds. *The Paradox of Constitutionalism: Constituent Power and Constitutional Form*. Oxford, 2008.

Lowe, Gregory Ferrell, and Per Jauert, eds. *Cultural Dilemmas in Public Service Broadcasting*. Goteborg, 2005.

Luhmann, Niklas. "Öffentliche Meinung." *Politische Vierteljahresschrift* 11 (1970): 2–28.

Lux, David S., and Harold J. Cook. "Closed Circles or Open Networks? Communicating at a Distance during the Scientific Revolution." *History of Science* 36 (1998): 179–211.

Lynch, Michael. *Art and Artefact in a Laboratory Science*. London, 1985.

Lyotard, Jean-François. *The Differend: Phrases in Dispute*. Translated by Georges van den Abbeele. Minneapolis, 1989.

Lyotard, Jean-François, and Jean-Loup Thébaud. *Just Gaming*. Translated by Wlad Godzich. Minneapolis, 1985.

Macfarlane, Alan. *The Origins of English Individualism: The Family, Property and Social Transition*. Oxford, 1978.

Mah, Harold. "Phantasies of the Public Sphere: Rethinking the Habermas of Historians." *Journal of Modern History* 72 (2000): 153-82.

Mamdani, Mahmood. *Citizen and Subject: Contemporary Africa and the Legacy of Late Colonialism*. Princeton, NJ, 1996.

Mandelson, Peter, and Roger Liddle. *The Blair Revolution: Can New Labour Deliver?* London, 1996.

Manheim, Ernst. *Die Träger der öffentlichen Meinung: Studien zur Soziologie der Öffentlichkeit*. Leipzig, 1933.

Mannheim, Karl. *Ideology and Utopia: An Introduction to the Sociology of Knowledge*. Translated by Louis Wirth and Edward Shils. New York, 1985.

May, Maisie. "Inoculating the Urban Poor in the Eighteenth Century." *British Journal for the History of Science* 30 (1997): 291–305.

McCabe, Colin. "Realism and the Cinema: Notes on Some Brechtian Theses." In *Popular Television and Film*, edited by T. Bennett, S. Boyd-Bowman, C. Mercer, and J. Woollacott, pp. 216–35. London, 1985.

McCarthy, Thomas. "Complexity and Democracy, or the Seducements of Systems Theory." *New German Critique* 35 (1985): 27–55.

McDonald, Andrew, ed. *Reinventing Britain: Constitutional Change under New Labour.* Berkeley, CA, 2007.

McKee, Alan. *The Public Sphere: An Introduction.* Cambridge, 2004.

McKeon, Michael. "Parsing Habermas' 'Bourgeois Public Sphere.'" *Criticism* 46 (2004): 273–77.

McLeod, Roy M. "Law, Medicine and Public Opinion: The Resistance to Compulsory Health Legislation, 1870–1907." *Public Law* (Summer/Autumn 1967): 107–28 and 180–211.

Meehan, Johanna, ed. *Feminists Read Habermas: Gendering the Subject of Discourse.* London, 1995.

Melton, James Van Horn. *The Rise of the Public Sphere in Enlightenment Europe.* Cambridge 2001.

Mill, John Stuart. *The Philosophy of John Stuart Mill: Ethical, Political, Religious.* Edited by Marshall Cohen. New York, 1961.

Miller, Genevieve, ed. *Letters of Edward Jenner.* Baltimore, 1983.

Mitchell, Trent A. "The Politics of Experiment in the Eighteenth Century: The Pursuit of Audience and the Manipulation of Consensus in the Debate over Lightning Rods." *Eighteenth-Century Studies* 31 (1998): 307–31.

Moers, Colin, ed. *The New Imperialists: Ideologies of Empire.* Oxford, 2006.

Morris, R. J. *Cholera, 1832: The Social Response to an Epidemic.* London, 1976.

Mouffe, Chantal. *On the Political.* London, 2005.

Müller, Jan-Werner, ed. *German Ideologies since 1945: Studies in the Political Thought and Culture of the Bonn Republic.* New York 2003.

Negt, Oscar, and Alexander Kluge. *Public Sphere and Experience: Toward an Analysis of the Bourgeois and Proletarian Public Sphere.* Minneapolis, 1993.

Nietzsche, Friedrich. *On the Genealogy of Morals.* Edited by Keith Ansell-Pearson. Translated by Carol Diethe. Cambridge, 1996.

Norris, Pippa. *Digital Divide.* New York, 2001.

Norval, Aletta. *Aversive Democracy: Inheritance and Originality in the Democratic Tradition.* Cambridge, 2007.

Nussbaum, Martha. *The Clash Within: Democracy, Religious Violence, and India's Future.* Cambridge, MA, 2007.

———. *Upheavals of Thought: The Intelligence of Emotions.* Cambridge, 2001.

O'Connell, Joseph. "Metrology: The Creation of Universality by the Circulation of Particulars." *Social Studies of Science* 23 (1993): 129–73.

Olafson, Frederick. *Heidegger and the Ground of Ethics.* Cambridge, 1998.

Olesko, Kathryn M. "Tacit Knowledge and School Formation." *Osiris* 2nd series 8 (1993): 16–29.

Oliver, Mark. *Can the Market Deliver? Funding Public Service Television in the Digital Age.* London, 2005.

O'Neill, Onora. "Practices of Toleration." In *Democracy and the Mass Media*, edited by Judith Lichtenberg, pp. 155–85. Cambridge, 1990.

Owen, David. "The Expressive Agon. On political Agency in a Constitutional Democratic Polity." In *Law and Agonistic Politics*, edited by Adrew Schaap, pp. 71–86. Aldershot, 2009.

Ozer, Mark N. "The British Vivisection Controversy." *Bulletin of the History of Medicine* 40 (1960): 158–67.

Paley, Julia. "Toward an Anthropology of Democracy." *Annual Review of Anthropology* 31 (2002): 469–96.

Parekh, Bhikhu. *Rethinking Multiculturalism: Cultural Diversity and Political Theory*. London, 2000.

———, ed. *The Parekh Report: The Future of Multi-Ethnic Britain*. London, 2000.

Patel, Raj. *Stuffed or Starved: The Hidden Battle for the World Food System*. New York, 2008.

Peacock, Alan. *Public Service Broadcasting Without the BBC?* London, 2004.

Pelling, Margaret. *Cholera, Fever and English Medicine*. Oxford, 1978.

Pestre, Dominique. "Pour une histoire sociale et culturelle des sciences: Nouvelles définitions, nouveaux objets, nouvelle practiques." *Annales* 50 (1995): 487–522.

Peters, Michael A., Alan Britton, and Harry Blee, eds. *Global Citizenship Education: Philosophy, Theory and Pedagogy*. Rotterdam, 2008.

Pickering, Andrew. *The Mangle of Practice: Timage, Agency, and Science*. Chicago, 1995.

Pilkington, Colin. *Britain in the European Union Today*. 2nd ed. Manchester, 2001.

Porter, Dorothy. *Health, Civilisation and the State: A History of Public Health from Ancient to Modern Times*. London, 1999.

Porter, Roy, and Dorothy Porter. "The Politics of Prevention: Antivaccinationism and Public Health in Nineteenth-Century England." *Medical History* 32 (1988): 231–52.

Porter, Theodore M. *Trust in Numbers: The Pursuit of Objectivity in Science and Public Life*. Princeton, NJ, 1995.

Poster, Mark. "Cyberdemocracy: The Internet and the Public Sphere." 1998. Available at http://www.hnet.uci.edu/mposter/writings/democ.html.

Prochaska, Frank. "Body and Soul: Bible Nurses and the Poor in Victorian London." *Historical Research* 60 (1987): 336–48.

———. "A Mother's Country: Mothers' Meetings and Family Welfare in Britain, 1850–1950." *History* 74 (1989): 379–99.

Rawls, John. *Political Liberalism*. New York, 1993.

———. *A Theory of Justice*. Cambridge, MA, 1972.

Raymond, Eric S., ed. *The New Hackers' Dictionary*. 3rd ed. Cambridge, MA, 1996.

Razzell, Peter. *The Conquest of Smallpox: The Impact of Inoculation on Smallpox Mortality in Eighteenth-Century Britain*. Firle, 1977.

Rheinberger, Hans-Jörg. "Gaston Bachelard and the Notion of 'Phenomenotechnique.'" *Perspectives on Science* 13 (2005): 313–28.

Rheinberger, Hans-Jörg, and Michael Hagner, eds. *Die Experimentalisierung des Lebens: Experimentalsysteme in den biologischen Wissenschaften 1850/1950*. Berlin, 1993.

Ricœur, Paul. *Lectures on Ideology and Utopia*. Edited by George H. Taylor. New York, 1986.

Riley, James C. *Sick Not Dead: The Health of British Workingmen during the Mortality Decline*. Baltimore, 1997.

Roberts, Marc J., Stephen R. Thomas, and Michael J. Dowling. "Mapping Scientific Disputes that Affect Public Policymaking." *Science, Technology, and Human Values* 8 (1984): 112–22.

Rogers, Carol L. "The Importance of Understanding Audiences." In *Communicating Uncertainty: Media Coverage of New and Controversial Science*, edited by Sharon M. Friedman, Sharon Dunwoody, and Carol L. Rogers, pp. 179–200. Mahwah, NJ, 1999.

———. "Science Information for the Public: The Role of Scientific Societies." *Science, Technology, and Human Values* 6 (1981): 36–40.

Rosenfeld, Michel. "Habermas's Call for Cosmopolitan Constitutional Patriotism in an Age of Global Terror: A Pluralist Appraisal." *Constellations* 1 (2000): 159–81.

Rouse, Joseph. "Beyond Epistemic Sovereignty." In *The Disunity of Science: Boundaries, Contexts, and Power*, edited by Peter Galison and David J. Strump, pp. 398–416. Stanford, CA, 1996.

———. *Engaging Science: How to Understand Its Practices Philosophically*. Ithaca, NY, 1996.

———. *How Scientific Practices Matter: Reclaiming Philosophical Naturalism*. Chicago, 2002.

———. *Knowledge and Power: Toward a Political Philosophy of Science*. Ithaca, NY, 1987.

Rupke, Nicolaas A., ed. *Antivivisection in Historical Perspective*. London, 1990.

Rusnock, Andrea. *Vital Accounts: Quantifying Health and Population in Eighteenth-Century England and France*. Cambridge, 2002.

Sandel, Michael J. *Democracy's Discontent: America in Search of a Public Philosophy*. Cambridge, MA, 1996.

Scambler, Graham, ed. *Habermas, Critical Theory, and Health*. London, 2001.

Scannell, Paddy. "Public Service Broadcasting and Modern Public Life." *Media, Culture and Society* 11, no. 2 (1989): 135–66.

Schaap, Andrew, ed. *Law and Agonistic Politics*. Aldershot, UK, 2009.

Scheuerman, William E. "Unsolved Paradoxes: Conservative Political Thought in Adenauer's Germany." In *Confronting Mass Democracy and Industrial Technology: Political and Social Theory from Nietzsche to Habermas*, edited by John P. McCormick, pp. 221–42. Durham, NC, 2002.

Schiera, Pierangelo. *Laboratorium der bürgerlichen Welt: Deutsche Wissenschaft im 19. Jahrhundert*. Frankfurt am Main, 1992.

Schlesinger, Philip. *Media, State and Nation: Political Violence and Collective Identities*. London, 1991.

———. *Putting Reality Together*. London, 1987.

Schmitt, Carl. *The Crisis of Parliamentary Democracy*. Translated by Ellen Kennedy. Cambridge, MA, 1985.

Shapin, Steven. "The House of Experiment in Seventeenth-Century England." *Isis* 79 (1988): 373–404.

———. "'The Mind Is its Own Place': Science and Solitude in Seventeenth-Century England." *Science in Context* 4 (1990): 191–218.

———. "Science and the Public." In *Companion to the History of Modern Science*, edited by R. C. Olby, G. N. Cantor, J. R. R. Christie, and M. J. S. Hodge, pp. 990–1007. London, 1989.

———. *A Social History of Truth: Civility and Science in Seventeenth-Century England*. Chicago, 1994.

Shapin, Steven, and Simon Schaffer. *Leviathan and the Air-Pump: Hobbes, Boyle, and the Experimental Life*. Princeton, NJ, 1985.

Simmel, Georg. *Soziologie: Untersuchungen über die Formen der Vergesellschaftung*, in *Gesamtausgabe*. Vol. 11. Edited by Otthein Rammstedt. Frankfurt am Main, 1992.

Skinner, Quentin. *Reason and Rhetoric in the Philosophy of Hobbes*. Cambridge, 1996.

Sköld, Peter. *The Two Faces of Smallpox: A Disease and Its Prevention in Eighteenth- and Nineteenth-Century Sweden*. Umeå, 1996.

Somers, Margaret R. "Citizenship and the Place of the Public Sphere: Law, Community, and Political Culture in the Transition to Democracy." *American Sociological Review* 58 (1993): 587–620.

———. *Genealogies of Citizenship: Markets, Statelessness, and the Right to Have Rights.* Cambridge, 2008.

———. "Narrating and Naturalizing Civil Society and Citizenship Theory: The Place of Political Culture and the Public Sphere." *Sociological Theory* 13 (1995): 229–74.

Sousa Santos, Boaventura de. *Toward a New Legal Common Sense: Law, Globalization and Emancipation.* 2nd ed. London, 2002.

Sousa Santos, Boaventura de, and Cesar A. Rodiguez-Garavito, eds. *Law and Globalization from Below: Towards a Cosmopolitan Legality.* Cambridge, 2005.

Spinosa, Charles, Fernando Flores, and Hubert L. Dreyfus. *Disclosing New Worlds: Entrepreneurship, Democratic Action, and the Cultivation of Solidarity.* Cambridge, MA, 1997.

Specter, Matthew G. *Habermas: An Intellectual Biography.* Cambridge 2010.

Squires, Judith. "Culture, Equality and Diversity." In *Multiculturalism Reconsidered.* Edited by Paul Kelly, pp. 115–32. Cambridge, 2002.

Stafford, Barbara Maria. *Body Criticism: Imaging the Unseen in Enlightenment Art and Medicine.* Cambridge, MA, 1991.

———. *Good Looking: Essays on the Virtue of Images.* Cambridge, MA, 1996.

Stevenson, Nick, ed. *Culture and Citizenship.* London, 2001.

Stewart, Larry. *The Rise of Public Science: Rhetoric, Technology, and Natural Philosophy in Newtonian Britain, 1660–1750.* Cambridge, 1992.

Stichweh, Rudolf. "The Sociology of Scientific Disciplines: On the Genesis and Stability of the Disciplinary Structure of Modern Science." *Science in Context* 5 (1992): 3–15.

Stiegler, Bernd. *Philologie des Auges: Die photographische Entdeckung der Welt im 19. Jahrhundert.* Munich, 2001.

Sturdy, Steve, ed. *Medicine, Health and the Public Sphere in Britain, 1600–2000.* London, 2002.

Tambini, Damien. "New Media and Democracy: The Civic Networking Movement." *New Media and Society* 1, no. 3 (1999): 305–29.

Tambini, Damien, and Jamie Cowling, eds. *From Public Service Broadcasting to Public Service Communications.* London, 2004.

Taylor, Charles. *Modern Social Imaginaries.* Durham, NC, 2004.

———. "Modes of Civil Society." *Public Culture* 3 (1990): 95–118.

Thompson, John B. *The Media and Modernity.* Cambridge, 1995.

Thompson, Noel. *Political Economy and the Labour Party.* London, 1996.

Thussu, Daya Kishan, ed. *Media On The Move: Global Flow and Contra-Flow.* London, 2007.

Tocqueville, Alexis de. *Democracy in America.* New York, 1945.

Tomlinson, Jim. *Government and the Enterprise since 1900: The Changing Problem of Efficiency.* Oxford, 1994.

Tönnies, Ferdinand. *On Public Opinion: Selections and Analyses.* Edited and translated by Hanno Hardt and Slavko Splichal. Lanham, NJ, 2000.

Toulmin, Stephen. *Return to Reason.* Cambridge, MA, 2001.

Tully, James. *An Approach to Political Philosophy: Locke in Contexts.* Cambridge, 1994.

———. *Public Philosophy in a New Key.* Cambridge, 2008.

———. *Strange Multiplicity: Constitutionalism in an Age of Diversity.* Cambridge, 1995.

Turner, Frank M. "Public Science in Britain, 1880–1919." *Isis* 71 (1980): 589–608.

Turow, Joseph. *Breaking Up America: Advertisers and the New Media World.* Chicago, 1997.

Vierhaus, Rudolf. *Deutschland im 18. Jahrhundert: Politische Verfassung, soziales Gefüge, geistige Bewegung.* Göttingen, 1987.

Villa, Dana. "Postmodernism and the Public Sphere." *The American Political Science Review* 86, no. 3 (September 1992): 712–21.

Waldenfels, Bernhard. *In den Netzen der Lebenswelt*. Frankfurt am Main, 1985.

Wall, Stephen. *A Stranger in Europe: Britain and the EU from Thatcher to Blair*. Oxford, 2008.

Warner, Michael. *Publics and Counterpublics*. New York, 2002.

Wear, Andrew. *Knowledge and Practice in English Medicine, 1550–1680*. Cambridge, 2000.

Weber, Thomas. *Gandhi as Disciple and Mentor*. Cambridge, 2004.

———. *Hugging the Trees: The Story of the Chipko Movement*. Harmondsworth, 1988.

Webster, Charles. *The Health Services since the War, II: Government and Health Care—the British National Health Service, 1958–1979*. London, 1996.

Webster, James G. "Beneath the Veneer of Fragmentation: Television Audience Polarization in a Multichannel World." *Journal of Communication* 55 (2005): 366–82.

Wetzel, Michael, and Herta Wolf, eds. *Der Entzug der Bilder: Visuelle Realitäten*. Munich, 1994.

Wigley, K. J. "The Development of the National Plan." *Journal of the Royal Statistical Society Series A* 129, no. 1 (1966): 6–25.

Williams, Raymond. *Television: Technology and Cultural Form*. New York, 1975.

Williams-Searle, Bridgett, and Harvey Amani Whitfield. "Introduction: Citizenship Struggles in North America and the Caribbean." *Citizenship Studies* 10 (2006): 1–4.

Winch, Peter. *Ethics and Action*. London, 1972.

Wittgenstein, Ludwig. *Philosophical Investigations*. Edited and translated by G. E. M. Anscombe. Oxford, 2002.

Wohl, Anthony S. *Endangered Lives: Public Health in Victorian Britain*. London, 1984.

Wollstonecraft, Mary. *The Vindication of the Rights of Woman*. Edited by Sylvana Tomaselli. Cambridge, 1995.

Wood, Patricia K. "Aboriginal/Indigenous Citizenship: An Introduction." *Citizenship Studies* 7 (2003): 371–78.

Young, Iris Marion. *Intersecting Voices: Dilemmas of Gender, Political Philosophy, and Policy*. Princeton, NJ, 1997.

Young, Robert. *Postcolonialism: An Historical Introduction*. Oxford, 2001.

Zerilli, Linda M. *Feminism and the Abyss of Freedom*. Chicago, 2008.

Ziman, John. "Public Understanding of Science." *Science, Technology, and Human Values* 16 (1991): 99–105.

CONTRIBUTORS

Georgina Born is Professor of Music and Anthropology at the University of Oxford. Previously, she was Professor of Sociology, Anthropology, and Music at the University of Cambridge. Honorary Professor of Anthropology at University College London and a Fellow of the Center for Cultural Sociology at Yale University, she is the author of *Rationalizing Culture: IRCAM, Boulez, and the Institutionalization of the Musical Avant-Garde* (Berkeley, CA, 1995) and *Uncertain Vision: Birt's BBC and the Erosion of Creativity* (London, 2004). Apart from her academic work, Born is also engaged in cultural policy and media policy work on the BBC, public service broadcasting, and the cultural sector in Britain and Europe, and gave evidence to the House of Lords Select Committee on the future of the BBC.

Steven G. Crowell is the Joseph and Joanna Nazro Mullen Professor of Philosophy at Rice University. Working in the field of twentieth-century European philosophy, especially phenomenology and the neo-Kantian tradition, he is the author of *Husserl, Heidegger, and the Space of Meaning: Paths Toward Transcendental Phenomenology* (Evanston, IL, 2001). His latest book is *Normativity and Phenomenology in Husserl and Heidegger* (Cambridge, forthcoming in 2013).

Christian J. Emden is Associate Professor of German Intellectual History and Political Thought at Rice University and a former Fellow of Sidney Sussex College, Cambridge. He is the author of *Nietzsche on Language, Consciousness, and the Body* (Chicago, 2005), *Walter Benjamins Archäologie der Moderne: Kulturwissenschaft um 1930* (Munich, 2006), and, most recently, *Friedrich Nietzsche and the Politics of History* (Cambridge, 2008). His current research is concerned with the visual culture of the natural sciences, and he is working on a book about Nietzsche's philosophical naturalism.

Gordon Graham is Henry Luce III Professor of Philosophy and the Arts at Princeton Theological Seminary. He is a Fellow of the Royal Society of Edinburgh and was previously Regius Professor of Moral Philosophy and Director of the Centre for the Study of Scottish Philosophy at the University of Aberdeen. He is the author of several books on aesthetics and ethics, including *Evil and Christian Ethics* (Cambridge, 2001), *Eight Theories of Ethics* (London, 2004), *Philosophy of the Arts*, 3rd ed. (London, 2005), *The Re-enchantment of the World: Art versus Religion* (Oxford, 2007), and *Ethics and International Relations*, 2nd ed. (Oxford, 2008).

Anne Hardy is Honorary Professor at the Centre for History in Public Health, London School of Hygiene and Tropical Medicine. An expert on the history of public health, she is the author of *The Epidemic Streets: Infectious Disease and the Rise of Preventive Medicine, 1856–1900* (Oxford, 1993), *Health and Medicine in Britain since 1860* (London, 2001) and, with Lise Wilkinson, of *Prevention and Cure: From Tropical Medicine to Global Public Health* (London, 2000). Currently, she is working on food, water, disease, and British society between 1880 and 1970.

Christopher Kelty is Associate Professor at the University of California, Los Angeles, with appointments in the Institute for Society and Genetics, the Department of Information Studies, and the Department of Anthropology. His research focuses on the cultural significance of information technology, especially in science and engineering. He has published widely on science and technology studies, specifically Internet culture and history, intellectual property, the public sphere, free and open source software, public domains, commons, authorship and ownership, and the history and philosophy of science and technology, in the United States, Europe, and India. He is the author of *Two Bits: The Cultural Significance of Free Software* (Durham, NC, 2008).

David Midgley is Reader in German Literature and Culture at the University of Cambridge and a Fellow of St. John's College. He has published several books on modern German literature, including *Writing Weimar: Critical Realism in German Literature, 1918–1933* (Oxford, 2000). He is currently writing a book on Alfred Döblin.

James Tully is Distinguished Professor of Political Science, Law, Indigenous Governance, and Philosophy at the University of Victoria, Canada. A Fellow of the Royal Society of Canada and the Trudeau Foundation, he previously held the inaugural Henry N. R. Jackman Distinguished Professorship in Philosophical Studies at the University of Toronto in the Departments of Philosophy and Political Science and the Faculty of Law. He is the author of A *Discourse on Property. John Locke and his Adversaries* (Cambridge, 1980), *An Approach to Political Philosophy: Locke in Contexts* (Cambridge, 1993), *Strange Multiplicity: Constitutionalism in an Age of Diversity* (Cambridge, 1995), and the two-volume *Public Philosophy in a New Key* (Cambridge, 2008). He also edited John Locke's A *Letter Concerning Toleration* (Indianapolis, 1982) and Samuel Pufendorf's *On the Duty of Man and Citizen according to Natural Law* (Cambridge, 1991), as well as, with Alain-G. Gagnon, *Multinational Democracies* (Cambridge, 2001).

Gary Wihl is the Hortense and Tobias Lewin Professor in the Humanities and Dean of the Faculty of Arts and Sciences at Washington University, St. Louis. He is the author of *Ruskin and the Rhetoric of Infallibility* (New Haven, CT, 1985) and *The Contingency of Theory: Pragmatism, Expressivism and Deconstruction* (New Haven, CT, 1994), and coedited *Transformations in Personhood and Culture after Theory: The Languages of History, Aesthetics, and Ethics* (University Park, PN, 1994). He is currently working on the interpretation of liberalism and constitutional change in nineteenth- and twentieth-century English and American literature.

Lord (Richard) Wilson was Master of Emmanuel College, Cambridge, from 2002 to 2012. He entered the Civil Service in 1966 as an assistant principal in the Board of Trade and moved to the Department of Energy, where his responsibilities included nuclear energy policy and the privatization of Britoil. From 1987 to 1990 he headed the Economic Secretariat in the Cabinet Office under Prime Minister Margaret Thatcher, and after two years in the Treasury was appointed Permanent Secretary of the Department of the Environment in 1992. He became Permanent Under Secretary of the UK Home Office in 1994 and Secretary of the Cabinet and Head of the UK Home Civil Service in January 1998. Upon his retirement from the Civil Service in 2002 he entered the House of Lords.

INDEX